THE POWER OF FEEDBACK

This follow-up to the 2003 edition of *Job Feedback* by Manuel London is updated to cover new research in the area of organizational management. This edition bridges a gap in research that now covers cultural responses to employer feedback, feedback through electronic communications, and how technology has changed the way teams work in organizations. *The Power of Feedback* includes examples of feedback from friends, family, colleagues, and volunteers in non-profit organizations. In this new book, both employers and employees will learn to view feedback as a positive tool for improving performance, motivation, and interpersonal relationships. Managers, human resource professionals, and students who will one day oversee teams will benefit from the research and advice found in *The Power of Feedback*.

Manuel London is Dean of the College of Business at the State University of New York at Stony Brook. He is also Director of the Center for Human Resource Management at Stony Brook. He received his PhD in industrial and organizational psychology from the Ohio State University and taught for three years at the Business School of the University of Illinois in Champaign-Urbana. He moved to Stony Brook in 1989. His research interests are in employee management and development, including career motivation, performance evaluation, feedback, and training.

David V. Day, Stephen Zaccaro, Stanley M. Halpin
Leader Development for Transforming Organizations: Growing Leaders for Tomorrow's Teams and Organizations

Stewart I. Donaldson, Mihaly Csikszentmihalyi and Jeanne Nakamura
Applied Positive Psychology: Improving Everyday Life, Health, Schools, Work, and Safety

James E. Driskell and Eduardo Salas
Stress and Human Performance

Sidney A. Fine and Steven F. Cronshaw
Functional Job Analysis: A Foundation for Human Resources Management

Sidney A. Fine and Maury Getkate
Benchmark Tasks for Job Analysis: A Guide for Functional Job Analysis (FJA) Scales

J. Kevin Ford, Steve W. J. Kozlowski, Kurt Kraiger, Eduardo Salas, and Mark S. Teachout
Improving Training Effectiveness in Work Organizations

Jerald Greenberg
Organizational Behavior: The State of the Science, Second Edition

Jerald Greenberg
Insidious Workplace Behavior

Itzhak Harpaz and Raphael Snir
Heavy Work Investment: Its Nature, Sources, Outcomes and Future Directions

Edwin Hollander
Inclusive Leadership: The Essential Leader-Follower Relationship

Ann Hergatt Huffman and Stephanie R. Klein
Green Organizations: Driving Change with I-O Psychology

Jack Kitaeff
Handbook of Police Psychology

Uwe E. Kleinbeck, Hans-Henning Quast, Henk Thierry, and Hartmut Häcker
Work Motivation

Laura L. Koppes
Historical Perspectives in Industrial and Organizational Psychology

Ellen Kossek and Susan Lambert
Work and Life Integration: Organizational, Cultural, and Individual Perspectives

Martin I. Kurke and Ellen M. Scrivner
Police Psychology into the 21st Century

Joel Lefkowitz
Ethics and Values in Industrial and Organizational Psychology

John Lipinski and Laura M. Crothers
Bullying in the Workplace: Causes, Symptoms, and Remedies

Manuel London
Job Feedback: Giving, Seeking, and Using Feedback for Performance Improvement, Second Edition

Manuel London
How People Evaluate Others in Organizations

Manuel London
Leadership Development: Paths to Self-Insight and Professional Growth

Manuel London
The Power of Feedback: Giving, Seeking, and Using Feedback for Performance Improvement

Robert F. Morrison and Jerome Adams
Contemporary Career Development Issues

Michael D. Mumford, Garnett Stokes, and William A. Owens
Patterns of Life History: The Ecology of Human Individuality

Michael D. Mumford
Pathways to Outstanding Leadership: A Comparative Analysis of Charismatic, Ideological, and Pragmatic Leaders

Kevin R. Murphy
Validity Generalization: A Critical Review

Kevin R. Murphy and Frank E. Saal
Psychology in Organizations: Integrating Science and Practice

Kevin Murphy
A Critique of Emotional Intelligence: What Are the Problems and How Can They Be Fixed?

Susan E. Murphy and Ronald E. Riggio
The Future of Leadership Development

Susan E. Murphy and Rebecca J. Reichard
Early Development and Leadership: Building the Next Generation of Leaders

Margaret A. Neal and Leslie Brett Hammer
Working Couples Caring for Children and Aging Parents: Effects on Work and Well-Being

THE POWER OF FEEDBACK

Giving, Seeking, and Using Feedback for Performance Improvement

Manuel London

Routledge
Taylor & Francis Group

NEW YORK AND LONDON

First published 2015
by Routledge
711 Third Avenue, New York, NY 10017

and by Routledge
27 Church Road, Hove, East Sussex BN3 2FA

Routledge is an imprint of the Taylor & Francis Group,
an informa business

Library of Congress Cataloging-in-Publication Data

London, Manuel.
The power of feedback : giving, seeking, and using feedback for
    performance improvement / Manuel London.
        pages cm
    Includes bibliographical references and index.
  1. Employee motivation.   2. Feedback (Psychology)
3. Performance standards.   4. Organizational behavior.   I. Title.
    HF5549.5.M63L663 2015
    658.3′14—dc23
    2014003252

ISBN: 978-1-84872-547-8 (hbk)
ISBN: 978-1-84872-548-5 (pbk)
ISBN: 978-1-315-81387-5 (ebk)

Typeset in Sabon
by Apex CoVantage, LLC

CONTENTS

CONTENTS

SERIES FOREWORD

The goal of the Applied Psychology series is to create books that exemplify the use of scientific research, theory, and findings to help solve real problems in organizations and society. Dr. London's *The Power of Feedback* is a great example of a noted scientist-practitioner pulling together the best of what academic research and work organizations can teach us about a problem that will touch just about everyone who reads this book—that is, seeking, providing, and using performance feedback.

Dr. London's book is divided into three sections. The first examines the way people perceive themselves, how feedback influences these perceptions, and how they perceive the givers of feedback. This section goes beyond the commonsense (and empirically supported) belief that people do not like to receive negative feedback, and shows how feedback can be incorporated into people's understanding of their own behavior. The second section details the many ways feedback can be collected, organized, and used. This section considers ways of giving those who provide and those who receive feedback tools and skills to make the process more successful. The final section of this book examines organizational, technological, and cultural trends that influence the process of giving and receiving feedback.

Dr. London notes that feedback is a constant, important, yet often unwelcome feature of our lives, both in the workplace and outside of work. His book lays out systematically what we know and what we need to know about ways to improve the provision and use of feedback, and shows how organizations can incorporate high-quality feedback into their strategies for developing a competitive edge. We are happy to add *The Power of Feedback* to the Applied Psychology series.

Jeanette N. Cleveland

Kevin R. Murphy

PREFACE

This volume is an update of the second edition of my book *Job Feedback: Giving, Seeking, and Using Feedback for Performance Improvement*, published by Lawrence Erlbaum in 2003. My editorial team, now at Routledge/Taylor & Francis, encouraged this current update. Much of the text is the same. We changed the title and revised the format to be more user-friendly. I replaced the academic parenthetical references throughout the text with notes at the end of each chapter, making the book easier to read while still providing access to the sources. I reduced the detailed descriptions of research, particularly older research, making the book more current. The principles of human behavior about feedback are still sound. The book is still research-based with updated information from the latest studies. I include current thinking about feedback in different cultures, applications of feedback through electronic communication, feedback to teams, and coaching to increase the value of feedback. I added more case examples from a variety of settings at work and outside of work, including feedback to and from one's family, friends, and volunteers in non-profit community organizations. My focus is on practical understanding and uses of feedback—both giving and receiving feedback to guide goal setting and improve performance.

Feedback is an anomaly. People have a general sense that feedback is good to give and receive. But many people avoid it like the plague. They are uncomfortable telling others they have done well, and they feel even more uncomfortable telling others they have performed poorly. Some people would just as soon not know how they did, and they dodge evaluations of their performance and opportunities to learn how they can improve.

This is not necessarily irrational. After all, sometimes people give feedback in a dysfunctional way—for instance, to deliberately hurt others' feelings and destroy their self-confidence. Or this may be the unintentional result. Others give or request feedback to influence how people see them.

Managers in various organizational settings rarely take time to give feedback. Most managers recognize that giving feedback is an important part of the manager's role, but they don't do it! They tend to let poor performance slide by rather than nip it in the bud. They ask me in puzzlement how to cope with poor-performing subordinates and how to improve marginal performers. Their subordinates complain that their managers rarely tell them how they are doing.

I know from personal experience that managers often shy away from giving feedback and have trouble dealing with subordinates' performance problems. I learned this when I was a manager of human resource and training units at AT&T and later in my current role as faculty member and administrator at the State University of New York at Stony Brook. I also found this to be true in my consulting work in large and small organizations in government and the private sector.

My interest in feedback arose from my early research on the employment interview with Milton Hakel and performance appraisal with Richard Klimoski during my days as a graduate student at Ohio State University. I especially wanted to know how people perceive and make judgments about each other. I incorporated this interest in my work on career motivation at AT&T with Douglas Bray. We defined three components of career motivation: career insight (having information about oneself and the organization), career identity (the goals one wants to accomplish), and career resilience (one's ability to overcome career barriers).[1] As such, feedback is an essential ingredient of an employee development program as people use information about themselves to formulate career goals.

Several years after studying career motivation and designing management development programs in ways that would strengthen managers' career insight, identity, and resilience, I began work with Arthur Wohlers and James Smither on a method to give managers information about how others see them. Called multisource or 360-degree feedback, this method collects ratings about managers from their subordinates, peers, supervisors, customers, and/or suppliers. The managers also rate themselves. The technique has several goals: It is a source of information to help managers determine areas for development. It is a way to communicate to employees what elements of management are important, and that different constituencies have different views of the manager's role. It contributes to a continuous learning environment. Annual (or more frequent) administrations of the survey call attention to managers' need to track their accomplishments and improvement in areas key to effective boss-subordinate, peer-peer, and customer-supplier relationships.

At the State University of New York at Stony Brook, I have continued my research on multisource feedback and applied the process in consulting projects in different types of organizations. I also began to flesh out the underlying psychological mechanisms and cognitive processes by which people use feedback. In a recent book, I examined interpersonal insight—how people evaluate and make decisions about others in organizations.[2] My model of how people process information about themselves and others suggests that some information is processed mindlessly.[3] The information might reinforce our existing self-image, but it doesn't suggest ways we can change and improve. Other information is processed mindfully. For this to happen, the information must set off an alarm in some way. This happens when unexpected performance results do not fit existing categories of the way we view ourselves. A process that guides or forces people to pay attention to feedback may also be a wake-up call. As we process the information mindfully we make attributions about its causes and ways we can control or improve our behavior. Hopefully, this leads to constructive strategies to enhance performance.

As I developed theory and conducted research on self and interpersonal insight, I realized that the concepts could be applied to improve feedback. I wanted to make my ideas practical and accessible to managers, human resource practitioners, and training professionals, as well as students in these fields. I thought that this should be especially important in today's increasingly changing organizations where high performance expectations and fair treatment are critical to success. In particular, I build on my work on career motivation, multisource feedback, and self and interpersonal insight to address how people give, seek, and use feedback and how to build better feedback systems. This is my goal in the present book. I believe that people can learn to be more insightful about themselves and better observers of others. I draw on theory and research to address issues of practical concern. In doing so, I hope to contribute to the development of sound performance feedback strategies in organizations. I examine the many ways that organizations and individuals benefit from constructive feedback. I view feedback as a key to effective performance management, and I show how feedback affects learning, motivation, and interpersonal relationships.

In this book, I cover the accuracy of feedback, the effects of feedback on performance, the measurement of contextual and task elements of performance, the unique value of peer feedback, methods for constructive feedback, coaching as a support to help managers use feedback to set goals and track progress, the use of feedback for self-development and continuous learning, personality variables (e.g., self-monitoring, conscientiousness, and emotional stability) related to seeking and using feedback, multisource feedback, and organizational factors that affect support for feedback. I examine methods for linking strategic planning with individual goal setting and development. I emphasize that feedback is not an isolated event but part of a strategic performance management process that starts with the organization's goals and includes the evaluation of performance outcomes in relation to these goals. Other topics are the emergence of globalization and cross-cultural factors affecting performance evaluations and the use of technology to collect performance data.

The chapters examine how people perceive and make judgments about themselves and others, the use of feedback surveys that collect data from multiple sources, feedback to teams, and feedback in multicultural organizations. I include theoretical developments in person perception and social processes that address how people make performance judgments and provide feedback and how people welcome, accept (or reject), and use feedback. I address the development of online feedback and career resources. I report research on the effects of feedback over time. I describe the use of coaches and psychologists to help managers and executives use feedback reports and examine feedback in global, multicultural corporations. I provide methods for encouraging continuous learning (becoming a self-developer) and creating a feedback-oriented organizational culture. I describe feedback in teams from a facilitator or supervisor to the team as a whole, and feedback from members to each other and the team. I discuss rater attitudes, rater similarity, and reactions to feedback (e.g., accuracy and perceptions of usefulness). I also offer examples of just-in-time, do-it-yourself multisource surveys available through the web, and feedback to geographically dispersed, "virtual" teams. I cover effects of feedback on performance improvement, the effectiveness of feedback and coaching, the use of coaches to deliver feedback, the value of self-evaluations, personality and feedback, the use of feedback as a method to convey valued competencies and performance expectations, and self-regulation and self-development as a basis for continuous learning.

This book is for managers, human resource professionals, and students hoping to be managers one day. I like to tell my students that all managers are human resource managers in that they oversee teams, choose team members, facilitate collaboration, evaluate performance, give feedback, and make decisions that affect team members. As such, they should have a good understanding of performance management, human resource management, career development, management development, and basic principles of industrial and organizational psychology. Overall, my aim in the book is to help readers understand how feedback operates and how to improve the ways they give and use feedback.

I am indebted to several colleagues whose work is represented here and cited at appropriate places. Edward Mone and I have written about how human resource systems can be designed to contribute to organizational change. Feedback is a central ingredient to our view of a comprehensive human performance system. I value Ed as a friend, colleague, and co-author, and I continue to learn a great deal from his organizational insights. James Smither and I have written a number of papers on multisource ratings, which shaped my thinking about this increasingly important management tool. Jim is an innovative and careful researcher who has taught me about melding research and practice. Gerrit Wolf, my colleague at Stony Brook, continues to be an inspiration for creative ideas about management. I have benefited from his optimistic, can-do philosophy. My thanks to Jonathan Laster for conducting interviews that led to ideas for many of the cases throughout the book. Last, but not least, I am indebted to my wife, Marilyn, and sons, David and Jared, who are never shy about giving me constructive feedback.

Manuel London

Notes

1. London (1985).
2. London (2001).
3. London (1995b).

Section I

HOW PEOPLE SEE THEMSELVES AND OTHERS

1

INTRODUCTION
The Power and Challenge of Feedback

Meaningful feedback is central to what we do on the job and in other aspects of our lives. Feedback guides, motivates, and reinforces effective behaviors and reduces or stops ineffective behaviors. Feedback tells us how close we are to our goals. Similarly, giving feedback is an important way to guide others' actions and decisions. Yet many people feel uncomfortable giving and receiving feedback. Indeed, the lack of feedback isn't unusual.

Managers and supervisors may give feedback as a way to reinforce their self-importance or manipulate how others see them. Givers of feedback may be destructive or hurtful intentionally or unintentionally. In addition, they may be biased by factors such as race, gender, or age. Receivers of feedback may be apprehensive about being evaluated, defensive in the face of negative feedback, and/or apt to ignore information that could help them.

People often use negative terms when they observe and describe others, while they use positive terms to describe themselves.[1] As a result, feedback may be disappointing and possibly detrimental. No feedback at all may be better in some cases. Feedback is not effective regardless of the content and manner in which it is given and regardless of the receiver's sensitivity to the information. Support mechanisms are needed to ensure that feedback is understood and used to set goals for improvement.

Such support mechanisms focus on the recipient's ability to comprehend the feedback, the recipient's sensitivity to feedback, the context, and accountability mechanisms. The recipient's ability to comprehend the feedback may depend on the extent to which the feedback conforms to the recipient's cognitive processing capabilities (e.g., it is not too detailed), causes the recipient to think about the task from others' perspectives, and can be readily applied to change behavior and improve outcomes. These conditions depend on the control and credibility of different sources and the clarity, reliability, and validity of the information they provide. They may also depend on standards and expectations for behaviors and the availability of coaching and role models for how to apply the feedback.

3

The recipient's sensitivity to feedback is the extent to which the recipient wants to learn and is able and motivated to process information from different sources. The context refers to what is happening in the environment and the demands and stressors experienced by those who give and receive feedback. Such conditions differentiate the recipient's role in relation to that of others and suggest reasons (and rationalizations) for differences in perspectives. Accountability mechanisms are ways to hold people responsible for giving and using feedback. These mechanisms may include requiring the recipient to explain and justify the use of feedback, reminders that people may have different viewpoints about the same event, expecting performance raters to provide accurate and meaningful ratings, and rewarding behavior change and improved performance.

Case: Lack of Feedback Is Not Unusual

Consider Sheila Monroe, an apartment rental property manager in her mid-30s who supervises 10 people. She describes her work as high-stress, balancing the need to please her employer (the rental management company), her staff, and the tenants. She has worked for her current employer for more than 5 years and says that the only feedback she ever received from her employer was the relaying of a letter sent by a tenant to the property management company about how helpful Sheila was in solving a problem. Other than that, she has not had a formal performance appraisal or any sort of feedback, positive or negative. She says that she has a strong work ethic and a desire to do her best on the job at all times. She believes this is why her manager has not felt the need to give her feedback. Her performance meets expectations and there have been no difficulties. Still she would appreciate more recognition of how hard she works and the success she has keeping her tenants satisfied. And she wouldn't mind some tips on how to do even better. She recognizes that she hasn't gone out of her way to ask her employer how she is doing and have a discussion about what she can do better, if anything.

Highlights of the Book

In this book, I examine how people give, seek, and use performance feedback. I describe processes by which givers of feedback perceive and judge performance, and I outline information processes by which receivers of feedback absorb (accept, deny, or ignore) and apply feedback. I consider formal sources of job feedback including performance appraisal, multisource (upward and 360-degree) survey feedback methods, and assessment centers. I also examine the ways individuals and groups receive informal feedback. This includes guidelines for how to give effective feedback under different conditions and how to hold people accountable for giving feedback.

I focus on the receiver of feedback by considering self-assessment, seeking feedback, and reactions to feedback. Several chapters provide surveys that readers can use to evaluate themselves. This includes self-assessment of performance and sensitivity to feedback from others. I emphasize that people need to be proactive in getting feedback, and I show how to increase feedback. I describe how employees can draw on co-workers as sources of feedback. I also show how to hold people accountable for using feedback.

I consider ways people can coach and develop others—in particular, how managers can coach their subordinates and how they can establish long-term, growth-oriented relationships that enhance individual and group performance. I give special attention to ways managers use feedback to increase coordinated behavior in groups and generate win-win resolutions to conflict. I also show how goal setting permits people to get feedback about their own performance relative to their goals.

Overall, I show how people can be more effective in gathering and processing performance information about others and feeding back this information in a way that is nonthreatening and leads to productive changes in behavior. Also, I show how people can gather, accept, and use meaningful feedback from appraisals, surveys, and informal discussions to change their own behavior. In doing so, the book suggests how professionals in the fields of human resource management and training can help people in their organizations give and use feedback more effectively.

Considerable work is done in teams and many organizations are global. I examine feedback in teams and cross-cultural (multinational) organizations. Also, since advancing communications technologies make feedback and development as close as accessible and portable as a wireless laptop computer, I examine how technology provides new means of collecting feedback and providing developmental resources. In addition, I consider how feedback is a means of communicating changing competency requirements as the nature of work evolves. I demonstrate how feedback programs are integrated into performance management systems to promote an organizational culture that supports continuous learning.

Feedback is important for people in most any job and organizational position. The book includes examples from different occupations throughout the text and also a special chapter on specific applications in different organizational contexts, including part-time and volunteer positions, and people in small businesses as well as large organizations.

The Psychology of Feedback

Industrial and organizational psychologists have devoted considerable attention to studying and guiding formal performance appraisal processes, but have given less attention to feedback delivery and use. However, psychologists have long recognized the value of feedback to enhance job challenge, increase motivation, and facilitate learning when the information is meaningful and given in a helpful way. Knowledge of results is a critical psychological component of motivation that stems from performance feedback inherent in the task or job. Moreover, feedback is an important element of career motivation. Insight about oneself and the environment affects the stability and direction of one's career behavior. Such insight stems from performance feedback and information about potentially fruitful career directions. Also, feedback is an important element in learning. We know that people learn by modeling others, trying new behavior, and receiving feedback on how well they are doing.

That people don't like to give negative feedback is not surprising. They know that the recipient is likely to be defensive or hurt. However, many people avoid even patting others on the back for good performance. Some managers seem to feel embarrassed or threatened about giving favorable feedback that a subordinate or co-worker deserves. Employees sometimes request feedback, but they usually don't do so when the results are likely to be negative and they can't avoid accepting blame.

Unfortunately, many managers don't know how to give feedback, let alone how to coach and develop subordinates. Some don't even see giving feedback as part of their jobs. Indeed, they may view performance discussions as a distraction from day-to-day operations. They decry the expense of individual development that may result from feedback discussions, and they fear losing an employee's loyalty and friendship from negative feedback. Managers' reluctance to give feedback is especially problematic in organizations faced with tight resources and employee cutbacks. Standards of performance are increasing in these firms, and more and higher-quality work is expected of everyone who remains. Marginal performance cannot be tolerated for long.

Elements of Feedback

Performance information may be *objective*, resulting from clearly visible performance output. Moreover, the amount and type of information may be under the control of the employees who can select the information they want about how well they are doing. On the other hand, performance information may be *subjective*, arising from formal and informal evaluations made by others. Employees may seek such information on their own. More likely, their supervisor or co-workers deliver the information, regardless of whether employees want it. Employees may be receptive or defensive depending on factors such as the favorability of the feedback, the source's intention to be constructive, and the employee's self-confidence. The source's willingness to give feedback depends on factors such as the source's ability to communicate, the source's comfort with giving a performance evaluation face-to-face or in writing, and the source's ability and desire to coach the employee in using the information to improve performance. Giving feedback may also depend on organizational expectations to deliver performance feedback as part of the management process.

Unfortunately, feedback has its dark side. For instance, managers may avoid giving feedback or may give destructive feedback deliberately. I cover the psychological, social, and situational antecedents of these all too common occurrences. I show how people give and seek feedback in ways that manage others' impressions of them. I relate destructive feedback to harassment and other forms of treatment abuse and discrimination on the job. I show how to encourage constructive feedback, develop functional feedback and growth-oriented interpersonal relationships, and discourage destructive feedback and dysfunctional interpersonal relationships.

I offer guidelines for improving the value of feedback and its use by recipients. Table 1.1 provides a summary of what you need to know about feedback. As I develop the points in Table 1.1 throughout the book, my goal is to help managers who struggle with the difficulty of discussing another's performance face-to-face with the individual. I show

Table 1.1 What You Should Know about Feedback

Key Points about Feedback

No one likes it . . .

- They don't like to receive it.
- They don't like to give it.

But . . .

- Feedback directs, motivates, and rewards behavior.
- Feedback is a dynamic, two-way interaction.

Key Principles for Giving Feedback

- Formative feedback helps people improve; summative feedback evaluates (grades) performance for use in making decisions, such as who deserves a pay raise.
- People don't react positively to feedback.
- People generally evaluate themselves highly.
- People make common attribution errors (attribute positive events to themselves and negative effects to factors or people beyond their control).

(Continued)

Table 1.1 (Continued)

Effective feedback is . . .

- Clear
- Specific (focused on behaviors and outcomes, not personality)
- Frequent
- Immediate
- Relevant to important task/performance behaviors
- Dynamic (changing over time as situational requirements and performance change)

Guidelines for Constructive Feedback

- Don't blame people for negative outcomes.
- Don't compare people.
- Focus on behaviors, not personal characteristics.
- Attribute good performance to internal causes.
- Recognize when a team should be praised.
- Be specific about ways to improve performance.
- Allow a controlled expression of feelings.
- Increase goal clarity.
- Challenge the recipient to do better.
- Increase the recipient's sense of independence and self-control.
- Encourage and reinforce a can-do attitude.

Receiving Feedback

- Behavior change is more likely when we accept others' evaluations.
- Self-perceptions, while lenient, can change with direct, frequent feedback.
- Personality affects how we react to feedback (people who are conscientious, low in anxiety, and high in self-efficacy are able to use feedback constructively).
- People seek feedback to gather accurate information, but also try to control what others think of them.
- Be alert to impression management behaviors, such as ingratiation, intimidation, self-promotion, defensiveness, and disclaimers.

Feedback to Teams

- Providing what a team needs depends on its stage of development.
- When the team is first formed, members need to know each other and feel motivated to work with each other.
- As the work unfolds, members may need help structuring the task.
- When the work is completed, members need encouragement to reflect on their accomplishments and what they learned about better ways to work together in the future.
- Develop a feedback-oriented culture: Seek and give feedback to the group as a whole, provide support for using feedback, thank each person; remind the team how much the group and the organization is depending on them.

---

how improved feedback processes can be integrated into more effective and comprehensive human performance systems. Psychological and organizational barriers to giving effective feedback are discussed. I show how to design feedback systems for collecting reliable and telling information about performance from multiple sources and viewpoints, and I present ideas for program development that can be used in managerial assessment and training.

I cover ways to provide interdependent group members with information that increases their coordination and cooperation. I also demonstrate how to hold managers accountable for giving and using feedback.

A Word about Legal Issues

Managers must be aware of the legal implications of feedback. The performance review process must be conducted in a professional and fair manner, focused on behaviors and outcomes (not personalities), and free of discrimination that is unrelated to job performance. Any performance appraisal system used to make an employment decision about a member of a protected class (e.g., based on age, race, religion, gender, or national origin) must be a valid system—that is, an accurate measure of performance associated with job requirements, or it may be challenged in the courts (in the U.S., based on Title VII of the 1964 Civil Rights Act, the Civil Rights Act of 1991, and the Age Discrimination in Employment Act of 1975). Rating systems that depend on subjective criteria and personality trait evaluations rather than evaluations of behavior may very well be worse than having none at all. Appraisals are subject to raters' subjective biases and prejudices. Appraisal systems linked to goal setting must be an *ongoing* procedure, such as the review process recommended here. If only an annual or semiannual review meeting occurs that covers only the most recent performance information, it may not be a valid system or one that provides acceptable justification for personnel decisions. In addition to frequent performance discussions, on-going documentation in behavior terms is recommended. However, remember that this material is discoverable in a court suit, so it must be accurate and factual. The supervisor should be clear with the subordinate at the outset of the performance period about how the appraisal will be used. Also, managers should review their appraisals of subordinates with the next level of supervision as a way of holding the manager accountable for a thorough and fair evaluation.

A related legal and social issue is sexual harassment. Harassment can easily masquerade as feedback. Sexual harassment involves sexual favors or the creation of an environment that tolerates unwelcome sexual advances or language. The organization should have a clear policy prohibiting such behavior. Moreover, the performance review guidelines and associated training should include reference to this policy and indicate that care should be taken to guard against creating a hostile environment in the review process. This includes any sexual advances, innuendos, or vulgar statements that the employee considers hostile or objects to.

Throughout the book, I offer some cases of people in different professions. What you need to do to do well in a job depends on your profession, of course. For medical professionals, for instance, this involves behaviors that focus on communication with patients, interaction with fellow health care professionals, especially between different disciplines (doctors working effectively with nurses), clinical competence, etc.[2] In many if not all professions, performance feedback is key to the role. Teachers, directors of plays and films, critics, building inspectors, financial regulators, and accountants all calibrate their work in relation to its outcomes and others' reactions to it, whether consumers, students, patients, audience members, clients, and so forth.

Also, keep in mind that feedback comes from many sources, some objective information and often subjective judgments. Newcomers can profit from feedback from co-workers. Co-workers have valuable experience about what is expected and what goals are reasonable. Feedback to newcomers to a situation may be social as well as task-focused. Co-workers can help newcomers understand what they need to do to get along, what actions will "work," and what actions will be perceived unfavorably.[3] The feedback can help newcomers build networks of co-workers who are collaborative and friendly.[4]

And note that feedback is important outside of paid employment. It applies to volunteers as well as to employees.

Case: Feedback to Volunteers

Morgan Thompson has volunteered at his sailing club for years. He served on the board, and for several years was president ("commodore") of the club. He noted that members of the club were quick to criticize him when things affected them negatively. Further, members who were critical of Morgan's decisions and actions rarely offered him assistance to correct the problem. Rather, they held Morgan, as leader of the club, accountable and responsible to solve the problem. Yet Morgan recognized that he could not easily give fellow members feedback. They were volunteers, just as he was, and paid dues. If he alienated them, even members who volunteered to accept particular roles in the club, they could pick up and leave, weakening the club's financial position.

Generational Differences

In giving feedback, givers need to take into account how receivers are likely to respond. People in different generations are likely to react differently to feedback. Indeed, there are generational differences in work orientation, performance expectations, and reactions to feedback.[5] Consider the following generations:

Baby Boomers (1946–1964): Goal-oriented, emphasize collaboration, team building, and avoiding conflict. They want feedback about team performance and how they can contribute to improving teamwork.

Generation X (1965–1979): Balance between work and life; they work to live not live to work; they find flexible work hours / job sharing appealing; they seek independence and autonomy. They value individual feedback and recognition.

Millennials or Generation Y (1980–2000): High sense of entitlement, want to bring about change and have an impact, view their work as an expression of themselves—not as a definition of themselves, seek continuing learning and will take advantage of training made available to them, want everything instantly, separate effort from reward—there is no such thing as pay for performance. They expect to be praised and rewarded regardless of whether their performance is ordinary or extraordinary. Millennials don't seek or accept feedback well. Professor Paul Harvey at the University of New Hampshire found that millennials have "unrealistic expectations and a strong resistance toward accepting negative feedback."[6] Millennials, today's 20-somethings, lack trust in authority yet have a strong sense of entitlement from their closeness to parents, an optimistic attitude, high tolerance, and a willingness, indeed desire, to compromise.[7] Watch an entertaining parody corporate training video entitled "Millennials in the Workplace" at www.youtube.com/watch?v=Sz0o9clVQu8.

New Silent Generation or Generation Z (2000/2001–Present): Not yet in the workplace; digital natives. They are used to physical and psychological distance in communication and work. They are likely to seek feedback through direct and indirect communications through a wide range of social media rather than direct, face-to-face communication with co-workers.

Overview of the Book

I divide the book into three sections. The first covers perceptual processes that influence how people perceive themselves and use feedback and how they perceive others as they prepare to give feedback. The second describes means of collecting feedback data (appraisals, multisource feedback surveys, and assessment centers) and ways to support people in using feedback (performance review and coaching) and hold them accountable for performance improvement. The last section examines current organizational and technological trends that influence feedback, ultimately leading to a feedback-oriented, continuous learning corporate culture.

The first section on person perception includes four chapters. Chapter 2 covers how and why feedback works. The chapter examines why some people are so uncomfortable about giving and receiving feedback. I enumerate the many potential benefits of feedback, distinguish between constructive and destructive feedback, and describe conditions that enhance feedback effectiveness. Chapter 3 covers how people evaluate themselves. I review the literature on variables that determine the gap between self-ratings and ratings from others. This feedback gap is supposed to signal the need for development. However, some people may not see the need for change when they evaluate themselves more highly than others evaluate them. I look at variables that determine the extent to which people evaluate themselves accurately, revise their self-perceptions, establish goals for performance improvement, and make learning an on-going process. Chapter 4 continues the discussion about person perception by turning to interpersonal dynamics associated with giving and receiving feedback. The chapter covers reactions to formal and informal feedback, self-regulatory mechanisms, feedback seeking, and impression management. Chapter 5 focuses on how people process information about others as sources of feedback. The chapter covers research on the accuracy of interpersonal perceptions. It describes cognitive processes people use to encode, store, and decode information prior to giving feedback. The chapter includes discussion of the effects on rater motivation, observation skills, information distorting biases, and empathy for others on rating accuracy.

The next section of the book describes methods for collecting feedback data. Chapter 6 describes traditional performance appraisal methods, including a variety of commonly used rating methods. The chapter even covers "ratingless" appraisals as a way to avoid labeling people with a numeric rating. Chapter 7 begins a discussion of multisource feedback surveys. These popular surveys collect ratings from a variety of sources—supervisors, subordinates, peers, and customers. The chapter explains why multisource feedback is used by so many companies as input for development. The chapter outlines the pros and cons of using multi-source feedback for development alone or for development and as a basis for administrative decisions. It also gives general guidelines for developing and implementing multisource feedback methods. The chapter considers how employees react to multisource feedback and the extent to which it relates to behavior change and performance improvement.

Chapter 8 describes assessment centers, computerized assessment, and business simulations as other sources of feedback. Chapter 9 shows how to support the use of feedback. It examines the manager's role as a provider of feedback. The chapter describes how people come to realize that they really do need to change. Goal setting is examined as a key factor in making feedback useful. Feedback is likely to have little value if people don't use feedback to set goals for improvement and then achieve their goals. The chapter also emphasizes the manager's role in performance management, recommending ways for supervisors to conduct constructive performance reviews with their subordinates.

The third section shows how to expand the power of feedback in light of differences between cultures, a focus on team and organizational performance that individuals contribute to, advancing technologies for the collection and communication of feedback, and ways to create a feedback-oriented, continuous learning organizational culture. Chapter 10 recognizes that organizations have become more global, expanding operations and forming partnerships around the world. The chapter reports research on cultural effects of performance ratings in multinational organizations. Chapter 11 covers feedback in teams. Teams have become an increasingly common method for getting complex, cross-functional work done in organizations because of the need for input from people with different skills. The chapter looks at how teams (including virtual teams with geographically dispersed members) form shared expectations and use feedback about individual team members' performance and performance of the team as a whole to meet the organization's performance goals. Chapter 12 describes the effects of changing technologies and jobs on feedback and development. It shows how computer-based technologies offer ways to collect and deliver feedback, set goals, receive coaching, and learn new skills. The book concludes with a chapter on how to develop a feedback-oriented corporate culture, ways to increase employees' feedback orientation, and methods to support continuous learning.

In summary, this book shows the value of meaningful feedback. Feedback is important for communicating changing job requirements and providing a basis for setting goals for performance improvement and career development. Feedback is essential for managing in times of increasing organizational complexity. It is important for strong self-esteem and accurate attributions of positive and negative outcomes. Also, it is vital for effective performance management—directing behavior, coaching, overcoming marginal performance, and reinforcing excellent performance.

Notes

1. Langer (1992).
2. Sargeant, MacLeod, Sinclair, and Power (2011).

3. Li, Harris, Boswell, and Xie (2011).
4. For instance, Morrison (2002).
5. See http://geography.about.com/od/populationgeography/qt/generations.htm and www.valueoptions.com/spotlight_YIW/gen_y.htm.
6. Marikar (2013, p. 16).
7. Marikar (2013, p. 16); Harvey (2013); MacKenzie (2013).

2

HOW AND WHY FEEDBACK
WORKS

Feedback is the information people receive about their performance. It may convey an evaluation about the quality of those behaviors and recommendations for improvement. Feedback is an important part of learning. For instance, test grades let students know what they have achieved and what they have to learn to do better next time. People at work give feedback to reinforce others' good behavior and correct their poor behavior. Customers give feedback to salespeople, directly letting them know how they feel or indirectly by not returning to the store.

The recipient of feedback judges its value and determines whether to accept and act on the feedback, reject it, or ignore it. Feedback has different purposes at different career stages. It helps newcomers learn the ropes, mid-career employees to improve performance and consider opportunities for development, and late-career employees to maintain their productivity. On the job, supervisors or managers are an important source of feedback because they establish performance objectives, track and evaluate progress toward those objectives, determine achievement of the objectives, and provide rewards for attaining the objectives. Other sources of job feedback are co-workers, subordinates, and customers. In other areas of life, we get feedback from our family, friends, and neighbors—feedback that is likely to be less systematic, more informal, and not necessarily wanted.

People are especially likely to need feedback when their actions need to meet certain standards, perhaps standards that are set by their employer or, in informal contexts, by their teammates.[1] People need feedback to calibrate how they are doing and what they need to do to improve. The question is whether the information is available. Some organizations have systems that give feedback—for instance, reports on performance. Some have expectations that others are supposed to provide feedback. It becomes okay to talk about how well activities went, like a post-game review with the coach.

People often don't like feedback, and indeed feedback can have deleterious effects. Negative feedback can be threatening, especially if it refers to our personal characteristics and generalities (e.g., "You're too timid," or "You're too aggressive," or "You need to be more assertive") rather than specific behaviors (e.g., "Yesterday, when you were talking about possible sales strategies, several other people wanted to give their opinions and I think they might have listened to you more carefully if you had given them a bit more time to have their say"). Even positive feedback can make people feel uncomfortable and maybe embarrassed—for example, telling them they are doing a great job in front of their teammates—or maybe confused by not being specific about what was so great.

This chapter describes why people feel uncomfortable about feedback.[2] You will learn about the benefits of feedback and some simple ways you can make feedback worthwhile. I draw upon the scientific literature to learn about the characteristics of feedback, feedback providers, and feedback recipients that determine when feedback is effective. Finally, I distinguish between constructive and destructive feedback purposes, styles, and behavior.

Feelings about Feedback

Consider how you respond to feedback. Do you like being told how well you are doing on a project? Even though you think you have done a good job, do you feel more confident hearing it from others? When you think you could have done a better job, do you still feel good when others think you did a good job? Is it important for you to know what people think about your work? Do you perceive receiving feedback as risky? Do you believe your boss would think worse of you if you asked him or her for feedback? Would you be nervous about asking your boss or co-workers how they evaluate your behavior? Do you feel it is not a good idea to ask your co-workers for feedback because they might think you are incompetent? Are you embarrassed to ask your co-workers for their impression of how you are doing at work? Would your co-workers think worse of you if you asked them for feedback? Do you believe it is better to try to figure out how you are doing on your own rather than ask your co-workers for feedback?[3]

Processing feedback can be an emotionally taxing process that could reduce its usefulness and increase the pain.[4] People have different ways of managing their emotions—some suppress them or fake them—for instance, agreeing with a feedback provider's unfavorable assessment but inwardly feeling hurt and vowing for revenge in some way or deciding to quit.[5] Avoiding or rejecting unfavorable feedback may be a way to relieve the stress rather than doing something constructive, such as learning new skills or simply doing things differently. When we receive feedback, we go through a series of steps in our minds. We focus on specific information we want to remember and interpret, perhaps paraphrasing it from our own viewpoint. We might give a label to what's happening. If the feedback doesn't jive with our self-perception or what we expected, we are likely to have a negative emotional reaction, including feelings of surprise, disappointment, and hurt.[6] We may blame ourselves or, more likely, attribute the feedback to causes beyond our own control—for example, thinking that the person doesn't know what he or she is talking about or that the problem is way beyond our control. We may make a quick judgment and then re-evaluate our reaction later after it had some time to sink in, possibly after we've heard the same message from others.

People feel more comfortable asking others for feedback who do not have power over them or are not in competition with them. These can't be just casual observers, however. These are people who have insight into expectations and what it takes to do well and can be trusted to give a fair opinion.

Even someone who shies away from seeking feedback directly may still crave it. Do you find yourself eavesdropping on other supervisors to get different points of view about your performance? Do you pay close attention to how your supervisor acts toward you to figure out where you stand? Do you keep your ears open in case your supervisor has any more information about your performance? Do you pay close attention to the feedback your supervisor gives to your co-workers?[7]

Feedback is a touchy issue in organizations. Of course, people like being told when they are doing well, but they probably don't take the risk to request feedback unless they are pretty sure the information will be positive. Indeed, they may ask for feedback in a way that ensures they get only favorable information. In general, people are apprehensive about being evaluated. They fear failure, and they would just as soon not know what others think of their performance rather than receive painful information, even if it could help them. Learning from feedback often requires overcoming a mental block—the tendency to rationalize, ignore, or avoid feedback.

Many people feel the same way about giving feedback as they do about receiving it. Some managers see little practical value in the performance feedback discussion. They foresee primarily aversive consequences from giving negative feedback. Managers generally view the feedback discussion as an unpleasant situation to be avoided, postponed, and handled hurriedly. So unless they want to deliberately abuse someone, they shy away from giving negative feedback. They know it puts the receiver on the defensive and leads to an uncomfortable situation at best. Being tactful and clear at the same time is difficult. They may also feel embarrassed about giving positive feedback. Feeling they are laying bare inner feelings, they worry that they will be perceived as ingratiating. They may believe that saying something positive now makes it harder to say something negative later. Or they fear that the receiver will expect a reward they cannot provide.[8]

Consider a few examples. Some of these are examples of feedback in action, some represent failures in feedback giving, some represent desire for feedback, and some represent problems of *not* giving feedback. A sales manager who recently lost his job in the latest company downsizing asked his boss, "Why me?" The boss gave him several examples of customers who had complained. The manager wondered why his boss didn't mention these problems earlier.

Here's another example: A supervisor wanted to let a subordinate know he did a great job on the project, but she didn't want the subordinate to expect a raise the supervisor couldn't provide. So she didn't say anything at all about the subordinate's performance.

Next, consider a graphics designer who liked working with a particular client because the client was clear about what she liked and didn't like. The client was usually satisfied, and told him so. Other clients would accept a job with little comment. But some of them would not return with new business, and the designer was never sure why.

Think about a company that started a new rating program that asked subordinates and co-workers to rate every manager each year. Managers in the company tended to ignore the feedback reports. They didn't have a chance to rate top management, and they saw no reason why they should pay attention to how their subordinates evaluated them.

A young manager with only 2 years' experience after college felt she should have a clearer career direction. She wished she had a plan that would move her ahead in the business. She didn't know what kind of future she had with the company. She envied a colleague in another department who had frequent discussions with her manager about career opportunities. Her friend had a good idea what she would have to do to be promoted, and she even had a career plan that indicated the types of assignments she should have during the next 5 years.

During difficult heart surgery, a surgeon, exhausted after several hours, shouted at the operating room team, "You need to be better prepared. This won't do," and proceeded with the surgery, saying little more other than what he needed. After the patient was stable and the resident took over, the surgeon steamed out of the operating room without saying a word.

One of the first lessons learned by newly appointed members to a quality improvement team was that total quality management requires data on customer satisfaction. The team developed indexes of performance quality and a tracking mechanism to collect and analyze the information.

Self-managing work teams in an automobile parts plant reviewed their production data at the end of each day. They tracked results weekly to evaluate fluctuations in performance and test the effectiveness of improvement methods.

On the soccer field, teammates congratulated each other after a tough win. Later in the locker room, all the coach said was, "Well, we squeaked by that one."

The minister thanked volunteers for helping in the soup kitchen and said nothing about the volunteers leaving dirty dishes piled up in the rectory sink.

Negotiation team members in a labor dispute met after each bargaining session to discuss the opposing team's reactions to offers and counteroffers presented during the session.

These examples show that performance feedback comes in many forms. Moreover, feedback is important to individual and group performance in different contexts. Now consider *why* it works.

Feedback and Goal Setting

What's more important, feedback or goal setting? Goals guide and motivate behavior to achieve a certain level or quality of performance. Feedback indicates how close we are to a goal and what adjustments we might need to make to reach that goal. However, you may be likely to ignore unfavorable feedback. Or it might reduce your motivation because it suggests that you cannot achieve a goal. If the unfavorable feedback indicates that more energy and effort could bring us closer to a goal, then the feedback will be useful. If it pinpoints skills and competencies we do not have that prevent us from achieving our goal, it can reduce our desire to achieve that goal. In the long run this might be fine if the feedback causes us to change our goals, reduce our expectations to a more realistic level, or set our sights on other achievements, whether a different career direction or specific behaviors and outcomes on a different task.[9]

Benefits of Feedback

Research on feedback indicates a number of reasons why it is so important to enhancing work outcomes. Feedback has a number of positive effects. Consider the following:[10]

- Feedback directs behavior—that is, it keeps goal-directed behavior on course.
- Feedback influences future performance goals, essentially creating objectives for achieving higher levels of performance in the future.
- Positive feedback is reinforcing in and of itself. Even if it doesn't lead to some material outcome, such as more money, people appreciate knowing when they have done well. Such feedback heightens their sense of achievement and internal motivation.
- Feedback increases people's ability to detect errors on their own. They know what performance elements are important and what

levels of performance are expected. As such, feedback sets standards of performance, and people learn to evaluate themselves against these standards.

- Feedback enhances individual learning. People realize what they need to know and what they need to do to improve. Seeking self-knowledge is a prerequisite for, and motivator of, growth and improvement.
- Feedback increases motivation by demonstrating what behaviors contribute to successful performance.
- Feedback helps people clarify their beliefs about the effects of their behavior. They learn the extent to which their good behavior contributes to rewards and their poor behavior contributes to being deprived of these rewards or being punished in some way.
- People learn what aspects of the situation beyond their control influence these outcomes. Feedback increases the salience of the information and the importance of the feedback process.
- People used to receiving feedback learn to seek it out. Also, they know how to ask for feedback they can use.
- In a group setting, feedback focuses group members' attention on the same performance elements and provides all group members with a common perspective. This is helpful when group members depend on each other to complete the task, have different roles, and want their teammates to like them.
- Feedback increases feelings of control and power. This applies to both the source of feedback and the recipient. Providers of feedback understand how information can improve others' performance. Recipients of feedback recognize how information helps them take control of their own performance.
- Regular feedback helps people feel they can cope with performance problems by being able to make incremental changes in their behavior and see the effects.
- Feedback increases people's feeling of involvement in a task. They recognize how they contribute to the task, and they feel a sense of task ownership and importance.
- In negotiations, feedback is a mechanism for evaluating offers.
- In decision making, feedback about the results of the decision helps groups and individuals recognize biases (e.g., the tendency to overly weight information that is worded negatively) and avoid these biases in the future.

In summary, feedback has value because it directs and motivates behavior. It has reward value in and of itself. It provides paths for career development. It contributes to increased self-awareness and willingness to engage in self-assessment. It enhances interpersonal relationships (e.g., between supervisor and subordinate, or between husband and wife). It fosters group development, and improves service quality and customer responsiveness. However, the benefits of feedback depend a great deal on how the feedback is delivered.

Constructive Feedback

Feedback is constructive when it offers concrete information that can be used. The intent is to help—that is, to maintain, correct, or improve behavior. It is provided in such a way that it is used by the recipient. It is clear and easily understood. Moreover, it is interpreted similarly by the source and recipient.

Here are some pointers to make feedback constructive:

- Constructive feedback is not necessarily positive. It may begin with positive feedback to capture the recipient's attention and involvement and then pinpoint specific behaviors that could be changed.
- Constructive feedback is about the recipient's behavior, not personality. It doesn't blame the recipient or threaten the recipient's self-concept.
- Constructive feedback takes into account the recipient's ability to comprehend and absorb the information. Too much information or data that are too complex may be distorted, ignored, or misunderstood.
- Constructive feedback happens in the moment when the event is fresh and not likely to be remembered differently by different people. It doesn't wait for the annual performance review. Stated another way, feedback should be timely so that the recipient knows just what behaviors and performance outcomes are in question. Feedback should occur immediately or soon after the behavior or performance about which feedback is given. Giving feedback should be a common practice, not an unusual occurrence that seems to have momentous implications.
- Constructive feedback takes the situation into account. The supervisor waits until behaviors can be discussed privately.
- Constructive feedback addresses elements of performance that contribute to task success and that are under the recipient's control.
- Constructive feedback comes from a credible source—someone who is taken seriously and believed to be accurate. Recipients will have a difficult time denying or ignoring such information.
- Constructive feedback is accompanied by explanation so that the recipient understands how it can be applied to improve task performance. Don't assume that the recipient will know what to do with the feedback.
- Constructive feedback includes support to help the recipient profit from the feedback. This might be training or special job assignments

that allow the recipient to practice and improve or just another chance to do things differently and better.

Here are characteristics of feedback that make it more meaningful and constructive, helping you determine how you can change and giving you the confidence that you can.[11]

- The source has knowledge about your performance (i.e., the source has credibility).
- The feedback specifies behaviors.
- The delivery is sincere and clear.
- The feedback is favorable—it recognizes what you do well.
- Any less than favorable feedback indicates what you need to do to meet standards.
- The source of feedback is available when you have questions or want follow-up opinions about how you are doing.
- The source encourages you to ask for feedback.

When these elements are present, you are more likely to want feedback, learn, and give feedback to others.[12]

Feedback can be made more useful and less likely to turn off the recipient if it focuses on strengths.[13] Industrial psychologist Herman Aguinis and his colleagues offered the following recommendations for a strengths-based approach for constructive feedback:[14]

- Focus on what the individual does well. Mention the strengths that contribute to that positive performance, and highlight positive results—for instance, "Your arguments made sense. They were clear and convincing. You provided the data to prove your point and you showed it on graphs that everyone could understand. You know how to communicate well even under stress. This certainly worked for us. You made the sale. Congratulations!"
- Closely link any unfavorable feedback to the individual's knowledge and skills rather than talents—for instance, "You seemed to lose the audience's attention for a while with all the detailed data. I suggest you watch the reactions of the people in the room when you are speaking to them. Be sensitive to their time and whether they care about what you're saying. Be ready to adjust your presentation, maybe skipping some detail and going directly to your main points." This is more constructive than saying, "People don't like to listen to you. You're a boring speaker."
- Adopt a strengths-based approach to suggestions for overcoming weak talents—for instance, "It's true you have an accent and people sometimes have a hard time following you. I know you are passionate about what you have to say. Why don't you speak more slowly?

22

Stop occasionally to ask if anyone has questions." This is more constructive than saying, "There is nothing you can do about your strong accent, so whatever you do, avoid having to give presentations, especially on important topics."

- Don't make snap judgments. Avoid giving feedback based on your initial reaction without knowing the person or the situation. Get to know the person's abilities, what the person needs to accomplish— or what you expect the person to accomplish—and the conditions under which the person is working. For instance, if you are working with a fellow volunteer for the first time, or an employee who was just assigned to your work group, take time to get to know the person. This may be obvious, but you may be frustrated by what you see the person doing wrong and want to correct the person immediately.

- If you are asking others to give feedback to you or to other people— for instance, asking them for comments on a survey that will keep their names anonymous—be sure to give instructions about focusing on events and behaviors, not general comments about the person's character. A meaningless and potentially damaging comment would be, "You're the worst customer service representative I've met. I don't know why the company keeps you on." A constructive comment would be, "When I had a complaint, you couldn't tell me how long it would take to fix the problem. This annoyed me." Or, "I went to you with a problem and your reaction was that nothing could be done. I would rather you told me that the situation was difficult for a particular reason and that there may be another way to solve the problem."

- Choose an appropriate setting when giving feedback. Don't give unfavorable feedback in front of others. This would only embarrass the recipient and make others feel uncomfortable, leading them to make judgments about you—that you don't care about others' feelings and this is something you might do to them someday.

- Select areas for feedback that can be addressed by adapting, doing things differently, or learning new skills. If you need to focus on a behavior that the person cannot easily change, be ready to provide some ideas for changing the situation or overcoming the weakness.

- Be specific and accurate. Avoid generalities and conclusions that are not necessarily true. For instance, don't say, "No one liked what you had to say," or "No one likes having you on their team." You don't know this is true and even if it is your opinion, it isn't helpful feedback. If this is what you want to say, think about why you want to demean the individual. It might show you more about yourself in this type of situation—for example, that you tend to take your frustrations out on others or that you like being superior.

- Focus on the consequence to others or to the organization. Explain why the person's actions and behaviors have an impact, perhaps reflecting on others.
- Follow up. Have a few follow-up meetings. Ask, "How are you doing? Did you have time to think about what I said? Have you tried doing things differently? How did it go? Are there ways I can help?"

Understandably, people hesitate to give negative performance feedback to someone they like. They may transmit bad news selectively by providing only neutral messages and avoiding unpleasant information. This decreases the possibility that feedback will be resisted, denied, or attributed to the person giving the feedback (e.g., "She never liked me!").

In general, people are more willing to give feedback and guide its effective use when the recipient can control the results, the results are positive, the source and recipient get along well, and the source and recipient agree.[15] Also, people are more willing to give feedback when the information is felt to be important by the recipient and source, the feedback is tied to rewards such as a pay raise, the source of feedback is dependent on the recipient in some way (e.g., for excellent performance), the source is responsible for providing the data (it is part of the source's role—for instance, what coaches and supervisors are expected to do), and there are positive norms in the organization for giving feedback (e.g., other managers do it and it is widely accepted as part of the management role).

Contrasting Constructive and Destructive Feedback

Constructive feedback is specific and considerate. It may recognize that some portion of the cause of poor performance is due to factors beyond the subordinate's control. Also, constructive feedback attributes good performance to internal causes, such as the subordinate's effort and ability.[16] This assumes, of course, that these attributions are appropriate. The feedback doesn't blame people for negative outcomes, and it recognizes people for their accomplishments. When a problem or weakness is evident, suggestions are made for improvement. Sample statements from the feedback source include, "I think there's a lot of room for improvement," "You did the best you could under the circumstances," or "You should give more attention to . . ."

Destructive feedback is the obverse, including general comments about performance, an inconsiderate tone, poor performance attributed to internal factors, and possibly threats. The feedback source might say, "You didn't even try," "You can't seem to do anything right," or "If you don't improve, I'll get someone else to do it."

Not surprisingly, people react more positively to positive feedback. People who receive more favorable feedback are more likely to accept the results as accurate, less likely to be defensive, and more likely to use the feedback for development. People who feel accountable for using feedback are indeed more likely to use it to guide their development.[17]

Feedback that focuses on a person's abilities and personality and not specific behaviors makes people angry and tense. The interpersonal relationship between the giver and receiver of the feedback becomes less collaborative. In the future when they disagree, they are more resistant to compromise. Indeed, the feedback may even lead to more conflicts in the future.

Abusive Behavior

We can learn about the nature and effects of destructive feedback from studies of abusive behavior. While abuse in the workplace may not be as blatant as that in other settings, it still occurs, and can be destructive to employees' careers and self-esteem. And of course, abuse can occur in other situations, whether at home, in the community, on the athletic field, or in a department store. It may even take the form of illegal behavior (e.g., sexual harassment or treatment discrimination). Profiles of domestic abusers include feelings of being weak and powerless. They are unable to tolerate frustration, have a low level of impulse control, frequently are overly dependent emotionally on their victim, and exhibit excessive jealousy. They have two sides to their personality: a nice person to the outside world (the pillar of the community) while exercising a form of domestic terrorism at home. Couples who deal ineffectively with conflict use aversive control strategies (e.g., criticism) as ineffectual ways to alter each other's behavior. Abusive, destructive behavior is learned, and often abusers come from families with a history of similar behavior.[18]

This pattern may hold for abusers in the workplace, including supervisors who give abusive feedback. The supervisor's power may lead the supervisor to manipulate the subordinate, losing sight of the subordinate's feelings and abilities. The hierarchical power of the organization means that supervisors who harass subordinates are in control of a variety of resources. This makes abused employees similar to other victims of abuse. The victim's oppositional or succumbing reactions reinforce the abuser, creating a gradually escalating series of punishing behaviors. Such a cycle may apply to supervisors who are insecure about their own power. Powerless authority figures use coercive methods to provoke resistance and aggression. This prompts them to become even more coercive, controlling, and restrictive. Such aversive control strategies tend to multiply over time and tend to be reciprocated, resulting in long-term costs and dysfunctional relationships.[19]

How Interpersonal Relationships Affect Feedback

Behaviors associated with constructive and destructive feedback depend on the nature of the relationship between the giver and receiver. Consider three types of relationships: those characterized primarily by control, reward, or affiliation.

- In *control-dominated relationships*, the feedback provider wants to control, or be in a position of power over, the recipient of feedback.
- In *reward-dominated relationships*, the feedback provider uses available rewards to affect the recipient's behavior.
- In *affiliation-dominated relationships*, the feedback provider wants to maintain a friendly relationship with the recipient.

Each of these dominant role relationships helps us understand different types of constructive and destructive feedback. Keep in mind that negative feedback can be constructive or destructive, depending on how it is presented. Also, positive feedback may be destructive under some circumstances—for instance, if the value of the positive behavior is minimized or undervalued by the source.

Now, let's consider each type of relationship. Characteristics of control include power, negotiation, demeanor, tone, and values. The control-motivated feedback provider who wants to be constructive empowers the recipient in ways they can both win. The provider is respectful and patient, talks about behaviors and possible alternative ways of acting, and leaves it to the recipient to try different actions and seek further feedback. However, the provider will return to the situation and behaviors in later conversations to evaluate how things are going.

However, the control-motivated provider who wants to be destructive is domineering. The provider behaves as if this were a zero-sum game in which only the provider or the recipient can win and one of them must lose. The provider is curt and attacks the recipient's personal characteristics, saying, for instance, "You need to be a team player," or "People can't work with you," not delving into any specific situations, behaviors, or ways to improve.

Characteristics of reward-dominated relationships are behavior continuity, confidence building, evaluation/reward, attribution, timing, and focus. The supervisor's intention in constructive, reward-dominated relationships is to encourage and reinforce a can-do attitude. The supervisor praises the subordinate, attributing favorable outcomes to the subordinate's behavior and ability and negative outcomes to environmental factors beyond the subordinate's control. Feedback is given soon after the behavior occurs, and the focus is the task itself. The supervisor's intention in destructive, reward-dominated relationships is to discourage the subordinate. The subordinate's confidence is diminished if not destroyed through belittling, disparagement, ridicule, and demeaning words and actions (e.g., labeling or name calling). The supervisor withholds positive reinforcement and gives negative reinforcement—focusing on what went wrong, not what went right. The supervisor attributes any positive outcomes to factors beyond the subordinate's control ("You were lucky," or "The situation worked in your favor *this time*"). The supervisor attributes negative outcomes to the subordinate ("You don't seem to know how to work with people"). Feedback is delayed and the focus is on the subordinate as a person rather than the task.

Characteristics of affiliation-dominated relationships are expression of feelings and, more generally, communication. The provider's intention in constructive, support-dominated relationships is a controlled expression of feelings. Communication is open, two-way, clear, frequent, and face-to-face. The provider reveals information about him or herself as a way to gain confidence and trust and provide a level playing field for honest discussion of the recipient's strengths and weaknesses. The provider strives to be fair and treat recipients equally. The provider gives the recipient considerable attention and may deliberately or unwittingly increase or foster learning.

But when the provider's intention is destructive in a support-dominated relationship, he or she will vent, personally benefiting from emotional catharsis regardless of its effects on the recipient. Communication is closed and one-way. Messages are oblique and confusing. In general, communication is infrequent and indirect. The provider makes hurtful statements in the guise of friendship—for example, "You need to know this for your own good." The provider is self-protective and secretive about his or her own characteristics, not wanting to reveal information that may suggest weaknesses and lack of dependability. The provider discriminates unfairly in evaluating and providing information to recipients, demonstrating personal biases that are unrelated to the needs of the task or organization. The provider provides the recipient with little attention and may deliberately or unwittingly prevent learning.

Characteristics of all types of relationships (whether based on control, reward, or affiliation) are *focus*, *behavior*, and *rationality*. Constructive relationships are typified by the provider's focus on the recipient. The provider is tolerant and supportive. Also, the provider's rationality is "20/20," meaning that the provider is aware of his or her intentions in giving feedback—the effect he or she wants and the recipient's likely reactions. Destructive relationships are typified by the provider's focus on him- or herself. The provider's behavior is intolerant and, in the extreme, abusive. And the provider's rationality is myopic—that is, generally short-sighted and careless as to the short- and long-term effects on the recipient. The provider is likely to attribute the feedback to the welfare of the

27

recipient ("I'm doing this to challenge you!"). Later, I will address ways to stop such destructive feedback and make feedback more constructive.

Case: The Value of Frequent Feedback

Polly Kramer is a director of human resources in her mid-50s. She described her work environment as super-high stress. For the last 3 years, she has worked for this fast-growing high-technology company. There are 40 people in her department, organized into six areas, each with a manager who reports to Polly. She said that feedback is typically precipitated by something that needs to be changed immediately. She meets at the end of every workday with her direct reports to recap the day's events, and then uses feedback to correct any behavior or action that needs to be changed. She feels strongly that the feedback should be immediate, so as "not to lose impact," and not wait until days later or a formal meeting to provide the feedback. This makes performance review and feedback easy to deliver. It's part of their everyday work environment. Her managers expect feedback, and often bring up issues themselves and give advice to each other. They focus on situations, behaviors, and decisions rather than personalities. Of course, personalities enter into how people handle different situations. But all her managers have learned to participate actively in these on-going performance discussions as part of the challenges to meet the needs of the rapidly expanding and changing business.

When Feedback Isn't Available, Self-Regulation Takes Over

Feedback increases performance by explicitly informing people of exactly how they performed. This helps people to compare their performance with their goals. They then are able to evaluate their past performance and the goal-performance differential to determine if future goals need to be altered. However, people often do not have formal feedback in their daily activities, and they need to rely on their own perceptions. They gain implicit feedback by performing the task and actively and continuously noting to themselves how well they are doing. This internal feedback is a substitute for external feedback, and can be reasonably accurate.[20] Self-monitoring is important to self-regulation. People observe their own performance, diagnose how well they are doing, determine how much further they have to go, and then adjust their thoughts about their own ability and goals for the future. In Chapter 3, I will say more about how people take it upon themselves to seek constructive feedback when it is not readily available.

Conclusion

Despite people's reticence about giving and receiving feedback, feedback has many benefits in directing, motivating, and rewarding job behaviors that are important to high performance. It is critical to the goal setting process as a way for people to track their progress and set new goals for further achievement. I described characteristics of effective feedback and ways to avoid destructive feedback. Lastly, I noted that when feedback isn't available, which is often the case, people evaluate their own performance.

This chapter raises the following points:

- People generally do not react positively to feedback. They are naturally apprehensive about being evaluated. Also, people worry about how others will react to feedback.
- Feedback directs, motivates, and rewards behavior. It is the basis for development and career planning. Moreover, it contributes to building effective interpersonal relationships.
- Effective feedback is clear, specific, frequent, and relevant to important job behaviors.
- Feedback is a dynamic process between source and recipient. Also, giving feedback affects both the source and the recipient.
- Constructive feedback attributes poor performance to external causes, such as situational factors beyond the recipient's control, when the external attribution is warranted. That is, it doesn't blame people for negative outcomes that are not their fault. Also, constructive feedback attributes good performance to internal causes, such as the recipient's effort and ability. It recognizes when an individual should be praised for positive outcomes.
- Destructive feedback can be abusive. While the word "abusive" may seem extreme as a description of workplace behavior, it occurs, and can be destructive to employees' careers and self-esteem.
- The nature of an interpersonal relationship determines how feedback is manifest. Constructive feedback in control-dominated relationships empowers the recipient and concentrates on ways the recipient and source can both win. It increases the recipient's sense of independence and self-control. In reward-dominated relationships, it encourages and reinforces a can-do attitude. It increases goal clarity and challenges the recipient to do better or overcome disabilities or barriers on their own. In affiliation/support-dominated relationships, it allows a controlled expression of feelings. It leads to increased mutual trust and confidence.
- When external feedback isn't available, people create their own internal feedback.

The next chapter provides the foundation for a better understanding of feedback. It examines factors that influence how people process information about themselves.

Notes

1. Krasman (2011).
2. This chapter is based on my earlier work, London (1995a).
3. Fedor, Rensvold, and Adams (1992) and Ashford (1986) used questions on these topics to measure employees' reactions to feedback.
4. Cannon and Witherspoon (2005).
5. Zhong, Cao, Huo, Chen, and Lam (2012).
6. Sargeant, Mann, Sinclair, van der Vleuten, and Metsemakers (2008); Sargeant, Mann, van der Vleuten, and Metsemakers (2009).
7. These questions were used by Ashford and Tsui (1991) to assess employees' feedback seeking behavior.
8. These findings come from Kopelman (1986), Meyer (1991), and Napier and Latham (1986).
9. Kayes and Kayes (2011); Latham and Locke (2006); London and Mone (in press).
10. These points are based on extensive and well-established literature that has been reviewed by Ilgen, Fisher, and Taylor (1979), Larson (1984), London (1988), and Nadler (1979).
11. Silverman, Pogson, and Cober (2005).
12. Whitaker, Dahling, and Levy (2007).
13. Aguinis, Gottfredson, and Joo (2012); Bouskila-Yam and Kluger (2011).
14. Aguinis et al. (2012).
15. Larson (1984) reported this.
16. Baron (1988).
17. For research on constructive feedback, see Facteau, Facteau, Schoel, Russell, and Poteet (1998), Leonard and Williams (2001), and Brett and Atwater (2001).
18. Bassman (1992) wrote a compelling book about abuse in the workforce. For early work, see Fleming (1979).
19. Kanter (1977); Jacobson and Margolin (1979).
20. Brink (2002); also Bandura (1986).

3

HOW PEOPLE EVALUATE THEMSELVES

In this chapter, I ask you to consider how you use feedback to shape your self-concept. The gap between self-perceptions and feedback from others should help you determine the need to behave differently. You are most likely to recognize the need for change when both your opinion of yourself and the opinions others have of you are consistent and pinpoint a weakness. However, you may not see the need to change when you disagree with the feedback you receive from others. This is when change may be needed most, but it is also when defense mechanisms, such as denial, come into play.

There is a conflict between the psychodynamics of defensiveness and growth. People who experience failure tend to inflate their self-perceptions as a way to salvage their self-concept.[1] People who experience success (e.g., receive a promotion) tend to agree with their co-workers' assessments of them.[2] That is, they are likely to see their strengths and weaknesses in the same way that others see them. People who perceive themselves more unfavorably than others evaluate them often have inconsistent levels of performance. They are concerned about improving their performance, but they are not likely to attempt hard tasks or set difficult goals.[3]

People who consistently perceive themselves higher or lower in performance than others rate them lack insight into their strengths and weaknesses. They are not likely to benefit from feedback, at least not immediately.[4] Over time, though, feedback can improve the accuracy of their self-image. Eventually, unfavorable feedback will decrease the extent to which one over-evaluates one's self-image.[5] You could say that the feedback wears down the defense mechanism. They realize it is easier emotionally to recognize their weaknesses and possibly do something about them. Until that point is reached, over-raters set goals that are too high for their capabilities. This actually increases their chances of failure and leads to unfavorable results. They may not see the need for training, for instance, until it is too late—until they have lost their job or asked to step down from a volunteer position.

31

People who under-evaluate themselves don't recognize their capabilities, perhaps because of low self-esteem. They tend to set goals that are too low for their capabilities. They won't get a chance to test their abilities and improve their self-concept.

Self-awareness is having an accurate understanding of one's strengths and weaknesses, usually indicated by agreement between evaluations of oneself and evaluations made by others. Self-concept is the view one has of oneself that results from self-awareness. In this chapter, I examine the extent to which people perceive themselves accurately. I look at the agreement between self- and others' perceptions and agreement between self-perceptions and the way people think others see them. I cover the meaning and emergence of self-perceptions by exploring research on the relation between feedback and self-awareness and self-concept. Next, the chapter considers personality characteristics related to how people react to feedback. Finally, I argue why self-assessment is so important to behavior change and personal growth.

Do You Evaluate Yourself Accurately?

A natural tendency is for people to over-estimate the quality of their own performance or the importance of their effort and contribution. Do you think you see yourself as others see you? Do you think you have an accurate view of your strengths and weaknesses? How you see yourself is important to you and the people with whom you interact. Your self-assessment helps you understand your work environments and the demands placed on you. However, if you are like other people, you will see yourself in a way that maintains your self-image. And that image is likely to be, to some degree at least, an over-estimate of your performance and effort. Let me explain.

Consider three types of agreement: (1) agreement between your self-perceptions and your beliefs about how others evaluate your behavior; (2) agreement between your self-perceptions and other's assessments of you; and (3) agreement between your beliefs about others' assessments of you and how others actually see you.[6] The elements of the first type of agreement tend to be highly correlated. That is, people think others see them in the way they see themselves. There is less agreement between actual evaluations by others and self-perceptions—the second type of agreement. The way people believe others see them and the way they actually do see them, the third type, tend to be modestly related. So self-appraisals and evaluations from others are generally not equivalent. As a result, we would not want to use self-appraisals as a substitute for ratings from others. Still, as we will see later, self-perceptions may be valuable for comparison purposes and as a way to diffuse defensive reactions to feedback.

Self-Other Agreement

People are generally lenient when evaluating themselves. So self-perceptions are not likely to be accurate predictors of feedback. People who evaluate themselves higher than others evaluate them (let's call them "over-estimators") are likely to be low performers. Individuals who evaluate themselves lower than others rate them ("under-estimators") tend to be mixed in their performance.[7]

How We Think Others See Us

People tend to think others see them in the same way they see themselves. However, there is less agreement between self-perceptions and the way others actually evaluate them. People form judgments about how others evaluate them by both the feedback they receive and how they see themselves. They filter feedback through their self-concept. This is why people over-estimate the agreement between their self-evaluations and how they think others see them. Not surprisingly, people who are more egocentric tend to think that others see them in the same way they see themselves. But if they believe that those rating them—supervisors, for instance—control valued rewards, such as pay raises, they are more accurate in judging how others see them. This might happen because people realize there will be a clear indication of how another person views them—that is, a pay raise (or not, as the case may be). In other words, people seem less likely to exaggerate in thinking about how others view them when there is going to be a concrete outcome resulting from the others' opinions.[8] Think about yourself. If you know you are going to receive some type of concrete evidence of how a significant other views you, whether that person is your boss or your intended spouse, does this influence how you see yourself or how you think these significant others see you—that is, before you actually receive some valuable outcome, whether it be a pay raise or a response to a proposal?

Some people have very strong self-perceptions that are carried over to a belief that others perceive them quite clearly and have good insight into their personalities. When asked to guess how others see them, these individuals think about how they see themselves. They evaluate their own performance and suppose that others will evaluate them similarly. Over the course of many interactions, an individual's self-perceptions may actually influence how others see him or her. This is especially likely for people with high self-confidence who convey to others what they think of themselves in a clear and convincing way. As an example, take John, a VP for marketing. He tends to have a favorable, if not inflated, view of his performance. He thinks others see him in the same way. How could

33

they not? As a gregarious individual, he is not above talking about his accomplishments.

When some people are asked to evaluate themselves, they think about how others react to them. Rather than look inward, they look outward. These individuals are likely to develop self-evaluations that agree with others' opinions of them. If they receive signals that they are highly regarded, they are likely to see themselves the same way. However, if they see signs that they are not highly regarded (e.g., they feel they are being ignored or they hear rumors that others think their work is lacking), they may come to doubt their abilities.

For example, consider Mary, the director of the office of finance for a municipal government agency. She is constantly concerned about the opinions of the various managers her office serves. She is delighted when she receives feedback that a report was well received. However, when there are problems—for instance, a report was unclear and led to many questions or a report was not completed on time—she tends to blame herself. While her profession demands close attention to detail, her colleagues feel that she is highly self-critical.

So there is likely to be a dynamic interaction between self-perceptions and others' opinions. Self-views can rub off on others just as others' evaluations can affect how people see themselves. Agreement between self- and others' opinions may therefore start out low but increase over time.

People tend to agree when it comes to evaluating another person. They see differences between others—that is, they can agree among themselves about others' behaviors. They observe the same behavior, consider the same available information, and come to the same conclusions. But people are less adept at recognizing how others see them. After all, they have a vested interest in their self-concept and in hoping that people evaluate them favorably. When they get feedback, they initially explain it in a way that agrees with their self-image. If the feedback persists in diverging from their self-image, their self-image may bend in the direction of the feedback or will provoke more intense defensiveness. This will happen more rapidly if the person giving the feedback is also making decisions about valued outcomes for the feedback recipient.[9] Has this ever happened to you? Have you changed your views of yourself generally or for a specific skill based on what others have told you or how they react to you?

Feedback that is misleading, incomplete, or not accurate will have dysfunctional consequences. For example, lenient (non-critical) feedback to people who over-estimate their performance will reinforce their positive self-image and maintain their low performance. Ambiguous or incomplete feedback to individuals with low self-image will not improve the view they have of themselves.

Case: Self-Insight from Observing Others

Amy Martindale is a minister in her early 30s. She is a full-time spiritual leader and a part-time graduate student working toward a doctorate in psychotherapy. She often encountered congregants who were not open to anyone's ideas other than their own. She used the phrase, "more about the giver than the receiver." She described receiving negative feedback from one of her congregants after a sermon. She felt the congregant didn't have the ability to understand the subject. In retrospect, she recognized that she has a tendency to push back when she is criticized. She said that, after all, she works hard to prepare and deliver a sermon, and finds listening to negative reactions difficult. She knows, though, that this goes with the territory—it's part of working for and serving a community. She wishes her congregants could learn to realize that their tone, words, and timing all make a difference in how she reacts to their reactions. Of course, she's the one being trained in psychotherapy, not them. So she tries to learn from her congregants and how she reacts to them as well as how they react to her.

Summary

People tend to evaluate themselves leniently in order to affirm or enhance their self-image. People interpret feedback through their self-concept. Still, self-assessments can help people interpret feedback. People tend to think that others see them the way they see themselves; however, people are really not very adept at recognizing how others see them.

Emergence of Self-Awareness

Self-awareness refers to having an accurate view of your strengths and weaknesses. This is important in understanding how people react to feedback. Feedback is supposed to increase your self-awareness. However, self-awareness and your resulting self-concept do not stem just from receiving feedback about your performance from others. Rather, they emerge from your exploration of your own perceptions and experiences. Carl Rogers had the idea that positive change results primarily from reducing the gap between how you see yourself and the way you experience the world.[10] Feedback will help you if you process the information in a deliberate, conscientious way and if the changes suggested by the feedback are consistent with organizational goals and needs. This sense making and change process resulting from feedback needs to be supported by empathetic understanding, positive regard, and genuineness from others—your boss, co-workers, a mentor, an external coach, or family and friends. Feedback is the starting point. Support from others helps you overcome resistance to feedback (rather than feeling threatened), helps you focus on behavior changes that are consistent with organizational objectives, and reinforces your efforts to change.[11]

Relation between Feedback and Self-Awareness

Self-awareness can be measured by a survey measurement technique called 360-degree feedback. This method, used by many businesses, collects performance ratings from peers, subordinates, supervisors, and sometimes customers (I describe this method fully in Chapter 7). Avon Corporation, the beauty products company, conducted a study of job performance self-awareness relationships using 360-degree feedback surveys.[12] Their 360-degree feedback rating form was based on six roles Avon's leaders are expected to play: learner, global partner, developer, strategist, achiever, and change agent. The survey asked raters about 19 sets of behaviors (competencies) and 75 specific practices linked to the six leadership roles. The 360-degree feedback survey was meant to enhance leaders' self-awareness about their fit with Avon's leadership model. The instrument was not used for promotion or compensation decisions. Raters completed it online anonymously. Studying data from a sample of 460 top leaders, Avon found that leaders' self-awareness was not high—that is, their self-perceptions did not agree with others' opinions of them. Most leaders rated themselves lower than their bosses rated them. However, the leaders' peers rated them even lower. The implication was that the leaders tended to think less of themselves as leaders than their bosses thought of them, but their peers were more critical of them. The study also showed that separate performance ratings associated with the company's leadership development were positively related to supervisor ratings on the 360-degree feedback instrument. Leaders who disagreed with their colleagues' ratings were likely to be rated below expectations on leadership development.

The lower ratings from colleagues surprised Avon because the culture in the company was generally affirming. However, apparently raters tended to be honest, not lenient, perhaps because the ratings were anonymous. Also, the tendency in the company was for leaders not to share their feedback with those who rated them. So if feedback is going to be used, it needs to be built into development plans and the leaders need to be held accountable for carrying out these plans.

Personal Qualities That Influence Self-Assessments

Individual characteristics may affect how people evaluate themselves. For instance, people tend to be more accurate in evaluating themselves when they are higher in intelligence, internal locus of control (the feeling that they can control what happens to them), achievement orientation (the desire for advancement and success), introversion, and sensitivity to others' feelings. Interesting, successful leaders tend to be more realistic and less lenient in evaluating themselves.[13] People are less accurate in evaluating themselves because they tend to be lenient, they tend to attribute poor outcomes to external conditions, and they need to impress others.[14]

The way people evaluate others is also associated with characteristics of the perceiver. The more similar the perceiver is to the person evaluated—for instance, in education, race, gender, and socio-economic background—the more accurate the evaluations. Not surprisingly, evaluators who know the person they are evaluating well—for instance, having worked together for several years—are more accurate than evaluators who see the person evaluated only in certain contexts (e.g., committee meetings) and not on a daily basis. As a result, subordinates may be able to evaluate their manager's supervisory behavior better than the manager's boss, who may not be as close to the manager. In addition, there is a higher relationship between self-perceptions and ratings by others in organizations that encourage supportive interpersonal relationships (e.g., evaluate managers on their teambuilding and communication skills) compared to organizations that pay little or no attention to interpersonal relationships and may even promote poor work group dynamics (e.g., through poor communication and inadequate explanation of role relationships).[15]

Readiness to Change

People need to be willing to respond to feedback—that is, ready to change their behavior and/or learn new behaviors. This is especially important in environments that are complex and change often. Your adaptability is likely to depend on your self-awareness—in particular, your beliefs about your own capabilities—your competencies and ability to learn new skills, your confidence about your ability to produce results and to inspire others, your willingness to think through problems, and your openness to learning generally. Some people have a passion for learning. They are intrigued by new knowledge and ideas and they try new activities. They are likely to sign up for online learning, purchase the latest book, and talk to others about new developments in their field.[16] In general, they are the ones to ask others how they are doing and seek advice about what they could do differently.

Mindfulness and Self-Knowledge

When it comes to knowing yourself, you are likely to have some blind spots. We all do. Unfortunately, not seeing ourselves accurately can have negative consequences. We may over-estimate our performance and then are surprised when we are passed over for promotion. Even when the outcomes are not as consequential, we miss opportunities to change our behavior. We fail to hear others' comments or see their reactions to what we do or say. This may contribute to making poor decisions later, thinking that everything is okay and making choices or taking actions that we eventually find are counter to what others hoped we would do. Underestimating our performance can also be detrimental. We may have done well in others' eyes, but having a low image of our performance can cause us unnecessary stress and may make us take actions that preclude opportunities that could have been open to us. For instance, we may turn down an offer to participate in a project, thinking that we are not up to the task.

Fortunately, there is a way we can improve our self-knowledge. This is called "mindfulness"—paying attention to our current experiences without evaluating them.[17] Being mindful without evaluating ourselves has two advantages: it gives us more and higher-quality information about ourselves and it overcomes our natural tendency to protect our ego.

Summary

Self-awareness emerges from an exploration of personal experiences and perceptions. Feedback is a part of this experience. Research has found that performance outcomes are related to self-awareness, measured by self-other agreement. Personal qualities, such as personality characteristics, are related to how people evaluate themselves and others. Next, consider how personality affects how people are likely to react to feedback.

Personality and Reactions to Feedback

Personality is likely to be related to the extent to which a person accepts, values, and uses feedback. Personality refers to controlled temperament or dispositions that influence the pace and mood of a person's actions. Personality is likely to be evident in the distinctive ways that people deal with others that recur in a variety of situations. In other words, people with certain personality characteristics tend to behave in the same, identifiable way almost regardless of the particular situation. So, personality is likely to affect how people react to feedback and their use of the feedback for development. Moreover, personality is likely to be related to job performance because it affects the difficulty of the goals people set and their motivation for achieving them.[18]

Before people use feedback to change their behavior, they need to accept and internalize the feedback. Recipients who are higher in flexibility and the desire to make a good impression are likely to have a positive reaction to feedback compared to recipients who are lower on general well-being.[19] People are more likely to be open to positive feedback than to negative feedback because they naturally want to create and confirm a positive image of themselves. For this reason, they are likely to be threatened by, and likely to reject, negative feedback.[20] However, they may not reject negative feedback if they believe that the long-term benefits outweigh the immediate negative feelings.[21] People who encounter negative feedback are likely to set goals for improvement while people who encounter positive feedback are less likely to set development goals—because they aren't motivated to change. People are more motivated to use feedback for development when they are conscientious, low in anxiety, high in self-efficacy (the belief that they can make positive things happen), and high in internal control (the belief that they bring about things that happen to them as opposed to believing that they are at the mercy of others' actions).[22]

In a study conducted in the U.S. military, officers received a feedback report based on ratings from their unit members. The officers rated their own use of the feedback 6 months after receiving it. Also, the officers completed a battery of personality measures. The study found that officers who were high in agreeableness were rated more highly. Officers who were low in neuroticism were more likely to be rated by a psychologist as motivated to use the feedback. Officers who were high in responsibility rated themselves as feeling obligated (accountable) to use the feedback results. Officers who were high in extraversion were more likely to indicate they sought additional feedback. Officers who were high in responsibility were more likely than others to state they were participating in developmental activities. Those who were high in conscientiousness were more likely to report that they improved as a result of the feedback.[23]

Consider the practical implications of the general finding that personality is related to reactions to, and use of, feedback. Coaches who deliver the feedback and help managers interpret and apply it need to customize how they deliver feedback based on the recipient's characteristics. Feedback providers need to be prepared to deal with recipients' defensive reactions to unfavorable feedback. They should be alert to the tendency many people have to evaluate themselves positively—the reason why self-perceptions are not highly related to ratings by others. In companies and other organizational settings such as the military, understanding managers' personality profiles may help their bosses and coaches to recognize who is most likely to be receptive to feedback. Managers who are low in conscientiousness, emotional stability, openness to experience, agreeableness, and/or extraversion may need more time and attention in helping them use feedback than managers who are high in these personality variables. Those who are low in these characteristics are likely to be defensive. Their supervisors and coaches can talk to them about the benefits of using feedback to set development goals and seek additional feedback on whether they have changed their behavior and improved their performance. Coaches can benefit from having training in psychology that will allow them to understand the relevance of personality and assess personality characteristics. Without experienced and knowledgeable coaches, feedback may be misinterpreted or fall on deaf ears.

Motivation to Learn

Learning goal orientation, an aspect of personality or personal disposition, refers to what the recipient of feedback hopes to gain and learn from the feedback. As a result, it is important as a predictor of reactions to feedback. Goal orientation consists of three components: (1) attain mastery—the desire to acquire new skills and knowledge and to improve one's competence, (2) prove—the desire to demonstrate your competence and to be perceived favorably by others, and (3) avoid—the motivation to prevent others from forming unfavorable impressions about your ability and competence.[24] A mastery goal orientation (which can also be called a learning goal orientation) tends to be positively related to feedback seeking, while a prove or avoid goal orientation tends to be negatively related to feedback seeking.[25] That is, people with a goal to learn and improve continuously for the sake of skill and knowledge development are likely to be favorably disposed to feedback and, indeed, will seek it out. However, those who want to avoid negative impressions or who want to demonstrate their competence to others will not be pleased about receiving feedback, especially if is unfavorable in some way. People who are high in prove goal orientation feel more positive emotions after receiving positive feedback from others and fewer positive emotions after receiving negative feedback from others.[26]

Self-Concept Moderates Reactions to Feedback

Negative feedback can start distracting emotional processes, such as frustration and anger, and distracting cognitive processes, such as rumination, thereby voiding the potential positive effects of negative feedback.[27] However, for some individuals, negative feedback can increase motivation to do well. This is especially the case for people whose self-described concept of intelligence is low but in reality they know they have intellectual ability.[28] These individuals can learn from negative feedback without a backdrop of having to defend their poor performance. People who would say that their level of intelligence is high would be likely to be damaged by negative feedback.

Summary

Personality is likely to affect how people react to feedback. For instance, conscientious, high-self-efficacy people are more motivated to use feedback. This will be useful information for coaches and supervisors who help people use feedback. One important characteristic influencing use of feedback is learning goal. People with a mastery goal welcome feedback to help guide their continuous development, while people with a prove drive want to be perceived favorably by others and people with an avoid drive don't want to call others' attention to their weaknesses for fear they will form unfavorable impressions.

Why Ask Employees to Evaluate Themselves?

Given the problems with self-assessments, why ask people to evaluate themselves? Self-assessment is valuable for several reasons: It recognizes that people find their own feedback regardless of whether others give it to them. They regulate their behavior and performance and track the extent to which they are achieving their goals. In increasingly turbulent organization environments, people need to sort out others' preferences and evaluative criteria. In addition, self-assessment helps reduce ambiguity in the environment (e.g., about performance expectations and one's capability to meet these expectations). People form perceptions of themselves based on direct or indirect feedback from others, objective performance standards or explicit performance expectations, and observations of how others behave and are evaluated. Thus, feedback provides comparative information to calibrate one's own behavior and feelings.[29]

Enhancing Self-Assessment Accuracy

Self-assessments are more likely to be accurate when they are based on objective, easily measured performance dimensions (e.g., number of units produced or communications ability) than on subjective and ambiguous dimensions (e.g., one's organization sensitivity). Also, as I emphasized earlier, self-perceptions are likely to be higher than evaluations from others.

There are a number of good reasons for encouraging accurate self-perceptions. Accurate self-assessment can increase the match between self- and others' assessment, making it easier for employees to understand and use feedback. Accurate self-assessments allow employees to see the extent to which they are meeting others' (e.g., their supervisor's) expectations or the performance standards. Accurate assessments can help set a realistic level of aspiration for future achievements. Employees can develop accurate beliefs about their ability to achieve more difficult goals, which in turn can increase their motivation, desire to devote energy to the task, and willingness to persist in goal accomplishment. However, these outcomes will not occur if employees fail to assess their progress on relevant behaviors or if they focus on irrelevant behaviors.[30]

These possible outcomes suggest several challenges to accurate self-assessment. Employees must gather information while dealing with randomness, conflicting cues, and ambiguity. They must obtain information while protecting their self-image as an autonomous and self-assured person.

Importance of information quality. People easily distort feedback. They tend to over-estimate their abilities and performance. Also, they are quick to recognize any flaws in the reliability or validity of information about their performance, particularly if the information is unfavorable. However, feedback is hard to deny or ignore when it is objective and easily measured and understood. You will think less of another's personal judgments than detailed descriptions of specific behavioral incidents.

Anticipated reactions to feedback. People decide whether to seek feedback, and they may have a choice of sources, including the possibility of asking several people, "How am I doing?" Individuals' feelings about their own likely reactions to feedback may guide these decisions. For instance, they may anticipate that unfavorable feedback will make them feel bad, and so they hesitate to seek the feedback unless they are relatively certain it will not be negative. When feedback is inconsistent, people's fear of negative information may outweigh their satisfaction with the positive information. However, when re-evaluating their self-assessment, the ambiguity in the inconsistent feedback provides justification for self-enhancement. The inconsistency gives them reason to focus on just the favorable feedback and deny or avoid the unfavorable feedback. So, receiving consistent information, or at least information that suggests agreement among evaluators, is important to avoiding biases that may affect reactions to the feedback and later revision of self-image.

Reactions depend on favorability of feedback and agreement. People protect their egos by selectively attending to and/or interpreting information in a way that allows them to maintain a positive self-image. The extent to which self-protection is necessary will depend on the agreement between self- and others' evaluations. Consider several possibilities:[31] One possibility is that both self- and others' evaluations are positive. This leads to favorable feelings and self-affirmation. Another possibility is that both self- and others' assessments are negative. While self-affirming, this may lead to discouragement, procrastination, or lack of action. A third possibility is that self-assessment is positive and others' assessment is negative. This is not unusual. Maintaining a favorable self-assessment in this case constitutes self-delusion unless the person receiving the feedback has a good justification for denying the data or attributing the unfavorable feedback to a cause other than him- or herself. If the unfavorable evaluation is justified and ignored, the dysfunctional behavior is likely to continue to the individual's detriment. Yet another possibility is that self-assessment is negative and others' assessment is positive. This is less common, of course, but when it does occur, it can be highly dysfunctional. Individuals in this situation are likely to set lower standards for themselves than they are capable of achieving, and they don't try as hard as they should.

Ways to improve self-other agreement. Changing an individual's self-image is not easy, particularly if the individual has been conditioned to think of him or herself in negative terms. An effort should be made to ensure that formal evaluations that occur annually or semi-annually are used as a basis for making important personnel decisions (e.g., pay raises and job assignments). This puts teeth into the performance feedback, making the evaluations salient and meaningful to the raters and recipients. However, feedback givers should consider that increased salience may increase the recipient's defensiveness and does not automatically lead to more accuracy in self-perceptions. Annual or semi-annual performance reviews are not a substitute for frequent, specific, and behaviorally oriented feedback throughout the year. This feedback, coupled with feedback from the formal reviews, will help to increase accuracy in self-perceptions.

Summary

Self-assessments are more likely to be accurate when they are based on easily measurable, objective criteria, not surprisingly. When self-perceptions agree with evaluations from others, people are more likely to accept the feedback. However, they may not learn from the feedback and change their behavior as a result. Favorable ratings suggest no change is needed. Unfavorable ratings may merely affirm the receiver's low self-perception. So the receiver may not take action to change behavior even though such action is called for. People who underestimate their performance in the eyes of others may adjust their self-perceptions upward but not change their behavior. People who over-estimate their performance (a frequent situation) may have trouble facing facts and may look for ways to deny or rationalize the negative, or lower than expected, feedback. Specific and frequent feedback is likely to increase the agreement between the feedback and self-perceptions and increase the likelihood that the feedback recipient will take action to change his or her behavior and improve his or her performance. However and unfortunately, feedback is likely to be infrequent and subjective, and therefore easily ignored or rationalized as inaccurate and not to be trusted.

Conclusion

Your self-concept stems from your perceptions and interpretations of your experience. Your self-concept may change through experiences that challenge your view of yourself and increase self-awareness. Self-other agreement on performance measures are part of that experience and influence self-awareness. Understanding self-other agreement and its contribution to self-awareness is likely to influence how you react to feedback. Personality factors, such as conscientiousness and mastery goals, may also influence your reactions to feedback. Here are the take-aways from this chapter:

• People are lenient when it comes to evaluating themselves. However, self-ratings are a reflection of self-concept, and may be related to leadership and managerial behavior, which in turn is likely to affect performance.

• Agreement between our self-perceptions and others' perceptions of us is important because we are more likely to change our behavior when we accept others' evaluations of our weaknesses. Our self-perceptions tend to agree substantially with the way we believe others see us. However, agreement between our self-perceptions and the way we are actually viewed by others is much lower. Nevertheless, self-perceptions can change with direct feedback.

• Our personality affects how we react to feedback. People are more motivated to use feedback for development when they are conscientious, low in anxiety, high in self-efficacy, and high in internal control.

• People are more likely to be open to positive feedback than to negative feedback because they naturally want to create and confirm a positive image of themselves. Conversely, people are likely to be threatened by, and likely to reject, negative feedback unless they believe they can benefit from it.

• People who are low in conscientiousness, emotional stability, openness to experience, agreeableness, and/or extraversion may need more time and attention in helping them use feedback than managers who are high in these personality variables. Those who are low in these characteristics are likely to be defensive.

• People who give feedback to others should consider how the recipient is likely to react to the feedback. This might be hard to do without a report about the recipient's personality. Still, over time, feedback providers (supervisors, friends, etc.) get to know the people to whom they are giving feedback. For instance, they have a sense of who is likely to be defensive and who is prepared to deal with unfavorable feedback. Feedback providers should be alert to the tendency many people have to rate themselves positively.

- A mastery or learning goal orientation refers to the desire to acquire new skills and knowledge and to improve one's competence and a readiness to receive feedback.
- The more self-perceptions agree with ratings from others, the more individuals are likely to see the feedback as valid.
- Self-other agreement may be enhanced simply by providing feedback more frequently and basing feedback on objective, measurable criteria.

In this chapter, I focused on how people react to feedback and how people who are giving feedback can understand feedback recipient's likely reactions to feedback. In the next chapter, I probe more deeply into the factors that influence how people evaluate others and can learn to give more constructive feedback.

Notes

1. McCall and Lombardo (1983).
2. McCauley and Lombardo (1990).
3. Bandura (1982).
4. Ashford (1989).
5. Atwater, Rousch, and Fischthal (1995).
6. Ashford (1989) conceptualized these types of agreement.
7. These conclusions come from research by Harris and Schaubroeck (1988), Atwater et al. (1995), Yammarino and Atwater (1997), Atwater, Ostroff, Yammarino, and Fleenor (1998), and Halverson, Tonidandel, Barlow, and Dipboye (2002).
8. These findings stem from work by Shrauger and Shoeneman (1979), Fenigstein and Abrams (1993), and Kenny and DePaulo (1993).
9. This was found by Fenigstein and Abrams (1993).
10. Rogers (1980).
11. Goodstone and Diamante (1998).
12. This study was reported by Cohen, Bianco, Cairo, and Geczy (2002).
13. Bass and Yammarino (1991).
14. These findings were reported by Mabe and West (1982) and Rousch and Atwater (1992).
15. These results are from Yammarino and Dubinsky (1992).
16. Lombardo and Eichinger (2000).
17. Carlson (2013).
18. Smither, London, and Richmond (2002).
19. Ryan, Brutus, Greguras, and Hakel (2000).
20. Kluger and DeNisi (1996).
21. Korsgaard, Meglino, and Lester (1997).
22. Colquitt, LePine, and Noe (2000).
23. Smither et al. (2002).
24. For research on learning goal orientation, see Elliot and Harackiewicz (1996), VandeWalle (1997), and VandeWalle, Brown, Cron, and Slocum (1999).
25. VandeWalle and Cummings (1997).

26. Botwood (2002).
27. Gerstenberg et al. (2013).
28. Gerstenberg et al. (2013).
29. Ashford (1989, p. 135); Wofford (1994).
30. These points and the challenges to follow were made by Ashford (1989).
31. These possibilities were identified by Ashford (1989).

4

UNDERSTANDING GIVING, SEEKING, AND USING FEEDBACK

There are many sources of feedback. At work, a source can be an impersonal monthly sales report picked off an in-house computer system. This would be an objective source of performance. But let's focus on feedback from people—one's boss, subordinates, peers, other employees, customers, or suppliers. This feedback may be direct—for example, a boss sitting down with you for an annual performance appraisal, or a co-worker commenting on a presentation you just gave. The feedback may be formal and evaluative, summarizing how you performed during the year, or informal and formative (i.e., developmental), giving ideas for improvement.

Sometimes feedback comes without asking. It might come in the form of the annual performance appraisal review or a feedback survey report. Other times, you may ask for the feedback. However, most people shy away from seeking feedback. When they do ask how they're doing, they may have an ulterior motive—for instance, to get someone to say something nice about them. They may wonder how asking for feedback will affect what the source will think and say. They may wonder whether their asking will highlight behaviors that may otherwise have gone unnoticed. They may ask in a way they hope will make a favorable impression on the source.

This chapter considers the nature of informal feedback, self-regulatory mechanisms that influence how you react to feedback, the extent to which people seek feedback on their own, and how feedback seekers try to manage the impressions other people have of them.

Case: Seeking Feedback

Gina Williams is a young entrepreneur. With an undergraduate degree in electrical engineering and a master's degree in software design, Gina, who is in her mid-20s, has already started two successful high-tech businesses. She started the first with several fellow students when they were sophomores. They sold it when they graduated, and Gina quickly re-invested her windfall in a new business, which she worked on while she was in graduate school. Gina develops products using a technique she learned when she was a freshman—lean start-up. Gina's products have been apps for smart phones. When she has an idea, she develops a prototype. She can envision different ways the app might be developed and used—all the services it can produce, the neat displays it might have, and the ease of access for end users. However, using lean start-up, she doesn't wait to have the full-fledged product ready. Instead, she develops a simple prototype and asks friends to try it. She puts an early version online and sends the prototype to a list of people she has been developing who like to fool around with new technologies. As these early adopters try her apps, she collects information on how they use them. She sends them brief online surveys to ask their opinions. Collecting this information over time has changed Gina's conception of her products. The apps are in a continued state of refinement, and the later "finished" products are always quite different from how Gina conceived of them when she started.

Informal Feedback

It goes without saying that employees should treat each other with respect while carrying out their roles on the work team. This ". . . can succeed only if colleagues are willing to have frank discussions to work through inevitable disagreements and misunderstandings. . . . In many companies, managers are afraid to offer frank feedback. As a result, problems are swept under the rug, tensions simmer, and talks that should have happened in the moment are delayed for months, until a performance review."[1]

Informal feedback about a person's job performance comes from numerous sources—supervisors, peers, subordinates, customers, and suppliers. Informal feedback in other areas of life also comes from numerous sources, and probably more often than you receive feedback on the job. If you are married or have a significant other, you probably receive feedback from him or her on a daily basis, and no doubt you give it too. If you have children, feedback giving and receiving is probably continuous. In other settings, like religious or community groups, feedback may be less direct if it comes at all. Societal norms prevent people from making unflattering comments directly to your face, and people are more inclined to talk behind your back, gossip that might come back to you from others. This feedback is likely to be hurtful and not informative about behaviors you could change. People are often reluctant to give positive feedback, thanking others in public for their good work, except in formal occasions when it is expected. This may be because people don't want to embarrass others or are afraid they will insult others by making positive comments about one person and leaving others out, no matter how unintentional this might be.

Actually, feedback in one form or another is just about continuous in that we observe and react to others as they interact with us. This is especially the case if you are in an environment where there are people with whom to discuss performance issues or at least observe reactions to one's behavior and performance. If you are not in that kind of environment, or if you are not interacting closely and in person with others, you are not likely to get a sense of how others feel about your behavior and abilities. People who spend considerable time working alone (e.g., telecommuters) may need to make special efforts to seek meaningful feedback. Similarly, their supervisors may need to make special efforts to keep open lines of communication about performance.

Informal feedback, which occurs in the moment following a problem behavior or a negative performance outcome, is likely to be more important than the once-a-year or semiannual performance review meeting in terms of improving work performance and attitudes.[2] As such, organizations should pay more attention to informal feedback when they design and implement performance management programs. Human resource departments tend to focus on the formal appraisal process (e.g., the appraisal form, guidelines for a feedback meeting) rather than day-to-day feedback. Managers need to learn the importance of being fair and accurate, and that not doing so is likely to diminish the value of the feedback by making employees angry and defensive. Also, managers need to be sensitive to employees' characteristics that are likely to affect their reactions to feedback. Employees will respond feedback differently—for instance, depending on their ability to see themselves as the manager sees them, their self-confidence in being able to learn and improve, the amount of support and coaching they need over time, and their concern about how the feedback will look to others if they find out what the manager said (which recognizes the importance of not giving negative feedback publicly). Managers need to be emotionally intelligent to understand not only themselves but also how others react to them.[3] In addition to training managers to give informal feedback, human resource departments should pay attention to training employees to receive feedback in a nondefensive way—to see feedback as valuable and to talk about ways to do better.

Managers are likely to give feedback informally to employees about particular behaviors or performance when several conditions occur:[4]

- The behavior is important to the manager—for instance, the manager sees the behavior as critical for the individual's or the team's performance.

- The level of performance is below standard.
- The low level of performance is unusual for the employee, who generally performs well.
- The manager views the employee as personally responsible for the performance outcome.
- The manager recognizes that part of his or her job as a manager is to give feedback, and this is expected in the organization.
- The manager likes the employee.
- The manager believes the employee will respond well to the feedback—will see it as constructive and will want to talk about ways to improve.

One-on-One Feedback

In one-on-one situations, people convey information about each other to each other. In the process, they express and fulfill their needs and expectations.[5] We learn from others when they make direct statements (e.g., "I don't understand what you mean" or "You need to work on that"), ask questions (e.g., "Why were you so rough on him?" or "Why didn't you let her get a word in edgewise?"), and react to you (e.g., look puzzled, surprised, or confused). Such feedback occurs spontaneously in any interaction.

We pay attention to how others act toward us and the casual, unsolicited feedback remarks they make.[6] Other cues are more indirect. For instance, we observe how quickly they return our phone calls, how often they come to us for advice, and how long we are kept waiting when we have an appointment. The danger is that we misunderstand or draw erroneous conclusions. This depends on our insight into interpersonal relationships in general, and the closeness of the specific relationship.

Insight into interpersonal relationships requires understanding the expectations we have for each other. People expect to hear about task achievement and competence from their co-workers, while they expect to hear about personal feelings and social relationships from their friends, some of whom may also be work associates. Over time as a relationship develops, people disclose more about themselves to others and they feel increasingly comfortable giving feedback. This is probably more likely to happen with peers than with supervisors or subordinates. The relationship becomes closer and more direct as people deal with problems and dilemmas. Self-disclosure, exploration, testing, and negotiation deepen over time. A well-developed relationship is characterized by spontaneity of exchange, efficient communication, and mutual investment.[7]

Mutual exchange relationships occur when both parties give and receive something of value. The development of interpersonal relationships depends on the expectation that continued interaction and commitment will be more rewarding than weakening or discontinuing the relationship.[8] Relationships between two people evolve as they develop expectations about whatever it is they are working on together, what the outcomes of the joint endeavor should be, and how they should work with each other. Social exchange is based on implicit obligations and trust. The value of the exchange may depend on the identities and status of the two parties relative to each other. Such a social exchange occurs between a supervisor and subordinate, as when a supervisor provides a subordinate with choice assignments or opportunities for career development. It occurs between spouses when each party offers to give and take, even if it's simple: "You do the dishes, and I'll drive the kids to school."

Developing the social exchange relationship requires knowing something about the other party in the relationship—what the other party needs and values and can benefit from and enjoy. So for instance, individuals may value information, influence, favors, or just friendship. Each party has expectations about how he or she can benefit and what can or must be rendered in return. However, these expectations and the timing of their delivery may not be specified. Neither party may know the extent of the other's expectations and whether they have been fulfilled unless they provide each other with feedback.

Interpersonal feedback can be an important part of mutual exchange and development of a close relationship. Close acquaintances and friends establish ways of providing each other feedback that give clear information that is accepted and constructive in suggesting ways to change behavior. However, relationships are fragile. Relationships that are not fully developed can easily unravel when explicit unfavorable comments take the recipient off-guard, cause embarrassment, or engender mistrust. Even in close relationships, a tactless comment can be insulting and undermine the relationship. Situational norms also influence appropriate comments. People who have worked together for years may feel comfortable discussing performance issues, but not personal behaviors, such as personal appearance.

Case: The Value of Frequent Feedback

Jack Wilson is an assistant district attorney for a large city. He is in his later 20s and was admitted to the bar just a year ago. He is one of several hundred attorneys in the district attorney's office. Jack describes his position as high-stress. He receives informal feedback weekly. His supervisor reviews his cases, examining their progress, including the strategies and decisions Jack made prosecuting cases. Jack finds these reviews to be constructive. He respects his supervisor, an experienced attorney, who has keen insights into tough cases,

The feedback is less evaluative than it is pointing out ways Jack can improve or simply giving him alternative ideas for handling prosecutions. Having frequent feedback like this is critical because Jack can do something about the cases at hand. If his supervisor waited for a formal review, there would be little Jack could do to improve. This was much better than Jack's first position with the department. He received little to no feedback from his supervisor and he was miserable. He felt he was inexperienced and out there on his own to sink or swim. This was learning the hard way. His current supervisor is open to talking about performance. Even when he loses a case, his supervisor helps him figure out what he can learn from the experience.

Summary

Informal feedback invokes a host of interpersonal dynamics that influence how you react to feedback. People develop expectations about each other. These expectations influence how honest and direct people are with each other and how much they are likely to learn about themselves. Social dynamics influence what people say and how they say it. As a result, people's reactions to feedback can be controlled or self-regulated. Next, I want you to consider the self-regulatory mechanisms that influence feedback interactions.

Mechanisms for Self-Regulation

Think about how you adjust your behavior in relation to how you perceive what's going on in your environment. Some people are more sensitive to others' behavior and feelings. Some are internally focused and try to elicit reactions from others that confirm their self-opinion. Others try to protect themselves against unfavorable information about themselves even at the expense of never learning about their strengths. Still others try to create situations that verify a negative self-image and prevent them from being successful.

Conscientiousness

People who are conscientious are likely to seek feedback to regulate their behavior. Conscientious people are organized, efficient, goal-oriented, and persistent. Also, they are likely to be better performers than those who are low in conscientiousness. People who are high in conscientiousness are likely to take on difficult, unattractive, but necessary tasks. Moreover, they are highly motivated and think constructively about what they can accomplish.[9]

Self-Monitoring

Some people are more sensitive to feedback and willing to respond to it constructively than others. These people are called *self-monitors*. Self-monitors are attuned to what the external environment requires and expects of them. They vary their behavior to meet the needs of the situation. Low self-monitors are influenced primarily by their attitudes, values, and related personality traits. They do not modify their behavior to adapt to changing situations or circumstances. High self-monitors are responsive to group norms, roles, and other features of the social situation, and as such, they display a variety of behaviors depending on the situation. They constantly compare and adjust their behavior to an external standard (the expectations or reactions of other people) or internal standard (one's own concerns and values). As such, high self-monitors are alert to feedback, attuned to the source's motivation and expertise in providing the feedback, and ready to change their behavior when the feedback is valid.[10] Are you high in self-monitoring? If you are, you would respond affirmatively to the following statements. These are from a survey that is used to measure self-monitoring.[11]

- I can make impromptu speeches even on topics about which I have almost no information.
- I guess I put on a show to impress or entertain others.
- In different situations and with different people, I often act like very different persons.
- I may deceive people by being friendly when I really dislike them.

Maybe you are low in self-monitoring. If so, you would probably respond positively to the following:

- I find it hard to imitate the behavior of other people.
- In a group of people I am rarely the center of attention.
- I am particularly good at making other people like me.

Self-Esteem

Another individual characteristic, separate from self-monitoring, is *self-esteem*—how positive one feels about oneself. High self-esteem enhances a person's adaptability and resilience in the face of barriers. Low self-esteem makes an individual vulnerable—that is, emotionally reactive, sensitive, and intolerant of barriers.

Do you wonder about your own self-esteem? People high in self-esteem respond positively to the following statements:

- I feel that I'm a person of worth, at least on an equal basis with others.
- I feel that I have a number of good qualities.

- I am able to do things as well as most other people.
- I take a positive attitude toward myself.
- On the whole, I am satisfied with myself.

People low in self-esteem respond positively to the following:

- All in all, I am inclined to feel that I am a failure.
- I feel I do not have much to be proud of.
- I wish I could have more respect for myself.
- I certainly feel useless at times.
- At times I think I am no good at all.

High self-esteem should moderate the high self-monitors' reactions to feedback. That is, high self-monitors who are high in self-esteem are likely to respond to feedback most constructively. Positive feedback bolsters their self-esteem, and critical feedback motivates them to change their behavior to match expectations (or at least try to do so). So if you are high in self-monitoring and self-esteem, you are likely to welcome feedback and use it to think about ways to change your behavior and improve your performance.

On the other hand, high self-monitors with low self-esteem are likely to be threatened by critical feedback and hence engage in self-protective, defensive mechanisms that limit the likelihood that they will obtain such feedback in the future (e.g., they don't seek feedback). Also, they tend to discount or ignore positive feedback. So they are unlikely to benefit from feedback and may suffer from fear of it.

Low self-monitors, regardless of self-esteem, are likely to be impervious to feedback (whether negative or positive, constructive or destructive).[12]

Self-Affirmation

People seek self-affirming information as a way to maintain the image they have of themselves. This may be initiated by an event that threatens the image in some way—for instance, receiving negative feedback in an area the individual believed was a strong point. Self-affirmation is a rationalization and self-justification process that happens through continuous interpretation of one's experiences until the self-image is restored. People with high self-esteem have more ways to maintain or restore their self-image than people with low self-esteem.[13]

Self-Protection Mechanisms

Self-protection mechanisms are ways people affirm their self-image. For instance, they may implicitly ask for distorted information, as when they ask for feedback in a way that prompts a positive response—for instance, asking, "Did I do okay?" That is, they ask in a way that compels others to say good things about them. People who use self-protection mechanisms receive less accurate information about themselves and, as a result, have less understanding of their abilities. Consider four types of self-protection mechanisms: *denial*, *giving up*, *self-promotion*, and *fear of failure*. Table 4.1 describes how these mechanisms are manifest in behavior.[14]

Table 4.1 Self-Protection Mechanisms

Denial

- Reacts negatively to feedback
- Blames others for failure
- Never admits mistakes
- Inhibits others' performance
- Rarely asks for feedback
- Does not give credit where it is due
- Has inflated perceptions of his or her own performance

Giving Up

- Abandons difficult tasks
- Avoids being compared with better performers
- Tunes out others who perform better
- Would leave a job because co-workers perform better
- Negative feedback lowers performance
- Dislikes better performers
- Does not try hard enough on difficult tasks
- Gives up easily

Self-promotion

- Makes sure others know about successes
- Asks for praise
- Concerned about status symbols
- Talks about own good performance
- Makes others feel compelled to say good things about his or her performance
- Admits one's own contribution to a group's success

Fear of Failure

- Points out own strengths when criticized
- Afraid of failure
- Gets upset by own poor performance

(Continued)

Table 4.1 (Continued)

- Tries to prevent others from doing well
- Tries to convince others they are wrong
- Tries to raise others' opinions of self
- Downplays own weaknesses
- Concerned about making the "right" career moves

Self-Handicapping

Self-handicapping strategies are another way people protect their self-image. People rationalize events in ways that are flattering to them. This allows them to increase their pride when they succeed and avoid shame when they fail. Self-handicapping ensures they will be able to interpret the outcome of their behavior in the most flattering way. For instance, they avoid information about their own abilities. They prefer not to know how they did, so they avoid feedback or avoid situations that will make it clear to themselves and others that they were responsible for a particular outcome. People who have low self-esteem are most likely to engage in self-handicapping. These individuals are unsure of themselves and would prefer not to know the truth about their abilities. This is especially likely when they doubt their ability to do something well or they believe the evaluator is likely to be highly critical of their behavior.[15]

Case: Fear of Failure and Desire to Achieve

Gore Teller is a 33-year-old journalist for an online news magazine. The magazine has received considerable attention for breaking some hot stories. However, Gore did not write those stories. He is known in his firm as "fast and furious." He can turn around an assignment more quickly than anyone else. If he worked in a factory, he would be called a rate buster—someone who works harder and faster than anyone else to produce more widgets. Gore's work is competent and reliable. His writing is clear and direct. And indeed he works hard, during many late evenings and weekends. His philosophy is that he may not be the most insightful or articulate journalist, but his success is rooted in his ability to produce sound articles. When he starts a project, he can hardly wait to turn it in. He wants his editors to see that he meets deadlines and has sharp focus on the story. He dreads getting stories with multiple edits in the file, particularly comments from his editors about what they liked or didn't like. When an editor returns an article with comments and suggestions, Gore gets

---

to it right away, responding to each of the comments and making corrections for a quick turnaround. He doesn't like to read his work once it's printed. He doesn't want to see how the editor re-wrote sections or deleted material. Gore relishes the work. But in the changing world of journalism and tight economic climate, he is always afraid that if he doesn't produce, he will lose his job, with editors turning to less expensive freelancers. Gore likes the security of a full-time position with benefits. He knows this is increasingly rare in his business, and he feels that his security is tied to producing. He knows that taking the time to refine his work, even to have others read it before he hands it in, would be valuable. But he doesn't have the patience, or doesn't want to risk his reputation for being fast and on-time.

Summary

Self-regulatory mechanisms influence our openness to feedback and the extent to which we shield ourselves from feedback. Some people are highly sensitive to the way others react to them. You may have strong self-esteem, and so you are open to new ideas about your strengths and weaknesses. Others are highly protective of their self-image. They seek self-affirmation and guard against negative feedback. While self-regulation helps us protect our self-mage, it prevents us from realizing our full potential. Having an accurate self-assessment is likely to help us recognize what we can do well and what we cannot do well, and therefore helps us direct our goals and behavior in ways we can be successful. However, as I pointed out in the last chapter, self-appraisals tend to be lenient. Moreover, some people describe themselves differently depending on the impression they want to create in a given situation. Also, supervisors may be lenient just because they think their subordinates will have a somewhat exaggerated view of themselves. This reciprocity coupled with self-protection may limit the value of feedback. In the next section, I consider the extent to which people actually seek feedback.

Asking for Feedback

As I stated earlier, the extent to which we seek feedback and how we seek it depend on our self-image and the mechanisms we use to maintain our self-image, as well as our purpose. Feedback seeking can be a way to gather accurate information about ourselves. It can also be used as an impression management technique specifically to influence what others think of us. In addition, feedback seeking can be used to protect our egos. When we ask for feedback, we consider the psychological costs and benefits. We consider the source's expertise, accessibility, quality of the relationship with the individual, and ability to affect positive and negative outcomes. People with high need for achievement and self-esteem choose sources high in expertise and relationship quality. Those with high performance expectations choose sources high in reward power. Also, those who need to improve their performance the most are least likely to seek feedback.[16]

Motivation to Seek Feedback

The motivation to seek feedback is not entirely straightforward. Feedback may be useful for correcting errors and reducing uncertainty, but it may be dysfunctional if it threatens our self-esteem. Low performers who need feedback most may be the most reluctant to seek it.

Many people actively seek feedback. The feedback may be obtained by monitoring the environment or by active inquiry. However, people worry about the effects of asking for feedback. Consider how you would respond to the following statements about the cost of requesting feedback.[17]

- If I asked my supervisor to evaluate my performance, he or she would become more critical of me.
- I would look incompetent if I asked my supervisor for additional information about my performance.
- I get embarrassed asking my supervisor for performance information.
- It takes too much effort to get my supervisor to talk to me about my performance.
- My co-workers don't tell each other how they are doing, even though they may talk about others' performance behind their backs.

Consider how often you directly ask others, "How am I doing?" How often do you talk to your supervisor about your job performance or ask for more performance information than you are given? How often do you ask friends or your significant other for feedback? People worry about the costs of asking for feedback in terms of the effort required, the possibility of losing face, and the amount and type of inferences required.

Acceptance of Feedback

When people receive feedback, they evaluate its accuracy. They make an attribution about whether the feedback applies to them or whether it is due to other factors (e.g., the source's motivation to hurt or praise the recipient, or situational conditions that were beyond the recipient's control). When people accept the feedback and attribute the cause to themselves, they are likely to set meaningful, realistic goals that have the potential of improving their performance.[18]

Several personality variables influence a person's feedback seeking and reactions to feedback. People who are low in self-confidence are likely to be apprehensive about being evaluated—for example, these individuals engage in ego protection mechanisms (discussed earlier in this chapter). They tend to deny or avoid negative feedback and in general try to control the feedback they receive. However, if you are high in self-confidence, you are likely to welcome feedback. You will tend to engage in self-assessment and self-regulation.

Generally, people who are high in self-esteem rate themselves high, especially when the appraisal is done on ambiguous performance dimensions. Those with a self-serving bias take credit for success and attribute blame to external causes. People who are high in internal control make more accurate attributions about their role in causing events and are willing to attribute negative events to themselves and positive events to others when appropriate. Those low in internal control are more likely to rate themselves leniently and protect themselves from criticism. People high in internal control recognize that they can effect positive outcomes; those high in external control believe that they have little control over outcomes.

Overall, people who are courageous enough to seek unfavorable feedback are able to increase the accuracy of their self-understanding. They are likely to accurately recognize how others view their work.[19] People who are high in self-efficacy—the belief that they can bring about positive outcomes in their lives—are relatively free from cognitive distractions, biases, and distortions; they should be better able to clarify role expectations by seeking information. Also, by seeking greater amounts of information, they should achieve greater role clarity and accomplish higher levels of performance. In contrast, individuals who are low in self-efficacy are likely to be distracted by intrusive negative thoughts and subject to negative cognitive biases and uncertainties about their abilities. As a result, they will not seek, and may even avoid, information that could clarify their roles and help them improve their performance.[20] People who are already likely to perform well (those with high self-efficacy) increase their advantage over time by integrating and interpreting information to clarify their role and improve their performance. They self-regulate goal-directed behavior by seeking feedback proactively. This is likely to generate a continuous increase in performance and provide a continuous advantage, thereby further enhancing self-efficacy. People who are low in self-efficacy do not seek information effectively by using both asking and observing.

Case: Nervous about Giving Feedback

Spencer Rascoff, CEO of Zillow, the online real estate web site, admits that he has difficulty giving negative feedback. "I hate delivering bad news, especially about people's performance. It's one of the hardest things for a manager to do. What's helped me get better at it is to focus more on the team. When I say to somebody, 'You're not performing up to the level that we need you to perform,' it's not an indictment of that individual as much as me showing the proper respect to the rest of the team."[21] When asked how feedback discussions typically played out before he became comfortable with these kinds of talks, he said, "I would get incredibly nervous and fall into the trap that most young managers fall into, which is that they are too vague in their feedback and so things are left to interpretation."[22] He learned that specificity and showing how the team depends on the employee moves the focus from the manager delivering the feedback to the performance-related behaviors that need to change.

Case: Giving Helpful Feedback

Deval Steiglist has been a high school art teacher for the last 22 years. In his mid-40s, he is also a portrait artist. Portraits require considerable attention to detail. Also, he knows that his subjects, who are clients, pay him high fees for quality products. They want portraits that are realistic yet flattering. Deval is talented, but painting is a painstaking process. He tries to instill this high standard in his students. He teaches in the same way he learned when he attended a prestigious art institute and then obtained his teaching license. He explains techniques and then gives students ample opportunity to apply them to different modes of visual art. His classes usually end in critiques. This was the nerve-racking part of Deval's own education, when the instructor and the class would review his work, sometimes still in progress. Often Deval would start over, comprehending the suggestions made by his teacher and fellow students and trying new approaches they recommended. This improved his technique greatly over time. It took Deval a good ten years before he felt confident to offer his services as a portrait artist. He recognizes that his students vary in talent. He also knows they are sensitive to criticism. A harsh comment can easily turn off a student who shows some talent. Deval tries to get to know his students, to see how they react to critiques. He has learned to make comments in a constructive way, never to deride a student's ability, or lack thereof, but to comment on the work itself and what the student can do to improve it within the student's capability. This too takes patience. Deval has developed a reputation as a supportive teacher who nurtures talent while instilling a love of art in students who are less talented.

Summary

People can learn a great deal about themselves by asking for feedback. However, this takes courage. As I stated in the previous section, people's self-protection tendencies often prevent them from asking for feedback and, when they receive it, reacting to it positively. People with high self-efficacy are likely to be more open to feedback and willing to seek it on their own. Being in an information-rich environment is important. Moreover, sometimes people need to be encouraged to seek clarifying information by both observing and asking for information. You should be alert to personal tendencies that influence your feedback seeking. Asking for, and receiving, feedback is influenced by how we want others to think of us. This is the topic of the next section.

Impression Management

Impression management refers to ways people try to influence others' perceptions of them. Consider the extent to which you do the following: play up the value of a positive event that you have taken credit for; try to make a positive event that you are responsible for appear greater than it actually is; try to take responsibility for positive events, even when you are not solely responsible; try to let someone know you were responsible for a positive event; try to look good in front of someone—for instance, your supervisor or your spouse.[23]

People try to influence others' impressions of them in a variety of ways. They may try it directly through such assertive behaviors as ingratiation (telling them how great they are), intimidation (letting them know how much influence you have over what happens to them), or self-promotion (telling them how great you are). Or they may act defensively through such behaviors as apologies ("I'm really sorry about that—you can blame me"), restitution ("I'll pay for that"), and disclaimers ("I wasn't involved at all"). Another way to manage others' impressions, or at least try, is associating or disassociating oneself with an event (e.g., "boasting" in a way that links you to a favorable event or disclaiming a link to an unfavorable event).[24]

When people seek feedback, they are often concerned about how asking for feedback affects what others will think. However, research has shown that seeking unfavorable feedback can enhance the source's opinions of you. They feel that you are bold enough to ask, knowing that you had an unfavorable impression, and they see that you care about their opinion and want to improve. However, seeking favorable feedback can decrease the source's opinions, making others think you want them to think highly of you by calling attention to your positive behaviors.[25] Before asking for feedback, you are likely to consider whether it is better to ask for feedback sooner after a favorable event than an unfavorable event, and when the source is in a good mood. You will probably care most about what others think of you when they control rewards—for instance, a supervisor—and when they give feedback publicly—for instance, in a staff meeting.

You are likely to ask for feedback from someone who matters to you—your manager, spouse, or a good friend—especially if you think you will receive a positive response. If you think you will receive negative feedback, you are not likely to ask someone who matters. You may ask someone who observed your behavior but who does not have reward power over you, maybe a co-worker in another department who happened to be present when you gave a presentation. You will also consider how to ask. You may try to ask for feedback in a way that calls attention to favorable aspects of your performance.

People tend to avoid seeking feedback when others are watching. Having an audience increases anxiety and nervousness from being evaluated, especially for people who are "publicly conscious"—that is, sensitive to how others react to them. They are hesitant because they perceive impression-management costs from asking how they are doing. They fear that seeking feedback will be perceived as a sign of insecurity, uncertainty, lack of self-confidence, or incompetence. Obviously, in a work context, employees are concerned about what their bosses think of them because their bosses control pay, promotions, job assignments, and other valued job outcomes. So they try to create a favorable impression by, for example, setting higher public goals and providing excuses and apologies for poor performance. If the organization's norms make feedback a frequent occurrence and it is okay to request feedback, then employees will be more likely to seek feedback.[26]

Be aware of your impression management behavior and the image you project. Size up your audience and the situation (how the people with whom you interact may influence your performance). Recognize the dangers of the strategy you have chosen. Also, realize that impression management is not a substitute for high performance—indeed demonstrating excellence is the surest way to make a good impression. Just be yourself. Don't try to be something you are not because people will see through the facade.[27]

Summary

The extent to which people ask for feedback is influenced by their desire for others to think highly of them. We all want to be liked and respected, and as employees, we want others, especially our supervisors, to evaluate our performance highly. We don't want to call attention to negative aspects of our performance even when we think we can benefit from learning how others see us. When we ask for feedback, we are concerned about how merely asking and thereby causing others to think about our performance may influence the impression they have of us. Many people's self-esteem is too fragile to take the risk. They care too much about what others think (sometimes for good reason—for instance, in the case of the supervisor who controls important outcomes, such as our salary increases and promotional opportunities, not to mention our very jobs). Seeking positive feedback can backfire, causing others to think we are courting favor. However, seeking unfavorable feedback can enhance others' opinions of us.

Conclusion

People's reactions to feedback may depend on the nature of the feedback (constructive or destructive) and the relationship they have with the feedback source. People seek feedback from a variety of informal sources during their everyday interactions at work. Mechanisms for self-regulation, such as the desire to enhance and protect one's self-image, affect a person's receptivity to feedback. In this chapter, a person's individual characteristics affect motivation to seek feedback and the likelihood that feedback will be accepted and used (e.g., a person's self-monitoring tendency). I also made the point that people should understand how they use feedback seeking as an impression management tool. So here are some conclusions:

- Informal feedback comes from numerous sources as we interact with others. We can view feedback within the context of one-on-one relationships, group dynamics, and negotiations.
- Norms guide the social exchange by imposing implicit standards about when and how the receiver of information must repay the source. Interpersonal feedback can be an important part of the mutual exchange and the development of a close relationship.
- People regulate their activities in relation to their perceptions. People vary in their sensitivity to others' behavior and feelings, desire to confirm their self-opinion, need to protect themselves against unfavorable information, and tendency to create situations that verify a negative self-image and prevent them from being successful.

- The way and extent to which people seek feedback depend on their self-image and mechanisms they use to maintain that self-image. Feedback seeking can be used to gather accurate information about oneself and/or as a technique to control what others think of you.
- Impression management techniques include such assertive behaviors as ingratiation, intimidation, or self-promotion and defensive behaviors such as apologies, restitution, and disclaimers. In general, people should be alert to their impression management behavior and the image they project.

Now that we have examined the value of feedback (Chapter 2) and how people evaluate themselves (Chapter 3) and react to feedback (Chapter 4), we turn in the next chapter to how people evaluate others.

Notes

1. Bryant (2014a, p. 4).
2. Farr (1996).
3. Goleman (2001).
4. Farr (1996).
5. I discussed this in London (1995b, Chapter 9).
6. Ashford and Tsui (1991).
7. Gabarro (1990).
8. Organ (1988).
9. We know this from the work of Barrick and Mount (1991) and Stewart, Carson, and Cardy (1996).
10. Reilly, Warech, and Reilly (1993).
11. These self-monitoring statements were developed by Snyder (1974).
12. These findings and the measure of self-esteem come from Fedor, Rensvold, and Adams (1992).
13. Steele, Spencer, and Lynch (1993).
14. The self-protection mechanisms are from my work with Arthur Wohlers: Wohlers and London (1989).
15. Tice and Baumeister (1990).
16. These results were reported by Ashford and Tsui (1991), Karl and Kopf (1993), Morrison and Bies (1991), and Morrison and Vancouver (1993).
17. I adapted these items from Fedor, Rensvold, and Adams (1992).
18. Taylor, Fisher, and Ilgen (1984).
19. Ashford and Tsui (1991); Harris and Schaubroeck (1988); Levy (1991).
20. Brown, Ganesan, and Challagalla (2001).
21. Bryant (2013, p. B2).
22. Bryant (2013, p. B2).
23. Ferris, Judge, Rowland, and Fitzgibbons (1994) suggested these tactics for impressing others.
24. Kumar and Beyerlein (1991).
25. Morrison and Bies (1991).
26. Gardner (1992).
27. Gardner (1992) made these recommendations.

5

THE SOURCE'S PERSPECTIVE

Now that I have discussed how people evaluate themselves as they receive feedback, let's consider how people process information about others as the source of feedback. Feedback is a dynamic process between source and recipient, and giving feedback affects the source as well as the recipient. For instance, supervisors say that they like subordinates to whom they give positive feedback and dislike subordinates to whom they give negative feedback.[1] Also, giving feedback may increase the ease with which supervisors recall specifics about subordinates' behavior. In addition, giving feedback may increase supervisors' feelings of control over subordinates, especially if subordinates actually improve their performance. However, supervisors may perceive they have less control over subordinates if the feedback is followed by declines in performance.

People realize when others prefer to avoid giving negative feedback. People who believe they are performing poorly use feedback seeking strategies that minimize negative performance feedback as a way of maintaining their positive self-esteem.[2] As a consequence, they receive less negative feedback than may be warranted. This makes worse an already poor interpersonal relationship. As the performance problem persists, the potential provider of feedback is likely to see it as more severe and become increasingly angry and resentful toward the potential feedback recipient.[3] When the feedback is public, feedback providers will try to be consistent, making it harder to correct the situation by giving accurate feedback.

In this chapter, I draw upon research in psychology that explains the accuracy of interpersonal perceptions.[4] I consider the cognitive processes of how people encode, store, and decode information prior to giving feedback. Also, I show how rater motivation, observation skills, information distorting biases, and empathy for others influence rater accuracy. I begin by turning to the basic psychological and cognitive processes that underlie evaluations—a field called *person perception*.

The Psychology of Perceiving Others

The social psychological processes of person perception explain how people form impressions of others and use this to provide them with feedback. Person perception refers to the processes by which we form impressions and make inferences about other people in response to the behaviors, words, and interactions we observe between ourselves and others and between other people. This occurs over time and culminates when one person (e.g., a manager) is asked to evaluate another (e.g., a subordinate or peer). The evaluation is likely to be subject to a number of factors that affect the accuracy and usefulness of the judgment for the purpose at hand. Person perception incorporates various levels of analysis, including the perceiver, the person(s) perceived, the relationships between them, and the situation. The perceiver's goals, motivation, and cognitive skills and processes need to be considered. Also, the perceiver is an active participant in the process, interacting with the individual evaluated, thereby inducing behaviors that are then incorporated into the perception and the favorability of the resulting judgment.[5]

Positive feedback produces good feelings. Negative feedback can produce emotional reactions such as anger and frustration, and these in turn have the potential to increase employees' counterproductive behavior, less helping behavior, and the likelihood of leaving the job, or at least thinking about quitting. This is particularly true if negative feedback is delivered in public and/or in an insensitive manner, even if delivered in private.[6] Negative feedback is necessary, of course, to improve task learning and performance. Supervisors can mitigate the negative emotions that result from receiving negative feedback and increase learning by framing the feedback in a positive way—for instance, encouraging the employee to learn from the experience. Also, managers should help employees cope with their emotions that come from hearing negative feedback. Managers can be sure their feedback is clear, explain behaviors that can improve performance, and continue to provide social support and advice. Also, managers should pay attention to where they give the feedback. Giving negative feedback to an employee in public—for instance, during a team meeting—is likely to cause the employee embarrassment and will increase his or her defensiveness and anger, reducing the likelihood that the feedback can be a learning experience.

The way we perceive others may be influenced by expected patterns of behaviors, called scripts or schemas. These are well-learned behavioral sequences that define typical reactions to environmental conditions. The schemas we hold about the way people should behave under certain conditions tell us what information and events to monitor. The initial information we get about a person and the situation suggests relevant schema. This causes us to arrive at conclusions that influence our later perceptions. Cues that distinguish one person from another are especially likely to gain our attention and prompt a schema. We are primed to use some schemas. For instance, people who view themselves as high achieving categorize others on the basis of competence, labeling them "competent" or "incompetent." We may use schemas that fit how we feel at the moment. Mood may affect the type of schemas used, their intensity, and/or the strictness with which they are applied. When we are in a good mood, we are likely to be favorably disposed to others and rate them positively. Conversely, when we are in a bad mood, we are likely to rate others more harshly.

Our cognitions about others are shaped by the previously formed schemas we have about traits, roles, situations, and events. So, for instance, the initial beliefs we have about a person may be shaped by whether the individual is tall and thin versus short and fat, African American versus Asian, or what have you. An event schema forms our expectations about people within that context—for instance, an interview. We "know" how people are supposed to dress and act in an interview. Deviations from expectation draw our attention, while we may not fully internalize perceptions of behaviors and responses to questions that are expected. Schemas are stereotypes that function in our minds as first impressions. They form our expectations and color how we interpret or selectively perceive forthcoming information about the individual. On the one hand, schemas have a valuable function in helping us sort through information and make judgments quickly. On the other hand, they may cause us to ignore valuable information that disconfirms initial impressions.

Schemas, combined with perceptions, lead us to attribute reasons for a person's behavior. We observe and interpret a behavior through the schema. Moreover, in the absence of specific observations, we infer knowledge, traits, dispositions (typical behavioral tendencies), intentions, and membership in one or more social categories, such as "outstanding performer."[7] Our first response in being asked to judge another person or event may be to take obvious features and categorize them according to our schemas. We do this automatically—that is, without much thought. Our motives and goals influence how much control we exert over the inference process.[8] If we see little cost to being inaccurate (e.g., we won't be held accountable for our judgment), we use schemas as shortcuts to make rapid evaluations. If we are motivated to be more precise in our judgments, then we may take more time and go beyond these shortcuts to collect information thoroughly and make judgments we can defend.

There are times and conditions when sometimes we are motivated to seek full information and process it carefully—for instance, when others tell us to take care or when we realize the importance of the judgments. Other times we are motivated to confirm our initial expectations or stereotypes, perhaps because we see no value in working harder to make a better judgment or because we want to confirm our expectations and support our stereotypes. After all, confirming our prior beliefs is reinforcing, and disconfirming them may be upsetting. Also, personal desires may enter into our judgments—for instance, not wanting to recognize that others are better at their jobs than we are. Our mood and emotions may influence our perceptions. For instance, we may be more positively disposed to others when we feel good about ourselves. So we are more likely to let our egos influence our judgment than we are to be dispassionate in evaluating others.[9]

The idea that person perception is embedded within a larger social context means that judgments go beyond the eye of the beholder to include the beholder's interactions with, and influence on, the person evaluated. The perceiver may wittingly or unwittingly affect the target's behaviors, by asking certain questions, making certain statements, or nonverbally provoking reactions that demonstrate what the perceiver wants to see. Game playing and positioning may affect judgments as the target tries to manage the perceiver's impressions.[10] This may be complicated further when people are asked to evaluate each other and set up implicit situations (for instance, tit-for-tat or "you scratch my back and I'll scratch yours") that suggest evaluations may be influenced by what people want and expect from each other, not what they observe.

A word about *stereotypes*: Stereotypes are exaggerated beliefs about a group. We may apply stereotypes as we identify a person as a member of the group. The mind typically activates stereotypes automatically. They are elusive in that they are sometimes hard to identify and even more difficult to influence or change. Also, they seem to pervade organizations and society. Usually, the stereotype deals with likeability or competence, but rarely both.[11] Unfortunately, stereotypes can be used to explain or justify inequalities in organizations. People can hold ambivalent stereotypes that include both negative beliefs and some positive beliefs (e.g., likeable but incompetent or the reverse), allowing people to deny being uniformly bigoted against a particular group while continuing to justify status inequalities. Since stereotypes can affect the actions of both the perceiver who holds the stereotypes and the target about whom the stereotype applies, the stereotype can have the *appearance* of truth and become a self-fulfilling prophesy. So, for instance, by believing a member of a certain group is incompetent and treating the person as such, the individual is less likely to have opportunities to learn and demonstrate competence.

Fortunately, we don't have to put up with stereotypes. Controlling stereotypes is both an individual and organizational responsibility.[12] Personal motivation to avoid stereotyping and organizational interventions can help alleviate their effects. Personal standards can override societal beliefs, and social norms and standards of fairness can undermine stereotypes. Organizations can help overcome stereotypes in performance appraisals, job assignments, and other job-related decisions in several ways. Managers can be held accountable for their judgments and decisions. People will be more deliberate in their evaluations when they know they may be required to justify their decision and when valued outcomes are at stake. Emphasizing the mutual interdependence between feedback provider and receiver can remind the provider that cooperation and fairness are important, thus lessening the possibility that a stereotype will influence the provider's evaluations. Another way to reduce stereotypes is to inform people about how they can stereotype others without even knowing it. Training in the unconscious mechanisms by which stereotypes operate can help people control their thinking and judgments.

In addition to trying to affect individual's thought processes and decisions, work organizations can examine managers' evaluations and decisions about subordinates and daily treatment of subordinates to determine if some groups are disadvantaged relative to others.[13] Employee attitude surveys and subordinate ratings of supervisors can be a source of data to ensure fairness. Consultants can be hired as objective third parties to interview employees about their treatment. Performance ratings and promotion decisions can be examined to ensure fair treatment. Also, managers should be frequently reminded that they are responsible for egalitarianism no matter how much pressure they are under to meet goals. The organization can demonstrate that differences between people are valued and that managers who have good records for hiring and promoting people of diverse backgrounds should be rewarded.

Perhaps people would have an easier time justifying their evaluations if they had a good understanding of how they form opinions about others. In general, people don't have a good idea about how they form impressions of others.[14] For instance, research shows low relationships between the attributes raters say are important in evaluating people and those that are derived from statistical analyses.[15]

As an example, say Margaret, a department supervisor, is asked to rate each of her nine subordinates on five dimensions of performance and then to give each person an overall performance rating. Let's say she has to do this twice a year, and she has done it now for 3 years. That gives us quite a lot of data to analyze. Let's also assume that the subordinates' jobs have remained fairly static over this time period and nothing has happened to change Margaret's mind about what dimensions of performance are most important to overall performance. When asked which dimensions she feels are most important (i.e., have more weight) in making her overall rating, Margaret will be happy to tell us. However, if we then analyze her ratings across the years, statistically predicting the overall rating based on the set of performance dimensions, the dimensions that have higher weights in the prediction equation are not likely to match those she says are important.

When raters, such as Margaret, are given these statistically derived weights, they develop a better understanding of how they evaluate others, and they are able to learn how to form more accurate judgments. Moreover, they are more insightful about the importance they place on specific performance dimensions after they have had time to practice in similar situations with clear feedback about the quality of their judgments.[16] Over time, as raters are given information about their cognitive processes, they can become fairly good at accurately identifying the weights they use and how they go about making decisions about others.

Summary

How we perceive others is heavily influenced by schemas—our prior conceptions and viewpoints that help us interpret our observations. This is a give-and-take process as we interact with other people and try to influence their impressions as they try to influence ours. Stereotypes derived from societal beliefs can be overcome or avoided by holding people accountable for their judgments. Organizations should hold managers accountable for their perceptions and evaluations of their employees, including documentation to support their evaluations. This would be easier, perhaps, if people had a better understanding of how they form their judgments. Of course, in non-work contexts, people are not likely to be held accountable for their judgments about others. (An exception would be a court of law.) Next, I consider how person perception processes affect evaluations.

Cognitive Models of Appraisal

Automatic versus Careful Cognitive Processing

When raters observe behavior, they usually compare it to preconceived impressions (images or schemata). If the performance they observe conforms to their expectations, their observations are automatically categorized and not considered further. This state of mindlessness is characterized by an over-reliance on categories and distinctions from the past. As a result, evaluators are oblivious to novel or alternative aspects of the situation.[17] Their observations fit into an existing cognitive category, and no additional thought is needed to interpret them. However, if their expectations were not met, then they need more careful (deliberate or controlled) cognitive processing to understand the observation. The raters then ask themselves a series of questions: Is there a need for more information? Might the observed outcomes be caused by the situation rather than the individual being evaluated? If yes, could the individual being evaluated have changed the situational conditions to alter the outcomes? The answers will determine whether the evaluators attribute the outcome to the situation or to the individual being evaluated. If the performance discrepancy is attributed to the individual, then the favorability of the observation will affect the favorability of the evaluation. If the observation is attributed to the situation, then the favorability of the observation will not influence the favorability of the evaluation.

People placed in the task of evaluating others are likely to start with the assumption that the behavior they observe is intentional. That is, they are biased against situational explanations. This occurs because the evaluation processes focus attention on the person who is evaluated. If this person is highly experienced, the evaluator is likely to assume that performance outcomes resulted from the person's actions, not particularities of the situation. However, experienced evaluators tend to recognize and take into account situational constraints that may influence performance. They also take into account the reasons the person they are evaluating gives for the performance outcome. Regardless of the reason, however, the more serious the performance outcome, the more evaluators are likely to attribute the outcome to the person evaluated rather than the situation.[18]

Raters' evaluations are influenced by social and situational factors.[19] For example, a supervisor's ratings of a subordinate are likely to be more favorable when the supervisor has more opportunity to observe the subordinate; close observation by the supervisor will motivate the subordinate to work harder. This may occur when the supervisor has fewer subordinates and so has more opportunity to know and work with the subordinate. Supervisors may be inclined to give more favorable ratings if they believe that unfavorable ratings are not worth the trouble because they make subordinates angry and defensive. Supervisors may rate subordinates more favorably when the subordinates convey a positive image of themselves and they seem to pressure their supervisors to provide equally favorable judgments or suffer their ire. Another reason for favorably biased ratings is liking the subordinate. Supervisors may be inclined to favorably evaluate subordinates they like, because not to do so would be incongruent, not to mention interfere with the friendship.

Evaluators' Motivation Can Influence Accuracy of Perceptions

A number of factors may decrease rater accuracy, such as rater biases, motivation (or lack thereof), and insufficient information. Evaluators who want to provide more accurate ratings (perhaps because they want to be able to back up their judgments in case of confrontation with an employee) and are trained in doing so are likely to pay more careful attention to how they observe, encode, recall, and integrate information about the person they are evaluating.[20]

If we know that rater biases and motivation affect evaluations, we can at least make evaluators aware of them and encourage them to seek more detailed and concrete information. Evaluations are not based solely on the evaluator's memory. Evaluations may be based on previously formed impressions instead of memory of recent observations. Therefore, the effects of preconceived impressions may be lessened if raters are requested to recall recently observed behaviors before making their ratings.[21]

Effects of Evaluators' Expertise

Expert evaluators have been trained to avoid biases and have experience making accurate judgments. Hence, expert evaluators are likely to agree with each other and agree with objective performance indicators. However, experts may disagree among themselves if they perceive situational characteristics differently—for instance, one evaluator believes that situational conditions were a major determiner of performance and another evaluator arrives at a different conclusion. Also, the way the expert evaluator recalls information may depend on the evaluator's similarity to the person evaluated. Thus, experts may be subject to biases and differentially influenced by situational conditions. Even trained raters may make the mistake of jumping to a conclusion with little investigation.[22]

Case: Useful Feedback from Co-workers

Mike Williams, 23 years old, is a new high school math teacher; he had been teaching for 1 year. He described feedback he received from an older, more experienced teacher about his meeting with students during his lunch break. She suggested, simply and obviously, that despite his zeal, he should not take his lunch break to meet with students. He should use his lunch breaks, free periods, and days when school is off for rest and contemplation about his teaching. By doing this, he would be able to make it through the day without being worn out or burned out. Another experienced teacher who was assigned to observe him during his first year observed that he was making it too easy for the students, spoon-feeding the material. The experienced teacher suggested that the students needed to learn to work through the problems on their own. This would make his job a bit easier, allow more material to be covered, and strengthen the way the students learned. Mike saw this as very constructive feedback and modified his teaching.

Attribution Biases

A common bias is attributing favorable events to ourselves and unfavorable events to factors beyond our control. Another is believing that other people have the same expectations, beliefs, and attitudes that we do. We tend to blame our poor actions on the environment. However, when other people behave the same way, we tend to attribute the behavior to their dispositions. Generally, we under-estimate the effects of situational conditions on others and over-estimate dispositional factors. A reason may be that we pay attention to our environment when thinking about ourselves and pay attention to others and ignore the environment when evaluating others. Additional attributional errors include assuming mistakenly that we behave the same way regardless of the situation, believing that others face the same situational conditions that we do, and thinking that we have enough information to form an accurate evaluation.[23]

Impression Management

As I described in the last chapter, people are concerned about managing the impressions others have of them. They do this by using such strategies as ingratiation, intimidation, exemplification (i.e., being a model of exemplary behavior and dedication), supplication (supplicants try to have others pity them and help them with their troubles), and face saving. Trying to affect the impressions others have of us is not unreasonable. It is natural to put our best foot forward. After all, we want social approval. Also, impression management tactics can be effective. People who try to manage the impressions others have of them receive higher evaluations. In addition, people are less critical of others who use impression management. People who are good at ingratiating themselves with others tend to be better liked. Unfortunately, being overly ingratiating is likely to make a negative impression on others.[24]

Nonverbal cues are important to the way we learn about others. Such cues include eye contact, facial expression, distance, and gestures. Some cues are inherent in a person's being, such as race and gender, while others cues are transitory and under the individual's control (e.g., gestures, eye contact, and interpersonal distance). People use these cues to manage the impressions others have of them. Also, impression management includes saying things that flatter others or oneself or conform to others' opinions.[25]

People are more likely to engage in impression management when they think it will be beneficial. So, managing a supervisor's impressions is likely to be viewed as important because supervisors control valued outcomes. However, managing subordinates' impressions is likely to be viewed as less important. This may change when subordinates are asked to provide upward ratings of the supervisor. However, if these ratings are solely for developmental purposes (i.e., managers can use them to identify areas for improvement, but the ratings have no direct consequences), then managers may not try to influence the impressions their subordinates have of them. Of course, the managers may feel differently if upward feedback is incorporated into the evaluation process and used to make salary or promotion decisions about the managers.

Summary

A number of factors influence how people make judgments about others. Evaluations are affected by social and situations factors, such as the opportunity to observe and the image people try to convey of themselves. Evaluators' motivation to pay attention, recall behaviors observed, and base their judgments on fact will influence the accuracy of their ratings. Even experienced raters and experts in their fields may be subject to biases. Also, ratings may be affected by the impressions others try to create. In the next section, consider a few more evaluators' characteristics that may influence their evaluations.

Individual Characteristics Affecting Evaluations

Our skills and personality tendencies influence how we perceive other people. This section discusses observation skills, self-monitoring tendencies (our sensitivity to the environment), and empathy as individual difference variables influencing person perception.

Observation Skills

Observation skills include gathering and recording data about another person's behavior without judgment or bias. Some people are better evaluators than others because they are able to monitor and recall cues in various situations. Good evaluators, whether they are evaluating others or themselves, are high in self-awareness, high in cognitive complexity, and socially intelligent.[26] Moreover, they are able to make swift and accurate judgments of other people. Admittedly, this is not the same as acquiring an in-depth understanding of those observed, but it is enough to predict future behaviors.

Self-Monitoring

As I discussed in the last chapter, high self-monitors are those who are sensitive to others' reactions to them. They have an understanding of others' behaviors. For example, high self-monitors are more accurate than low self-monitors in making judgments about others' emotions. Being high in self-monitoring helps people in situations that call for interpersonal sensitivity, such as gender-nontraditional jobs (e.g., men in the nursing field). These employees must perform well, but also must show that they belong in the role. They benefit greatly from the adaptive self-presentation skills of high self-monitoring.[27]

Empathy

Empathy is the ability to understand others' feelings and emotions. People who are high in empathy can take the perspective of others and understand the situations in which they find themselves while remaining at a social distance from those observed.[28] Such individuals are able to distinguish between factors in the environment that influence a person's behavior and aspects of the person's past that influence his or her behavior. Empathy is not just a matter of intelligence. People are likely to be empathetic in understanding the emotions of those they know well.[29]

Case: Avoiding Confrontation

Katherine Settler is the director of student services in a private girls' high school. She has worked in the school for 20 years, as a teacher during the first 15. In her current administrative role, she supervises a staff of seven—four guidance counselors, two registrars, and one clerk. She admits that she does not give her staff much performance feedback. She says she tends to go with the status quo—leave things alone if they are working. She intervenes only when necessary. She mostly gives status reports of what has been done and needs to be done. This is because it is hard to get good people, and trusts the people she has, giving them the freedom to do what they need to do. She says that in truth, she would just as soon avoid any confrontation. She can see ways some of her staff members could improve. When she approaches this at all, which is seldom, she makes minor changes in work flow, such as when the office is open to students, how students make appointments, when course schedules are sent home, and such, rather than addressing any individual's specific performance.

Conclusion

I began this chapter by examining the meaning of person perception and exploring what people know about how they evaluate others. I described some cognitive models to help understand the performance appraisal process in light of possible situational constraints and motivational dynamics that influence rater accuracy. I considered how impression management influences evaluation and self-perception processes. I also considered how individual characteristics, such as observation skills and empathy, influence judgments of others.

Here are the major learning points from the chapter:

- The way we perceive others is influenced by our goals, motivation, and cognitive skills. Also, it is influenced by how we interact with others, eliciting responses and making judgments about those responses, possibly causing situations that confirm our initial beliefs.
- Cognitive schemas (preconceived beliefs or stereotypes) affect how we interpret information about others. Schemas help us sort through information and make judgments quickly, but they may bias our perceptions, causing us to ignore valuable information.
- We can control our own and others' stereotypes. We can be aware of them and how they influence our judgments. Also, organizations can train managers to avoid rating errors and hold them accountable for their judgments.
- We are not good judges of our own evaluation processes.
- Cognitive processes of person perception indicate that when we observe another's performance, we compare it to our expectations. If our expectations are met, we automatically process and categorize the information, and the observation is not considered further. If our expectations are violated, we initiate more controlled and thoughtful processing that may lead to a change in our perspective and evaluation of the individual.
- Our evaluations of others will be more accurate and probably more favorable when we have had more time to observe others.
- Our skills and personality tendencies may influence how we perceive other individuals. However, while appraisals tend to be biased, they can be made more accurate with the right support.
- In asking for, and giving, feedback we intentionally or unintentionally manage the impressions others have of us.
- Our observation skills, self-monitoring tendencies (sensitivity to the environment), and empathy affect how we evaluate others. Observation skills can be learned and improved.

Now that I have set the stage by examining how people form impressions of themselves and others, the next section of the book begins a review of sources of feedback. These are ways people and organizations provide feedback formally and informally, and ways individuals should consider in their search for constructive feedback.

Notes

1. Larson (1984).
2. Larson (1988).
3. Baron (1988).
4. This chapter draws from London (1995b, Chapters 3, 4, and 6), and London (2001, Chapters 1 and 2).
5. Klimoski and Donahue (2001).
6. Belschak and Den Hartog (2009).
7. Nickerson (1999).
8. Klimoski and Donahue (2001).
9. Klimoski and Donahue (2001).
10. Kozlowski, Chao, and Morrison (1998).
11. Fiske, Xu, Cuddy, and Glick (1999).
12. Operario and Fiske (2001).
13. Operario and Fiske (2001).
14. Reilly and Doherty (1989).
15. Nisbett and Wilson (1977).
16. Reilly and Doherty (1992).
17. Langer (1992); Sanders (1993).
18. Murphy and Cleveland (1991).
19. Judge and Ferris (1993).
20. Salvemini, Reilly, and Smither (1993).
21. Woehr and Feldman (1993).
22. Funder (1987); Zalesny and Highhouse (1992).
23. Herriot (1989).
24. Wayne and Kacmar (1991); Dobbins and Russell (1986); Gardner (1991).
25. Gifford (1994).
26. Boice (1983).
27. Anderson (1990); Anderson and Thacker (1985).
28. Stinson and Ickes (1992).
29. Stinson and Ickes (1992).

Section II

SOURCES OF FEEDBACK INFORMATION AND SUPPORT

6

PERFORMANCE APPRAISAL METHODS

Feedback is central to tracking performance—knowing how you are doing, what you need to do to improve, if anything, and how close you are to your goals and meeting performance expectations that others, such as your supervisor, have of you. Formal feedback at work usually comes in the form of the annual performance appraisal. There are other sources of feedback too, more informal and less systematic sources. Feedback can be visible in the tasks we do as we see the pace and quality of our work. It can come from reports, such as monthly sales figures. It also can come from other people—supervisors, subordinates, peers, and customers. This chapter concentrates on the traditional supervisor performance appraisal rating. I describe rating methods and also cover "ratingless" appraisals as a source of feedback. Also, I cover self-assessment as a way to highlight the responsibility you have to track your own performance and use feedback from others for your professional development and performance improvement.

Dimensions of Performance

Think of two types of performance: the tasks you are expected to do and what you do that goes above and beyond your formal job description. Going above and beyond is called "organizational citizenship behavior" or "contextual performance." It includes actions that (1) show your dedication to work, such as suggesting improvements, demonstrating initiative, and taking on extra responsibilities, and demonstrate functional participation; (2) show your dedication to your company, such as staying with the organization during hard times, favorably representing the organization to outsiders, demonstrating loyalty and obedience, and participating in community volunteer initiatives with your co-workers; and (3) show your dedication to others, such as cooperating with others, assisting or helping co-workers learn skills you know well, and courtesy. Task performance consists of activities that you are responsible for doing according to your job description.

A third element of performance that can be construed as separate from task and contextual performance is *adaptive performance* or learning. This is the proficiency with which you change your behavior to meet changing situational demands. Adaptive performance consists of activities that handle emergencies or crisis situations; demonstrate physically orientated adaptability; solve problems creatively; learn work tasks, technologies, and procedures; demonstrate interpersonal adaptability; display cultural adaptability; handle stress; and/or deal effectively with unpredictable or changing work situations. These actions have elements of task performance in that they encompass behaviors geared toward completing a task. They also have elements of interpersonal citizenship.

Handling stress is contextual—that is, it supports the social, organizational, and psychological context of work—but overlaps interpersonal and organizational citizenship and task performance. It includes such behaviors as remaining composed when faced with difficult circumstances or demanding workload (perhaps an element of job-task conscientiousness), not overreacting to unexpected news or situations, managing frustration by directing effort to constructive solutions instead of blaming others (perhaps an element of interpersonal citizenship), demonstrating resilience and professionalism in stressful circumstances, and acting as a calming influence that others look to for guidance.[1]

Elements of contextual performance vary in their importance to overall performance depending on the job. For example, organizational citizenship performance is important in customer service and sales jobs where employees have considerable personal contact with people outside the organization. Therefore supervisors place more importance on representing the organization in a favorable way in this type of job than in others. In support jobs, such as information technology client support, the main function is to help other people get their work done. Here, interpersonal citizenship performance is important.

In summary, performance appraisals may require supervisors to evaluate an employee's performance in contextual, task, and adaptive elements of performance. Jobs vary in the extent to which each of these categories of performance is relevant. If you are a supervisor or manager, you should understand the relative importance of these different job elements to the particular job they are evaluating. This also implies that how you help your team members perform better will depend on the job. For example, task structure may be needed on jobs for which task dimensions are predominant, while social support may be needed on jobs for which contextual or adaptive dimensions are predominant.

This also implies that you should collect appropriate information about the relevant job elements as you are preparing to evaluate your subordinates' performance. Task performance information may be easier to observe and interpret than contextual performance information.

The former may be available from objective data about the quantity and quality of service delivered or widgets produced by the employee or the employee's department. The latter may be available by talking to people and observing interpersonal interactions.

Once you understand the nature of the job and the sources of information, the information needs to be collected in a systematic way, provided as feedback, and integrated into the organization's performance management process for use in making compensation, job placement, and training decisions and assignments.

Rating Dynamics

As a manager, you are the traditional source of performance appraisal and feedback for the people who report to you. Most organizations require at least one annual appraisal and feedback discussion. During the one-on-one discussions with your team members, you explain the appraisal method and your evaluation, often in the form of ratings and written comments, discuss the results—accomplishments and areas for improvement—and request that the subordinate sign the form to attest that you explained the appraisal and reviewed it with the subordinate. Some appraisal forms may provide space for the subordinate to write his or her own opinion. The annual performance appraisal may lead to some change in compensation. Feedback about performance and implications for improvement and career development should be separate from discussions about pay in order to avoid or reduce your and/or your subordinate's defensiveness and focus attention on performance issues.[2] Some organizations suggest or require more frequent appraisals and feedback discussions that do not have implications for pay. I don't delve into rating methods and performance appraisal forms because this is part of an organization's performance management process. There are many excellent textbooks on appraisal methods.[3] I will provide just a few basics about rating formats and multisource (360-degree) feedback surveys.

Alternative Rating Formats

The traditional rating form consists of a series of items, each of which is rated on a numerical scale with scale points described by adjectives, such as "very good" or "exceeds expectations." The rating task isn't easy, and so it is not necessarily all that accurate. "Raters are faced with observing, storing, recalling, integrating, and judging the effectiveness of behaviors for a number of ratees. Finally, they must translate this judgment onto a rating scale."[4] Compound this with rater biases, lack of enthusiasm, and the time period covered by the review. Rater inaccuracies and disagreement among raters evaluating the same individual are not surprising under these circumstances. The fewest rating errors occur when scale formats include concrete, behavioral descriptions that are understandable, observable, and important to the job. Items that are general, focused on personal characteristics, unclear, judgmental, and/or not critical to the job are likely to result in the most rating errors. Rating scales that are based on job analyses with input from people doing the job are likely to be clearest and acceptable to the raters and the recipients of the feedback. The items may be phrased as behavioral expectations—that is, what the employee could be expected to do. Or they could be behavioral observations—examples of actual employee behaviors observed by the supervisor.[5]

A "Ratingless," Narrative Appraisal

Some authorities recommend eliminating ratings altogether. For instance, Herbert Meyer, a former human resource executive at General Electric and later professor of psychology at the University of South Florida, believed that attaching a numerical score or overall adjectival grade (e.g., "satisfactory") to the review is demeaning and unnecessary.[6] Any administrative actions, such as a salary increase or a promotion, communicate an overall appraisal better than a rating. Meyer recommended that supervisors write narratives—general descriptions with behavioral examples—but not provide numerical ratings. The narratives become written feedback.

Self-Appraisals

Meyer also considered the value of incorporating self-appraisals into the performance appraisal discussion. The subordinate takes the lead in the appraisal process. The supervisor's role is to give the employee recognition and suggest changes in behaviors or activities. He wrote,

> The appraisal feedback interview is a very authoritarian procedure—a parent-child type of exchange. Most modern organizations are moving away from authoritarian management toward an involvement-oriented working environment. A performance review discussion based on the subordinate's self review fits an involvement-oriented climate much better than the traditional top-down performance review discussion. It also has the advantage of forcing the manager into a counseling mode, rather than serving as a judge. Research has shown that performance review discussions based on self-review prove to be more productive and satisfying than traditional manager-initiated appraisal discussions.[7]

Supervisors are likely to need training in how to be a "counselor" and react to problems, such as how to deal with subordinates who have an inflated self-evaluation or, conversely, an unnecessarily self-deprecating view.

Meyer suggests that the conventional, one-way approach to feedback is sometimes appropriate when the subordinate is dependent on the supervisor, as is the case for new employees, trainees, or people in highly structured jobs. As subordinates become more experienced and the relationship grows between the supervisor and subordinate, self-appraisals are likely to be more valuable. They increase the subordinate's dignity and self-respect; place the supervisor in the role of counselor, not judge; enhance the subordinate's commitment to goals and development plans that emerge from the discussion; and avoid the subordinate reacting defensively. However, several problems with self-review should not be ignored.[8] It violates traditional mores about the proper relationship between boss and subordinate. Its value may be limited by a self-serving bias that inflates self-appraisals, especially if the appraisal is to be used for administrative purposes rather than solely for development. Since people tend to rate themselves leniently, by completing the self-rating, they are essentially preparing in advance for the feedback discussion. The self-appraisal may crystallize their position, and this could increase the potential for an adversarial discussion. Also, supervisors may be lenient because supervisors are sensitive to subordinates' self-judgments and prefer to avoid confrontation.

The Cost/Benefit of Appraisals

In many organizations, performance appraisals and feedback discussions are done poorly, and, because managers shy away from giving feedback, appraisals may not be done at all. Clearly, documentation of performance is needed to support personnel decisions, such as compensation and promotion. Documentation is especially needed when the decisions are negative and the organization needs supporting material to justify a decision that may be protested by the people affected. Also, performance appraisals can be central to stimulating feedback. However, the formal process, and especially the process of ranking employees, can engender defensiveness and hard feelings. Clearly, this reaction will not contribute to a feedback-oriented, continuous learning environment. Other processes, such as 360-degree feedback (see the next chapter) or continuous quality improvement processes (see Chapter 11 on teams), may reduce the need for formal appraisals.

The primary issue in these discussions is not how to identify and plan for future skill development but rather how to negotiate agreement with the employee that the rating is correct and acceptable enough to justify a decision, such as the merit pay outcome. If the employee cannot accept the decision and believes it is less than what it should be, the employee is likely to withdraw in some way. This issue is about more than dealing with defensive behaviors. Disagreement may occur if there has been little prior communication or feedback with the employee.

Perhaps a contingent approach should be taken to the conduct of feedback discussions. For example, some subordinates are less defensive when their supervisor begins a performance review discussion by asking for their self-evaluation. In other cases, delegating feedback may be better (e.g., have a coach or human resource manager deliver the news). Yet, in other cases, the supervisor should consider ways to convince the manager—positioning the positive, flattering feedback first and providing the flattering. In general, more research is needed on conducting constructive performance appraisal discussions.

Case: Performance Appraisal Ratings

Jim Schneider is a 39-year-old manager of the online marketing department for a regional specialty food chain. He started with the firm 2 years ago after working in online marketing for a wine distributor and, before that, a "big box" electronics store. He supervises a staff of three web designers and programmers, who are all in their early 20s and fresh out of college with degrees in information systems and digital design. His staff also includes four customer service representatives and one clerk. They are located in the firm's headquarters north of Boston. The firm has 22 stores across the region, and employees more than 400 people who are in a wide range of positions, including buyers who work at headquarters, to district managers, store managers, stock and checkout clerks, and truck drivers. Also, of course, the firm has several key officers, including the chief executive officer, whose family owns the business, the chief financial officer, a vice president of operations, a vice president of sales, a human resource director, and their staffs. The human resources department has a formal performance appraisal process. Once a year, Jim is expected to complete a performance appraisal form for each of his employees and then meet with each person to review his or her performance and set goals for next year. The form is the same for everyone in the company except the officers. It is a simple online form asking for ratings on five performance dimensions: meeting goals, performance quality, willingness to work cooperatively with others, attendance, and overall performance. Each dimension is rated on a 5-point scale from low to high. Jim can write any comments he wishes for each one of these ratings. After he meets with each employee, the employee signs that he or she reviewed the performance rating. Jim recognizes that having a record of each employee's performance is important. He doubts that this annual review and attaching a number to each one of these ratings mean much. His view of a "5" may not be the same as another manager's, or the employee's for that matter. Some of his programmers are dedicated and work extremely hard, often putting in overtime. They seem to be more concerned with web design and technology than they are with the company's food business, but Jim understands that this is only natural. Jim also feels that the nature of their work is constantly changing as the business has grown, largely due to his own expertise in applying online marketing techniques that he has learned over the years. He feels that the performance appraisal he receives from his manager, the VP of sales, doesn't mean much in terms of the value he has contributed to the firm. His bonuses have been good since they are tied to online sales. His technical staff receives bonuses that are tied to company performance, not their individual initiatives. Overall, Jim wonders if the appraisal process and compensation could be more effective.

Summary

There are a number of different rating formats. The most common method, a simple graphic rating scale, may not yield as precise and accurate ratings as other methods, such as ratings of dimensions that are defined by specific behavioral examples. Appraisals don't have to even include ratings, especially if the prime purpose is feedback for professional development and performance improvement. Self-appraisals can be very useful as a way to reduce the feedback recipient's defensiveness. While self-ratings tend to be inflated (as discussed in Chapter 3), self-assessment engages people in the process of their own performance review. Some people are more critical of themselves than others are of them when it comes to discussing their performance for purposes of guiding their development rather than giving them a salary increase. In general, managers need to give feedback in ways that are palatable to the receiver—that provide recognized and accepted justification for decisions and offer clear directions for development. This may mean positioning the feedback in a way that the recipient can digest it. As such, the particular rating format may be less important than what is done with the information, including how supervisors deliver the feedback and what the recipients do with the information to guide their performance improvement and career development. Still, ratings serve a purpose in demonstrating that administrative decisions are performance-based.

While performance appraisal and feedback are related but distinguishable processes, the quality of the appraisal and the context in which appraisals are made are likely to affect their value in giving feedback and improving performance. The next section indicates ways to reduce rater errors and generally improve the quality of performance appraisals, which in turn should improve their value for feedback.

Toward More Valuable Performance Appraisals

A variety of constraints make performance appraisal difficult for managers.[9] Time constraints make it hard to record relevant behaviors as they are observed. Memory constraints make it hard to recollect all relevant information when completing a performance appraisal form. Managers who have a number of subordinates are likely to spend more time with some of them than others. As such, managers are not able to engage in systematic observation of relevant information for all of them. For some subordinates, managers have an overload of information and may have trouble sorting through it all and focusing on critical areas of performance. For other subordinates, managers have too little information, or uneven information in that the manager's attention may be centered on a highly negative or positive situation. Subordinates may draw their manager's attention to certain information—for instance, sharing positive events and making light of negative events. Subordinates help managers make sense of situations and can, in the process, affect the manager's perceptions of the reasons for the events. Subordinates can attribute negative outcomes to factors beyond their control and positive outcomes to their own actions. Unless managers gather more data on their own, they are likely to trust their subordinates' explanations. Conflicting information may lead managers to draw erroneous conclusions. For instance, having some positive and negative information about a subordinate may lead to the conclusion that the subordinate is an underachiever with high potential but low motivation, or that inconsistent negative outcomes must be due to external causes.

The performance appraisal process takes place within the context of the social interaction between the manager, each subordinate, and the team of subordinates. The manager needs to maintain and enhance these relationships while at the same time evaluating each individual's accomplishments. The social dynamics are likely to influence the evaluation judgments. In addition, performance appraisal is complicated by multiple goals—distinguishing between subordinates to pay the best performers more, and identifying strengths and weaknesses for development. The pay decision requires making overall judgments about each subordinate's accomplishments and then comparing subordinates. The development evaluation requires a comprehensive review of each subordinate separately, looking at skills, knowledge, and behaviors that contribute to performance outcomes. Also, as I discussed in the last chapter, the evaluator's motivation may affect the evaluation process. Some managers are willing to invest more time, emotional energy, and cognitive effort in the appraisal task than others. The less information the manager has and the more pressing the demand for a judgment, the more likely the manager's appraisal will be affected by the stereotypes, leniency, halo, or other rater errors.

Changing organizational conditions are likely to influence the quality of appraisals.[10] Flatter organizational structures mean that managers have more subordinates reporting to them and less time to work with each. An emphasis on teamwork de-emphasizes individual differences in performance and emphasizes team relationships and work quality of the team as a whole, and individual performance appraisal may be viewed as hurting teamwork. New work arrangements such as telecommuting and geographically dispersed work arrangements make collecting performance information difficult. Fortunately, new information technologies allow collecting and recording high-quality data from multiple sources and maintaining records over time.

The most significant barrier to enhancing accuracy of performance ratings is the inability to identify factors that predict raters' ability or motivation to provide accurate ratings. Raters' motivation and sensitivity to how others are likely to react to them are likely to influence their ratings. In addition, raters tend to make a number of common errors. These should be recognized and steps should be taken to reduce or eliminate them through training.

Common Rating Errors

Managers' judgments of others' performance may be affected by a variety of perceptual errors. These common biases are often evident in performance ratings, although they may pervade narrative descriptions of performance even when ratings are not made. They are important for you as an evaluator to recognize since they will ultimately affect the feedback you give to others whether at work or in other situations.

- *Leniency.* The tendency to give overly favorable evaluations on all performance dimensions regardless of actual performance.
- *Severity.* The tendency to give overly negative evaluations on all elements of performance.
- *Halo.* The tendency to allow perceptions of one element of performance to influence evaluations of other, unrelated elements of performance.
- *Similarity.* The tendency to give overly favorable evaluations to others who are similar to you on characteristics that are unrelated to performance (e.g., age, race, or gender).

- *Central tendency.* The tendency to give mid-range evaluations on all elements of performance.
- *First impression.* The tendency to allow one's first impression of the person you are evaluating to influence your evaluations.
- *Recency effect.* The tendency to allow a recent incident to influence judgments of performance for the entire performance period.

Such errors suggest the need for training to reduce managers' errors of judgment and increase their rating accuracy.

Learning to Be a More Accurate Evaluator

One approach to improving evaluations is to alert people to common errors of judgment so they can spot them in how they evaluate others and guard against them. Other approaches change the evaluation method rather than the evaluator. Appraisal methods that have clear performance dimensions expressed in behavioral terms are likely to reduce rating errors. In general, the more ambiguous the performance dimensions and the less they relate to observable job behavior, the more raters' biases affect the ratings. Other approaches try to make managers better observers of performance, assuming that if they have clear recollection of job behaviors and they have a clear understanding of performance standards then their judgments will be relatively bias-free.

Observation skills training. Here are some ways to improve observation skills: (1) give observers prior experience in judging the topic and object of interest; (2) use good actors as models; (3) make the discriminations as discrete and defined with familiar terminology as possible; (4) allow judges to see the context that may have provoked the observed actions; and (5) allow observers sufficient time to observe.[11]

Training to reduce evaluation errors. Training methods to increase objectivity in performance judgments might include training people to observe cues, ask for additional information, and search for disconfirming evidence. People can learn to ignore biases, such as confirmation bias (leaning toward one perspective, seeking support for our initial view, and avoiding disconfirming evidence) and hindsight bias (believing that the world is more predictable than it really is because what happened often seems more likely afterwards than it did beforehand).[12] Also, people can learn how to conceptualize and process perceptions so they think carefully about what they perceive and the judgments they make.

Frame of reference training. Another training approach entails giving raters a frame of reference to evaluate the accuracy of their ratings as part of the training, in addition to lecture and discussion of job behaviors and rating dimensions. This might include practice in differentiating among ratees (rather than focus on rating errors). This may be accomplished by lecture and discussion of job behaviors and rating dimensions, general performance examples, rating practice, and general rating feedback.

Case: Sound Performance Management

Jean Sharp, age 31, has been a dental hygienist for the past 12 years. She has two children, 6 and 8, and she works 20 hours a week for a local dentist in a busy office. She has been working for this dentist for only 6 months. She has worked in two other offices, moving each time to earn a bit more money and have more flexible hours. In her previous jobs, she never had a formal performance appraisal. Her current employer, Dr. Paul, believes that performance management is important to the efficiency of his office and his bottom line, and he evaluates each of his four employees semiannually based on his perceptions and any input he has received from his patients. He uses a simple evaluation form that he found on a dental professional association web site. The form includes items that pertain to the health care provider's manner as well as the quality of her work, which Dr. Paul observes firsthand when he follows her routine cleanings with a brief check-up. Jean had never had a performance review from the other dentists she worked for. She was impressed that Dr. Paul took the time to meet with her privately for 30 minutes. Dr. Paul explained the process and the criteria he uses to evaluate his employees and why he believes this is important to his practice. He also said that he would cover areas of strengths and areas for improvement. He complimented Jean on the quality of her work, no doubt due to years of experience. He said that through overhearing her in her office, he felt that she talked to patients incessantly about her personal life, including problems with her children, her husband, and others in her family. Patients couldn't respond, of course. She conveyed the impression that she was unhappy with her life in many ways and this depressed patients. Talking to patients a bit was fine, but Dr. Paul preferred that she limit her conversation to pleasant, more innocuous topics, such as the weather or, better yet, recommendations about proper dental hygiene. Jean was taken aback. No one had ever criticized her performance in this way, particularly hinting that her personality, which she thought was outgoing and social, was a detriment to her work. She felt Dr. Paul was being too critical and not fair. Dr. Paul calmed her down, assuring her that she should just think about this and see if he might be right. He was sure her performance would be fine if she just gave this some thought. He offered to pay for a webinar training session for health care providers that he thought would be useful. It was all about bedside manner, but applied equally to this situation.

Conclusion

This chapter reviewed traditional approaches to performance appraisal—in particular, supervisor ratings. I described rating formats. However, I suggested the use of ratingless, narrative appraisals to avoid threatening "grades." This is especially valuable after an organizational downsizing. The supervisors may benefit from detailed, constructive feedback, but not ratings that label people and may be unnecessarily harsh. Also, I also recommended incorporating a self-appraisal into the performance review process. To summarize the major points from the chapter:

- The supervisor is the traditional source of performance appraisal and feedback, and the appraisal process usually involves a feedback discussion with the subordinate—thereby mandating explicit feedback if conducted properly.
- Some organizational policies and cultures support serious attention to feedback and development by making them an important (expected and rewarded) part of the way organizations operate.
- Rating formats can be designed to accentuate a focus on behaviors (rather than general opinions of personality, for instance). Such rating scales enhance rater accuracy and generate constructive information.
- Ratingless appraisals can avoid the defensiveness that often accompanies grading and focus the recipient's attention on behaviors and directions for development and performance improvement.
- Self-appraisals should be incorporated into the performance review process. Beginning a performance review with a self-appraisal increases the recipient's involvement in, and commitment to, the process and diffuses the recipient's defensiveness.
- Raters' motivation to provide ratings they can defend, situational conditions that allow time to observe behavior, and raters' self-monitoring tendency (sensitivity to how others react to you) affect ratings.
- Evaluators should be alert to common errors in evaluating others' performance, such as leniency, halo, central tendency, similarity, and recency. Be alert to these common rating errors to guard against them.
- Appraisal methods that have clear performance dimensions expressed in behavioral terms are likely to reduce rating errors.

The next chapter turns to another source of feedback: multisource ratings. These so-called 360-degree feedback processes collect ratings from peers, subordinates, customers, supervisors, and self. This can be a useful supplement to supervisory ratings, and a valuable tool in helping the employee to plan development activities.

Notes

1. Johnson (2001).
2. Lawler (1999).
3. London and Mone (2009).
4. Steiner, Rain, and Smalley (1993, p. 438).
5. For more details about performance appraisal scales, see a good text in human resource management, such as Cascio (2012).
6. Meyer (1991).
7. Meyer (1991, p. 68).
8. Blakely (1993).
9. Barnes-Farrell (2001).
10. Barnes-Farrell (2001).
11. Boice (1983).
12. Russo and Schoemaker (1992).

7

360-DEGREE FEEDBACK

360-degree feedback, also called multisource feedback, refers to performance ratings made on surveys completed by others. Raters may be subordinates, peers, team members, supervisors, internal customers, external customers, or others. Virtually all Fortune 500 companies use this method—some to give managers feedback for their development, others as part of the formal performance appraisal process to make administrative decisions such as pay increases or promotion.[1] Usually multisource feedback is collected for managers or supervisors, but it could be collected for any employee, with the raters depending on the employee's role in the organization. Multisource ratings are not always collected from all possible sources. For instance, sometimes just upward ratings are collected (i.e., subordinates are asked to rate their supervisor).

Multisource ratings are collected through surveys using computer, telephone, in-person interviews, or paper-and-pencil questionnaires. In Chapter 12, I will say more about how to use electronic technologies to collect performance ratings from multiple sources. A 360-degree survey may be administered annually or more often. For example, a division of Motorola collects ratings quarterly by computer for automatic averaging of scores and providing feedback reports to managers. Multisource feedback is growing in popularity and importance as a method for evaluating employees and providing them with input for development.

There are several reasons why multisource feedback is such a popular method for evaluating performance. The feedback contributes to individual development by providing information on worthwhile directions for learning and growth. It builds self-awareness, which in turn increases self-reflection and perhaps a greater understanding of others and how they react to you. This, in turn, could prompt managers to think more about the potential consequences of their actions toward others. Managers may feel accountable to respond to others' ratings of them. When administered over time, the survey results provide a way for managers to track changes in their own performance as they try to react to previous feedback and change their behavior.

From an organizational perspective, multisource feedback promotes organizational development by specifying dimensions of managerial behavior that are important to the organization's management. In this way, it clarifies management's performance expectations. It recognizes the complexity of managerial performance—that performance is viewed differently by different constituencies and that managers need input from these different sources for a comprehensive view of their performance.[2] The supervisor does not have sufficient information or perspective to be the sole reviewer. Supervisors are often reluctant to evaluate subordinates honestly. They want to avoid having to confront the subordinate with negative information.[3] Also, managers may need to behave differently with subordinates, peers, supervisors, and customers. Managers confronting organizational change recognize the importance of being attuned to the changing expectations of multiple constituencies, and they realize that this requires continuous learning.

In this chapter, I describe how multisource feedback is used for development and to make decisions about people. I review how people react to multisource feedback and the extent to which it relates to behavior change and improvement in performance.

Multisource Feedback as a Process

Multisource feedback should be viewed as part of an ongoing performance management and development process, not a discrete, stand-alone event.[4] Even if the multisource survey results are not used to formally evaluate managers, it is still part of the performance monitoring and improvement process. This includes setting performance goals, finding areas for improvement, taking action to learn and practice new skills and behaviors, and tracking different elements of performance from different perspectives (subordinates, peers, supervisors, customers). Multisource feedback is best used as a support mechanism for gaining input about your performance. You could regularly ask your boss, peers, and subordinates for input, but this takes time, and you may not get honest feedback when you put people on the spot. Also, you may not ask the right questions or receive the answers in an objective way. Using a 360 survey, all managers are evaluated in the same way on the same set of performance elements for the same purpose. You can compare your results to average scores obtained from others and from scores you received in the past. Of course, you need to interpret your results and judge their value. Did raters within a group (e.g., all subordinates) disagree and by how much? What does this disagreement say about the value of the average rating? Has the agreement among raters increased over time, perhaps because you are more consistent in your management style as a result of the multisource feedback? Is being more consistent important? Maybe you need to vary your behavior because your subordinates have different needs. Perhaps you have attended a management style course that provides a context for evaluating your subordinates' needs and managing in relation to their individual differences in capability and motivation. Ongoing feedback will help you determine how your behavior is perceived and whether your personal goals for development are paying off. Multisource feedback becomes a calibrating vehicle within this overall performance-management/development process.

Guidelines for Designing and Implementing a Multisource Feedback Program

Here are some steps to follow to develop a multisource (360-degree) feedback survey for your team or organization.

Involve Employees in Program Design

Employees should be involved in identifying and describing items that will be used in the rating process. They can flesh out performance dimensions set by top management and write comprehensible items to reflect these dimensions. Also, their involvement will increase their sense of ownership of the process. Furthermore, managers are more likely to accept the results when they know the items reflect performance dimensions that are important to the organization and meaningful to the people making the ratings.

Identify Item Content and Rating Format

The performance dimensions that are rated should be derived from analyses of current jobs with input from employees as well as top managers. Items should be worded in terms of behavioral frequency (how often . . .) or evaluations (e.g., 1 = poor, 5 = great). Ratings are likely to be most reliable when the items refer to objective or observable behaviors instead of individual qualities (e.g., traits such as trustworthiness and responsiveness). Here are a few examples of possible items:

- Jointly sets performance objectives with you.
- Supports you in developing your career plans.
- Motivates you to do a good job.
- Gives you authority to do your job.

- Provides the support necessary to help you do your job (e.g., advice, resources, or information).
- Understands the work to be done within your work group.
- Is available to you when needed.
- Encourages innovation and creativity.

Many scale formats are possible. One is a simple Likert scale, which asks for ratings of each item on a numerical scale ranging from, say, 1 to 5 points.

Rater Anonymity

The process should ensure raters' anonymity. This means guarding the ratings, probably by having an outside consultant code and analyze the data and prepare feedback reports. Such reports are usually computer-generated, particularly if the survey is on an optically scanned sheet, on a computer disk, or on a computer program tied to a local area network server or mainframe. Handwritten comments need to be typed to disguise the handwriting. Managers should not receive subordinate ratings if there are too few peers or subordinates (e.g., four or fewer) since this might suggest the identity of the raters.

Rater Training

All employees should be trained in how to rate accurately and what constitutes constructive comments. Also, recipients should be trained in how to use the data. Survey instructions should be clear. Employee briefings should be held to explain the reason for the ratings, how the data will be aggregated, and the nature of the feedback reports. Rater training should make raters aware of rating errors (e.g., leniency, central tendency, and halo—rating all elements of performance alike).

Feedback Report

Table 7.1 is a simplified feedback report for a few items.

An interpretation guide would ask the manager receiving the report to compare his or her self-ratings to the average subordinate ratings. The number of responding subordinates is an indication of the representativeness of the results across the work group. Data would not be presented if four or fewer subordinates responded to an item. The "norm" provides a comparison to how managers were perceived overall by their subordinates. The guide would include information about training and developmental experiences available that would be useful for each category of items.

Table 7.1 Sample Feedback Report

	Mean		Range		Number of Respondents Responding to Item	Norm[1]
	Self-Rating	Subordinate Rating	Low	High		
1. Jointly sets performance objectives with you.	5	3	1	4	7	3
2. Supports you in developing your career plans.	4	4	2	4	8	4
3. Motivates you to do a good job.	6	5	3	6	8	4
4. Gives you authority to do your job.	5	4	3	5	8	3
5. Provides the support necessary to help you do your job (e.g., advice, resources, information).	6	4	2	5	7	4

[1]Norm is the average of subordinate ratings for the item across all managers in the unit.

Using Multisource Feedback for Development and Administrative Decisions

Multisource feedback may be used solely to guide the recipient's development. Alternatively, it may be used by upper management to make decisions about the person rated, as well as to help the person identify areas for performance improvement and career development. By the way, multisource feedback can also be used to evaluate organization change and development by averaging results across managers in a department or the organization as a whole and examining levels of performance and changes in performance over time.[5] As a tool for organization development, multisource feedback can be used in team building discussions about the overall quality of management in the organization. Following changes over time across the organization can demonstrate the overall benefit of feedback to the organization as it promotes a feedback-rich climate.

Most companies use multisource feedback solely for development. Increasingly, however, companies are also using the results to make administrative decisions about managers.[6]

Use for Development

When multisource feedback is used for development alone, the managers who are rated are generally the only ones receiving their results, unless they choose to share the results with others. This highlights the importance of managers using the information for their own development. The organization takes responsibility for a rating process that protects rater confidentiality, for a computer-generated report of the results, for help in interpreting the reports, and for training and development opportunities. Recipients of the feedback must take responsibility for interpreting their results and using the information to guide their development and performance improvement.

Use for Administrative Decisions

Increasingly, organizations use multisource feedback for administrative purposes, such as merit pay and advancement decisions.[7] This makes the feedback all the more salient to the individuals receiving it. But the process is likely to feel threatening to managers, especially to those who are worried about the quality of interpersonal relationships they have with their colleagues. Such managers will say that they don't trust the process.

The Pros and Cons for Using 360 Feedback for Administration and Development or Just for Development

There are several reasons why multisource feedback should be used for development and not for administrative decisions.[8] Since ratings are provided anonymously, raters are less likely to be lenient when they know their ratings will not be used to make decisions about the managers they are rating. Keeping the results confidential promotes psychological safety, which, in turn, encourages managers receiving the feedback to be less defensive. When managers are asked to rate themselves, which is usually the case, managers are able to compare their self-concepts with how others see them and explore reasons for any differences. Executives may believe that having to base decisions on the results detracts from their own judgment and accountability—essentially reducing their discretion over key personnel decisions.

Executives may not be prepared to discuss the feedback results with their subordinate managers. Also, managers may feel uncomfortable talking to their supervisor about how others view their performance, finding the situation threatening and stressful.[9] It may take time for the organization to develop a culture that supports feedback. Using 360 data for decisions may prompt the recipient to be defensive and decrease the chances for using the data constructively, and may even cause dysfunctional relationships, as might happen if managers avoid feedback discussions or construct rationalizations to save face. This is more likely to happen if the data are used to make decisions about managers who have to explain their results to their boss. The credibility of multisource feedback results may be in question if raters have a vested interest in the results, as they would if their manager's annual bonus depends in part on subordinates' ratings and subordinates want their manager to be treated well in hopes that they, in turn, will also be treated well. Managers may try to influence how their subordinates rate them by implying rewards for positive results. Also, if subordinates or others (peers or customers) are chosen by the managers, they may not select impartial people.

There are, however, some good reasons for using multisource feedback to make administrative decisions. Important personnel decisions, like termination, promotion, and compensation, should be informed by different perspectives. This is especially important when supervisors don't have daily contact with the managers who report to them (e.g., in flat organizational structures in which executives have many managers reporting to them) and when performance cannot be easily quantified by means of some objective measures. Other reasons are simply that if good information is available, then it should be used to help in making better personnel decisions to benefit the organization. Knowing that ratings will be used in this way may encourage people to be more exact in their judgments, particularly if they might be called to task to explain them (less so if they are not). Executives are likely to gather information about managers from different sources before making decisions about them anyway. Multisource feedback formalizes and standardizes this process for all managers, not just for those executives who would like information for a special reason. Therefore, raters may be less biased than they might be if an executive approached them about a certain manager—for instance, telling the executive what they think the executive wants to hear. Overall, using data to make decisions increases the likelihood that managers will take their results seriously and use them to change their behavior and improve their performance.

Ultimately, the use of 360 feedback will depend on the organization. Probably, the most productive way to introduce the process is to use it first for development alone. Then, after employees become used to the technique and the resulting data and receiving feedback becomes routine, the organization can begin to incorporate it into administrative decision making. This may take several years. In any case, as emphasized in the next section, all raters and those rated should be clear about the purpose of the process.

Ways to Increase the Value of Multisource Ratings

There are a number of ways to limit rater distortion and increase the value of multisource feedback results for development and administrative decisions.[10] Survey results can be examined to determine the average ratings and variation in ratings across raters. Systematic biases, such as leniency, can then be identified. Giving raters feedback about distortion in data from prior ratings, or at least alerting them to possible rater errors, can encourage them to avoid these errors in the future. Raters can be given other performance data (e.g., objective measures such as sales) for comparison to their ratings to help them understand how well their judgments relate to these other measures.

In general, it is important to clarify for the raters and the managers receiving the results how the data will be used—for development and/or administration. This should be clear before the ratings are collected. Ratings that focus on managerial behaviors can be collected, say, every 6 months for purposes of development. Ratings that focus on managerial outcomes tied to organizational and departmental goals can be collected once a year for purposes of administrative decisions.

When implementing a multisource feedback survey process for the first time, organizations would be wise to use the results for development only for the first several years. In that way, defensiveness and impression management game playing are less likely to enter the equation, and participants will feel less threatened by the process. Use for development will create a continuous performance improvement mindset that recognizes the value of feedback. Over time, as employees, managers, and executives become more comfortable with the process and having discussions about the feedback results, the organization can change the policy (with plenty of advance notice and discussion) and begin using the data to make decisions, possibly collecting separate data focused on outcomes for decisions and maintaining a behavior-focused survey for development. Newcomers to the organization should be introduced to the process slowly, perhaps collecting development ratings about them for 2 years before collecting outcomes ratings about them for use in pay or promotion decisions.

There are ways to minimize rater effects and to increase the value of multisource feedback. The way the process is introduced in the organization—slowly and with clear explanation—is meant to enhance its value. The very process of averaging ratings across multiple raters within roles is meant to provide more accurate evaluations than would occur if one rater (e.g., the supervisor alone) made ratings and provided feedback.

As I suggested earlier in this chapter, when starting a multisource feedback process, use the information just for developmental purposes. Two or three rating cycles may be needed for raters and managers to become comfortable with the process, which means several years if the process is administered annually. After that time, the policy can be changed to incorporate the results into making decisions about the managers who are rated. Generally, managers tend to be more accepting of multisource feedback when the organization provides training to help managers improve on the performance dimensions that are rated.[11]

The use of computer or telephone to administer a multisource rating survey is increasingly common. In computer administration, the survey comes on a disk or can be downloaded online. Raters complete the questionnaire on the computer and send back the disk or, in the case of online, return the data directly via the computer. The telephone can be used to record responses, too. In this case, the survey comes by mail. Raters dial a given number and then key in their numerical response corresponding to each question. Raters can request that a printout of their responses be sent immediately to their printer so they can check their answers. Of course, the questions can actually be delivered on the telephone by a computerized voice. These high-tech methods have many advantages over paper-and-pencil surveys. As technology develops, they are becoming increasingly cost-effective. Results are computed automatically.

Use of Comments

Multisource feedback surveys usually have some space for open-ended comments. Managers often say that this qualitative information is the most useful, and they tend to rate them heavily in determining areas for improvement.[12] One reason for the compelling nature of verbatim comments may be that they are easy to interpret. They don't require digesting numbers and comparing scores. Recipients may feel that the evaluators wrote comments about areas that were of most importance to them, so they deserve attention. Also, since the raters took the time to formulate and type in specific comments, the recipients feel obligated to take them seriously.

If managers are going to place so much value on open-ended responses, then there should be ways to ensure that the comments are meaningful. Comments that are more behaviorally descriptive provide a better basis for figuring out what to improve.

Case: Resistance to 360

Doris Kleinman, age 52, was a senior vice president in charge of women's sportswear for a major, high-end clothing line. Her responsibilities included design, oversight of manufacturing, which was mainly in Asia, distribution, marketing, and sales. More than 300 people reported to her in different regions of the country and across the globe. She was one of five senior VPs in the company for different lines of clothing under the same brand. The garment industry is tough. It is fast-paced, and Doris needed to be aggressive and demanding to meet targets. This was especially the case during the economic downturn and increased competition from online market- ers. Most of the company's sales were from major department stores and the company's own brand stores in major shopping centers around the U.S. and in Europe. Doris and the other top officers of the company met monthly with the CEO, CFO, VP of human resources, and other key personnel. When the CEO called in an external con- sultant to develop and deliver a 360-degree performance appraisal process for all managers, starting with the top officers, Doris fought against it. She was used to being measured, daily, monthly, quar- terly, and annually. Each element of her position included objective indicators of all sorts, especially sales and bottom-line profitability, which were compared to sales and profits last year on the same day. However, the process the consultant described would collect percep- tions from the managers who reported to Doris and from her clients. Doris knew that the managers in her department were under high pressure and they saw her as a task master. Also, Doris didn't want to upset her clients, who tended to be buyers in department stores and regional managers of the company's own brand stores. Would they want to be positive to please Doris? Would they feel this was an imposition on their time, when all they really cared about was bottom-line performance, just as Doris did? Doris said this wasn't the best time, and the CEO should delay until the economy improved and people were under less pressure. Other VPs didn't feel as strongly as Doris, but they expressed reservations too. The CEO, however, wanted to show that he cared about style of leadership and provide development opportunities for all managers. So the CEO reached a compromise. He would begin the process by participating himself. He would ask his managers to complete the form about him. He would also ask for input from his board of directors, some key cli- ents, and even financial analysts who followed the garment industry and several investors who owned large proportions of stock in the company. The consultant would gather the data from interviews and surveys and meet with the CEO to provide feedback. He would then share the results with the officer team and describe his feelings about the process. Then the team would decide if they would participate. Doris felt this was fair.

Processing Multisource Feedback

Developing and administering multisource ratings are one thing; making them effective is another. The content of the ratings, how the feedback is delivered, and support for its use in setting goals for development and behavior change are all critical to making multisource feedback worthwhile. This is especially the case because multisource feedback can be difficult to interpret and opens the door to distorting or ignoring the information.

Here I emphasize the importance of having specific information, consider defensive reactions to multisource feedback, outline alternative modes of delivering multisource feedback, review psychological processes that encourage constructive use of multisource feedback, and suggest ways to make multisource feedback a part of the organization's culture.

Specificity of Information

The more the information is specific and reflects the nature of the task, the more compelling it is.[13] Information that reflects actual job behaviors is likely to be easier to understand and less threatening than descriptions of personal characteristics.

Feedback results may be accompanied by normative information—the average score for each item across all managers rated. This provides a basis of comparison of the individual ratings. For example, knowing that I received an average of 3.89 (on a 5-point scale ranging from 1 = low to 5 = high) from my subordinates on giving feedback would have different meaning if I knew that the mean rating received by supervisors in my organization (across, say, 50+ supervisors) was 2.75 or was 4.66. I would know I was doing better or worse than average.

Rather than presenting managers with data on how they were rated, a less specific form of feedback is to provide managers with a summary of the average ratings across the department or the entire organization. Thus, these employees receive only normative information. Such information may be a helpful and nonthreatening guide to managers in considering issues in their own departments. It can be valuable as an ice breaker in a team meeting aimed at discussing ways to improve interpersonal relationships, by asking the team to consider the extent to which the results apply to them. However, it lacks specificity, and it is easy to rationalize unfavorable results by arguing that they apply to others, not to our department.

Of course, feedback may also be informal, coming from others directly (through statements of others' opinions about your performance) or indirectly (through hearsay or other evidence of how others evaluate your performance). You may welcome such information and even seek it, or perhaps you may not want it at all. People may seek feedback for the purposes of creating an impression on others rather than learning how others feel about them. Moreover, informal feedback may be ambiguous.

Or it may focus on personal qualities (you learn you're "hard to get along with") rather than behaviors or actions (you "don't listen to others' ideas"). The more ambiguous and general the information, the less valuable it will be.

Toward an Impartial and Dispassionate Reaction

Recipients can easily be defensive when confronted with multisource feedback. In requesting informal feedback, recipients can ask only sources they know will be favorable. The recipient of multisource ratings can focus on the highest ratings regardless of source and performance dimension. If the feedback report includes the range (lowest and highest ratings) as well as the average for each source, then it is easy to focus on the top of the range. External attributions can be made for the lowest ratings ("There will always be some people who are unhappy," or "Low performers can't be expected to be honest"). Alternatively, the recipient can concentrate on the source or performance dimensions providing the highest ratings, rationalizing that these sources/dimensions are the most important.

The most constructive way for recipients to use feedback suggests the following guidelines: Review all the information thoroughly and objectively. Examine each piece of information; consider overall strengths, and enumerate the most serious weaknesses. For each source of multisource feedback, list the five highest and five lowest ratings, compare the list between sources, and identify the strengths that should be enhanced and the weaknesses that should be reversed. Diagnose whether the areas for improvement are *motivational* (need to devote more time and energy to the area; need to overcome discomfort or dislike of the behavior; need for incentives to reward the behavior) or *ability* (need to learn how to do the behavior). Set goals for learning (training courses; special job assignments). Make commitments for changing behaviors. Review the feedback and refine the performance improvement goals with one's supervisor. Compare feedback from the next rating period to the previous rating period to determine whether the changed behavior has an effect on the ratings. Finally, evaluate changes in unit performance to determine their links to development, behaviors, and rating changes. These guidelines are easier said than done, given people's tendency to be defensive.

Ways to Deliver Multisource Feedback Results

The way multisource feedback is delivered will affect how much attention the recipient gives to it and the likelihood of defensive reactions. Consider the following possibilities:

One-on-one delivery of results from a consultant. The consultant, an expert in performance improvement (perhaps an industrial/organizational psychologist or a human resource specialist), ideally from outside the company, reviews the results with the individual. This minimizes the threat and forces the recipient to consider all the results. The consultant may also help the recipient use the feedback to set goals for performance improvement.

One-on-one delivery of results from the immediate supervisor. Knowing that your supervisor not only sees your ratings but also reviews them with you makes them highly salient. This enhances the threat and increases the chances for defensiveness. However, if the supervisor knows how to review the feedback objectively and constructively by tying the results to directions for improvement, the outcome can be beneficial. If the supervisor attributes blame and merely demands improvement, then the subordinate may be particularly defensive.

Desk-drop. The feedback may come in the form of a computer print-out or an online report. Written guidelines for using the feedback may be provided. However, whether the recipient reviews and uses the information is totally up to the recipient. When the feedback is meant solely for the recipient's development and no one else in the organization will see it, the only incentive for reviewing the information is performance improvement. However, the easiest defense is not to look at the information at all. If recipients know that their supervisor will also see the results, however, there is more incentive to at least know what they are in case the supervisor brings them up.

Group session with general discussion on use. The recipients convene in a group to receive their individual results, usually delivered in a sealed envelope, and hear from a consultant or human resource specialist about ways to interpret and use the results. Recipients then have a chance to examine their individual results and ask general questions for clarification (e.g., "What does it mean if I rated myself lower than my peers and subordinates did?").

Group session with general discussion and targeted discussion about each individual. Here, the foregoing procedure is followed except that each person is given everyone else's ratings as well as his or her own. This may occur after a leadership development simulation as part of a course when the participants are all from different organizations. The simulation is followed by a chance for the trainers to rate the participants and for the participants to rate each other. The results are shared as a means of starting a discussion about each individual. Fellow participants share their reactions as a way to help each other. This information is hard to deny at the time it is given, but easy to forget after the course.

Designing Survey Feedback with Psychological Processes in Mind

Attention to and acceptance of multisource feedback can be enhanced by building in reinforcement mechanisms. These mechanisms are part of several well-understood psychological processes, which include the following:

- *Information processing*—The questions asked (items rated) communicate what performance dimensions are important in the organization.
- *Reward mechanisms (expectation that behavior change leads to valued outcomes)*—People pay attention to behaviors and outcomes on which they are measured and reinforced.
- *Impression management*—People want others to think well of them. Knowing that others will be evaluating them explicitly drives attention to the behaviors evaluated.
- *Social comparison*—People want to know their performance in comparison to others. The availability of comparative data (i.e., how others did on average) makes the results more salient, but may also focus attention away from one's behavior to one's self-concept. Helping the recipient compare the results to his or her past results may be more productive.
- *Goal setting*—Goals and feedback are mutually supportive. Goals help feedback work, and feedback helps goals work. Using the feedback to set goals translates the feedback into action.
- *Frequent feedback*—Some firms use multisource feedback quarterly, collecting the data and generating reports via computer.
- *Social learning*—People model others' behavior when they see it is valued and rewarded. When top managers seek and use feedback, others will too.
- *Commitment mechanisms*—People develop commitment to new behaviors when they are do-able (i.e., the individual sees the behaviors as possible and realistic) and when rewards and valued outcomes can be anticipated (a process known as prospective rationality). The rewards might be social and self-administered (e.g., a stronger sense of belonging) or material and visible to others (a salary bonus; an awards dinner). Also, people develop commitment to behaviors that they are making a substantial investment of time and money to develop (a process known as retrospective rationality). For instance, they express commitment to goals that they agree to in public (e.g., during a team meeting). To deny the commitment would be inconsistent with their self-image as an effective, rational person.

107

Case: Do It Yourself 360

Carmen LaCross is a 30-year-old executive in a public relations consulting firm. She oversees four account managers and seven consultants who advise corporate and individual clients on how best to get their name before the public in positive ways. Sometimes their work involves repairing reputations that have been damaged by a scandal or corporate misstep of some kind, not unusual in today's world of social media and unethical or unseemly behavior. Her clients depend heavily on her and her staff's ability to act quickly and positively. Their media contacts and know-how are critical. Carmen is one of more than 20 team managers in the firm across the country who have similar teams supporting a client base. Carmen specializes in sports team and player PR, which is an exciting yet high-pressure world, to say the least. Carmen is highly respected within the firm and the industry for being a young, aggressive professional who knows how to get the job done. Carmen believes that one of the secrets to her success is listening and caring about what others think of her and her team. She developed her own online survey to ask clients and contacts outside the firm and her manager and colleagues (the other PR executives in the firm) about her performance. She uses Survey Monkey, readily available online, to ask specific questions about particular actions and events, especially after a major PR campaign is completed or underway. She drafts questions to meet the situation and she sends the survey to those who were involved or who observed what went on and would have an informed opinion. Carmen got the idea from the firm's annual 360-degree survey process run by the human resources department. Carmen is asked to provide a list of names of people who should receive the online survey. The survey is sent to Carmen's supervisor, her subordinates, clients, and contacts. Also, Carmen completes the survey for herself based on her perceptions of her performance. A consultant the firm hires then meets with Carmen to review the results. Carmen finds the results useful although general. Respondents can write comments that sometimes provide helpful hints for improvement. However, Carmen impressed the consultants several years running when she described how she has used her own, tailor-made 360 survey to ask specific questions that give her specific ideas for doing better to meet client needs.

Conclusion

Multisource feedback is growing in popularity as a method for evaluating employees and providing them with input for development. It captures information from multiple constituencies and focuses your attention on your role from different perspectives. Multisource feedback builds on psychological processes that model, reinforce, and integrate feedback for development and performance improvement. Here are the main conclusions from this chapter:

- Multisource feedback can be used to guide development and make administrative decisions.
- Multisource feedback is valuable for your professional development because it provides comprehensive information from different perspectives. It builds your self-awareness, which in turn increases self-reflection and suggests directions for behavior change.
- Managers generally feel accountable to respond to others' ratings of them. That is, they want to demonstrate that they used the ratings and that, as a result, they improved their performance over time.
- Multisource feedback is valuable for development because the ratings are provided anonymously. Keeping the results confidential promotes psychological safety and reduces defensiveness.
- Multisource feedback can also be valuable for administrative decisions. Important decisions should be informed by information from different perspectives, especially when supervisors don't have daily contact with the managers who report to them.
- Ratings can be improved by being sure the areas of performance that are rated are specific and clear, the raters and recipients understand how the results will be used, and the recipients are encouraged to review their results in detail and consider their implications (i.e., the feedback reports are delivered in ways that promote close attention—e.g., with the support of the recipient's supervisor or an external coach).
- The multisource results should provide comparative data to demonstrate change in ratings over time, and encourage the use of the results to set goals for performance improvement and development.
- Multisource feedback is unlikely to be useful without coaching and support to help recipients pay attention to the results. Companies using multisource feedback should invest in follow-up coaching and facilitation to help recipients accentuate the positive and identify developmental needs.
- Multisource feedback is more valuable to people who care about how others view them and generally have a positive attitude about feedback.
- People who receive negative feedback from one or more sources may need more support and attention from a coach or supervisor to help them confront the unfavorable results rather than deny or ignore them.
- Organizations should track the success of the multisource feedback process over time, recognizing that it has multiple purposes and recognizing that the effects take time, often years.

Multisource ratings are just one source of systematic feedback. The next chapter considers sources of performance feedback under controlled conditions, specifically assessment centers and business simulations.

Notes

1. Church (2000).
2. Latham and Wexley (1981); Tsui and Ohlott (1988).
3. Fried, Tiegs, and Bellamy (1992).
4. London and Tornow (1998).
5. Bracken, Timmreck, Fleenor, and Summers (2001).
6. Timmreck and Bracken (1997).
7. London and Smither (1995).
8. London (2001).
9. Dalessio (1998).
10. London (2001).
11. Maurer and Tarulli (1994).
12. Rose and Farrell (2002).
13. Kluger and DeNisi (1996).

8

ASSESSMENT CENTERS AND SIMULATIONS

This chapter focuses on certain methods that give people feedback about their skills and capabilities: assessment centers, computerized testing and assessment, and simulations. These offer participants a chance to try new behaviors and learn about themselves. Some organizations use these techniques as part of development programs. Such programs are available in a number of forms to anyone who wants to enroll in them. They may be run by universities, leadership development institutes, and training firms. Companies may have their own programs customized to the needs of their employees and the objectives of the organization.

Assessment Centers

Assessment centers evaluate participants' skills and abilities. Assessment centers are sometimes used to evaluate job candidates in the employee selection process. But they are also used to evaluate current employees, especially those being assessed for possible promotion. An assessment center may also be used solely for development purposes. The results provide diagnostic feedback that will help participants identify directions for development in areas that will be needed in managerial positions at higher organizational levels.

The assessment center (which does not refer to a place, but a process) includes such exercises as the in-basket (written material requiring prioritization and responses), an interview, business games, a leaderless group discussion, and a variety of psychological and achievement tests. Assessment centers are expensive to develop and operate, and they cannot be implemented without a good deal of work and investment. The exercises can be administered online, reducing costs. They are a way to assess general managerial skills and then consider directions for development. This may cost several thousand dollars per participant.

The goal of an assessment center is to collect and integrate diverse information about a participant. The exercises represent typical job duties and are meant to assess dimensions of behavior important to job performance. For instance, a sales assessment includes simulations of sales situations. A managerial assessment center includes techniques to evaluate behavior in boss/subordinate relationships. Multiple assessors observe and evaluate participants on the performance dimensions. Narrative reports are written and tests are scored, some automatically if the simulations, games, and tests have multiple-choice responses and are administered online. When trained assessors observe participants in person, the assessors rate the participants on the performance dimensions, discuss their ratings with other assessors, and try to agree on ratings.

Developmental assessment centers are those used primarily, if not solely, for development of the participants rather than as input to decisions about them. The results are reported to the participants by an assessor or a psychologist. During the feedback session with the participant, the assessor reviews the meaning of the results and offers guidance for development. Suggestions for development may recommend building on one's strengths rather than eliminating weaknesses. Some elements of managerial performance cannot be learned easily, such as decision making. Others are learned more easily, such as communication skills. Developmental assessment centers provide feedback that *encourages* people to engage in activities that make them more eligible for promotion into management.

Case: Developmental Assessment

Christine Monroe, a 24-year-old account executive in an international corporate software company, was in her second year of a management development program. Hired after graduating summa cum laude from an Ivy League school with a B.S. in computer science and a minor in business, Christine had already been in two positions with the company: the first 6 months in the systems design area and the last year and a half in client project development and oversight in an account executive position, overseeing two subordinates who were experts in systems architecture. Christine's job was to work with clients on their specific needs, and with the assistance of her two subordinates, develop and implement configurations of the company's software to meet the client's needs. As part of her management development program, Christine recently attended a 3-day assessment center with 11 other high-potential managers during which she completed personality and career interest inventories and participated in several business simulations. One simulation was a business game that pitted three teams of four people each against each other to evaluate a set of data reflecting alternative business strategies and to make investment decisions. Another simulation

---

was working on a presentation and delivering it to the group of participants to convince them to allocate money to a particular charity. Another exercise asked her to review a set of memos and reports, prioritize them, and write notes to a supervisor and others expressing her priorities and recommendations. The participants were observed by several managers, who made notes about everyone's performance. A week after the assessment center, Christine met with one of the managers who observed her during the assessment process. He provided her with a report that reflected her collaboration, decision making, leadership, organization ability, adaptability, and several other characteristics that are important to management. The report stated that her strengths were in the areas of communications skills and ability to organize complex material quickly and make reasonable decisions. She also learned that she could be more collegial by listening to her co-workers' ideas and being flexible in considering different ways a group might proceed rather than coming to a conclusion and imposing it on the group. The manager who delivered these results stressed that the report was meant only to help her—it would not be used to make decisions about her future with the company. She and the manager discussed ways she could test different behaviors on the job. Christine was at first taken aback by the statement of some weaknesses. She was not used to hearing that she needed to improve in any way. She was assured by the manager, who promised to follow up with her in 2 months to see how she was applying what she learned about herself.

Summary

Assessment centers use activities and exercises to examine participants' behaviors under controlled conditions that are standardized for all participants. The advantage is that the behaviors are based on performance dimensions that are important to the job, and that cannot easily be measured through non-behavioral methods, such as paper-and-pencil or computer-based tests—for instance, communications, organizing, and interpersonal skills, including resolving conflict, negotiating, and persuading. Also, assessment centers can be constructed to measure behaviors in situations that are typical of positions (e.g., higher-level managerial jobs), and so the results reflect the participants' potential to handle situations that may not be typical of their current positions. In assessment centers, trained observers carefully record their observations during the exercises and then later rate behaviors and write in-depth qualitative reports on each exercise. These data are then combined across exercises and assessors to generate a useful report about the participant's managerial abilities and potential to perform well at higher levels. The data are often used to make selection or promotion decisions about people. However, they are also valuable for development, and indeed, some companies use assessment centers to provide participants with feedback about their strengths and weaknesses as input for development, not decision making.

Comparing Assessment Center Feedback to 360-Degree Feedback

Although their outputs are similar, assessment centers and 360-degree feedback surveys differ in several respects. Assessment centers are expensive tools for selection and development. 360-degree feedback surveys are less expensive and often used just for development. Assessment centers measure competencies required in jobs for which the participant is aspiring, while 360-degree feedback measures current performance.[1] Assessment centers use specially trained assessors who should be aware of, and try to minimize, common rating errors. 360-degree survey raters have interacted with the manager who is being rated for considerable time, and will continue to do so, while the assessment center assessor may not spend any personal time with the manager. Given that both tools may be used to measure the same behaviors and competencies, research is needed to examine their relationship.

The Boeing Company studied whether assessment center ratings used for selecting first-level managers are related to 360-degree evaluations used for managerial development.[2] The company's assessment center used a structured interview and a coaching simulation, and produced ratings on interpersonal skills, positive work orientation, working together, basic abilities, oral communication, planning and time management, and problem solving. The 360-degree feedback ratings were used solely for feedback to the managers to support their development (i.e., the results were not used to make administrative decisions about them, unlike the assessment center). Rater sources were the participant, the immediate supervisor, direct reports, co-workers, and customers. Items that were rated reflected behaviors associated with company values, such as leadership, integrity, quality, customer satisfaction, people working together, a diverse and involved team, corporate citizenship, and enhancing shareholder value. The company found high interrater agreement across the different assessment center exercises and within the different rating sources for the 360 feedback ratings. As expected, the factor of "working together" from the assessment center was positively related to the 360 dimensions of "leadership" and "a diverse and involved team." The assessment center factor "interpersonal skills" was positively related to survey ratings of "leadership." Managers' ratings and, to a lesser extent, co-worker ratings from the 360 survey were more strongly related to the assessment center results than were the 360 ratings from direct reports and customers. Even stronger relationships were found between the assessment center ratings and the average of manager, customer, and peer ratings on the 360 survey than for other combination of sources on the survey, indicating that averaging results across some sources may enhance the ability of the 360-degree survey to capture the performance measured in the assessment center.

This study from Boeing suggests that assessment center measures can be valuable sources of early feedback, particularly for assessment centers used in the selection process. Feeding the assessment results back to the participants, at least to those managers selected as first-line supervisors, can pinpoint areas for their development. Their later success can be tracked on 360 surveys, which, in turn, can provide tracking information for the managers to calibrate the success of their development efforts.

Another study was conducted by a large wireless communications company that had gone through a change in leadership.[3] The new CEO wanted senior executives to be evaluated using an "objective" method from outside the organization for developmental purposes. A one-day assessment center with four simulations was designed by an outside consulting firm for this purpose. The four simulations included a coaching interaction (participants prepared feedback and then met with a role player who assumed the role of the manager in need of coaching), a peer interaction (they prepared for and conducted a meeting with a role player who assumed the role of a peer from another division); a new product rollout (participants wrote their recommendations for a set of new products and then discussed these with a role player who assumed the role of an assistant director); and a business plan presentation (participants presented their findings and recommendations for a new product and an overview of the state of their region to two role players who assumed the role of board of directors members). The assessment resulted in an evaluation of 11 competencies. Participants received a summary report of their results in one-on-one feedback sessions.

About 9 months after the assessment center, the senior managers participated in a 5-day training workshop to learn about and discuss the organizational vision and mission developed by the new CEO. As a prelude to this process, a 360-degree survey was conducted for feedback to participants during the workshop to help them focus on their readiness to implement the behaviors needed for the new mission and vision. The survey was administered over the Internet. The same 11 competencies measured in the assessment center were also rated in the 360-degree survey. The results were fed back to the managers in one-on-one sessions with experienced executive coaches as a start to establishing a personal development plan.

The results showed that two competencies—high-impact communication and people development—were significantly related between the assessment center and the 360-degree feedback survey. This suggests that the assessment center and 360 survey were best at measuring these competencies. Ratings from the managers' supervisors correlated most highly with the assessment center ratings, similar to the Boeing study. Overall, supervisors seem to be most accurate among the various sources of ratings, perhaps because they have the best opportunity to observe, they have experience evaluating performance, and they may not be influenced by political factors or leniency or severity errors that may affect self-, subordinate, and peer ratings. Subordinate ratings on the performance dimension of high-impact communication correlated as highly with the assessment center ratings as the supervisor ratings on this dimension, possibly because subordinates have considerable interaction with the senior managers compared to peers and are able to evaluate communication skills accurately. Peer ratings of organizing and planning were more highly related to the similar performance dimensions evaluated in the assessment center, perhaps because peers are directly impacted by the senior manager's organizing and planning skills.

The results of these two studies suggest that assessment center and 360-degree feedback results are most likely to coincide from the perspective of the manager's supervisor. The results also suggest that 360-degree feedback results should not be automatically averaged across all raters, but that results from different rater groups should be examined, and their validity determined, separately. Recipients of feedback results from assessment centers need to understand the perspective of the results— that assessment center results seem to reflect their boss's perspective, but may reflect subordinate or peer perspectives for certain dimensions. If you are receiving 360-degree feedback, you need to understand that different sources have different perspectives.

Next, consider other assessment methods as sources of feedback—in particular, computerized assessment, business simulations, and organization analysis.

Computerized Testing Assessment

Another method for identifying skills and proficiency levels that is increasingly available and cost-effective is computerized assessment. This method uses computers to present items customized to the participant's ability, measure a variety of responses (e.g., time to respond to different situations), and, if appropriate, provide feedback at various points in time. It uses computer technologies, including a CD-ROM with full-motion video. For instance, managers being tested may be presented with several video scenarios of a boss and a subordinate involving, say, the need for conflict resolution, delegation, and/or coaching. After watching each scenario, managers are asked to answer multiple-choice questions. Responses may indicate different styles of management, which in turn can be demonstrated on follow-up videos that reveal the outcomes of different choices. As such, the method presents realistic, clear information; allows people to see how others might react to their behavior and decisions; repeats similar situations across participants; can vary the difficulty and complexity of the simulations; offers immediate and repeated feedback; and records precise information about the participants' performance (e.g., it can also determine whether the participant responds to an issue before viewing other pertinent information). It is most valuable for assessment of skills not easily or inexpensively measured via traditional in-person exercises or paper-and-pencil tests.[4]

Games and Simulations

Business games and simulations are often incorporated into training programs as a way to communicate changing business strategies and directions and help participants assess and build their strengths and weaknesses in relation to these strategic directions. Assessment centers use short business games and simulations. Here, I am addressing in-depth simulations of a longer duration, sometimes several hours or even days. These techniques are sometimes referred to as "practice fields" in that they help individuals and the organization as a whole learn and develop. They are valuable because managerial action in the real world may be too slow, ambiguous, and even risky to learn by doing.[5] Feedback from a simulation can be fast and clear. Moreover, a simulation is a safe place where managers may practice decision making and experiment with new styles of management. Participants have a chance to do, think, and feel; and feedback is an important part of the learning. Of course, the simulation must be realistic enough to be engaging, but not so complex that it is threatening. Several examples follow.

A Computer-Based Simulation

A telecommunications firm engaged consultants to deliver a new leadership training and development program that would communicate a vision for the organization and encourage managers to take more responsibility for leadership, as well as increase managers' knowledge and understanding of the industry.[6] The program was designed for the firm's 350 top managers. About 16 managers attended each two-and-a-half day session. One and a half of the days were dedicated to a simulation that modeled new global alliances, joint ventures between cable and telephone companies, and linkages with computer network providers and other industries, such as publishing and entertainment.

The computer-based game (which took 18 person-months to develop) had four teams of usually four participants each enter decisions on new products, marketing, salesforce, customer service, and operations. Participants were assigned roles, such as VP of marketing and VP of new product introduction. Each team could launch up to 12 products. Each team worked in a room with a PC networked to a central file server. Each team established its own strategic plan and goals at the start. Printable screens provided the teams with support data. Each round of the simulation required that the team search for data and decide about such issues as new products, pricing, and budget allocations between departments. Decisions were made about each function performed (e.g., marketing, customer service, operations), which in turn had implications for quality and market results. The teams could cooperate by licensing new products to other teams or investing in national advertising. At the end of each round, the key results were summarized and the teams were encouraged to compare each other's performance. The simulation provided a shared experience and an opportunity for discussion. Participants received feedback about their behavior and also learned how to step back from situations and hold process discussions.

Looking Glass

Perhaps the best-known realistic simulation is Looking Glass, Inc. Looking Glass was developed by the Center for Creative Leadership (a nonprofit organization established by the Smith Richardson Foundation to study issues of management and leadership). Looking Glass is a fictitious organization in the glass business. The simulation assigns roles to up to 20 participants, ranging from president to plant manager. After reading extensive materials on the firm (e.g., an annual report, financial data, job descriptions, and recent memos), the participants interact as they deal with the more than 150 problems embedded in the material. The simulation is used as a part of a week-long leadership development program by the Center for Creative Leadership. Participants can enroll in these programs as individuals or as part of a corporate group.

Case: One Person's Experience with Looking Glass[7]

Allen Bruce was a successful manager with a bright future in a growing firm. A bachelor in his mid-30s, he thought of himself as someone who was friendly and good with interpersonal relationships. He was shocked when he learned from an associate that he had a reputation of being "threatening" to work with and that others saw him

---

as an ambitious, somewhat self-serving person with little concern for others. After discussing this discrepancy between how he saw himself and how others seemed to see him, his boss recommended that Allen enroll in the leadership development program run by the firm that incorporated the Looking Glass exercise.

At the start of the workshop, Allen suggested to the other participants that they have a pre-simulation meeting. After reviewing the materials, Allen came to the first meeting well organized, with special interest in a memo from the company president that the three divisional directors of sales and marketing, of which Allen was to be one, get together to coordinate solutions to common problems. Allen's goal was to formulate a plan that would bring about dramatic improvement in Looking Glass's operations, and he planned to take the initiative to get things moving.

During the simulation, participants were assigned to office space. Phones rang, people talked, and mail was delivered. Allen began by calling the president as a way of making himself visible "upstairs." He then attended a products division meeting, but didn't contribute much because he was preoccupied by his own plans. He later pigeonholed another participant, Carl, who played the role of Looking Glass's vice president, and suggested that all the company's problems were due to inefficiency from lack of coordination, and he wanted to be given the authority to work with the other directors to develop a comprehensive plan to clean things up. Carl agreed, but during a subsequent meeting with the other directors, Allen had trouble convincing them that they really needed sweeping change.

Allen then worked in his office to draft an email to the president that outlined a re-organization of the firm that would address the principal problem, as Allen saw it. But he received no response. The president had spent the day emphasizing cost containment, and even sent a memo to the staff indicating that all recommendations should address cost cutting. Allen then shared his plan with the vice president, Carl. He suggested that Allen revise his plan to limit it to sales and marketing. This might make it more palatable to the management committee that would be meeting shortly.

Before the meeting, Allen telephoned one of his fellow regional directors, Wendy. She had seen Allen's plan and indicated she didn't think there was any support for it in the management committee. In fact, she informed him that the committee members had already ruled out his plan. Allen didn't see how Wendy would know that unless she had access to the president. Allen told her it was quite a shock to him to find that someone he trusted was a "back stabber." Allen felt better later when he learned from Carl that his re-organization plan had received "some consideration" from the management committee and that the sales and marketing areas would be re-structured in some way.

Allen later confronted Wendy with his feeling that Wendy and the other regional director took the essence of his plan for their own plan. Wendy was astounded that Allen would think she and others had spent their time plotting against him. Wendy said that she had been working on a "little agreement for transfer pricing," and this is what Carl referred to when he implied that parts of Allen's plan would be implemented. Allen was embarrassed and wondered how his imagination could have made him so paranoid.

The simulation ended in mid-afternoon. During the evening and following day, Allen participated in three debriefing sessions. The first two were general sessions with all the participants to discuss the experience as a whole and the performance of each division as a unit. During the third session, each participant's individual performance was discussed. Four main points emerged with the help of a facilitator and the other participants. Allen realized that he had a tendency to manipulate people. He sometimes invested too much in his own plans at the expense of what others were trying to do. He was a skilled communicator and wanted to cooperate with superiors, but he was less concerned about building rapport with peers and subordinates. Finally, he discovered that he tended to attribute to others the same manipulative motives that he himself had as a way to justify his own actions.

Allen showed resilience in accepting this new self-awareness. He admitted that the messages were not easy to hear, but that they were useful. He felt that he got what he came to learn.

Conclusion

Assessment centers are an excellent development tool because they provide in-depth information under standardized conditions. Increasingly sophisticated computerized assessments and business simulations can also provide meaningful feedback. The value of the feedback, however, lies in using it to set development goals. These standardized, realistic methods may be particularly valuable at the start of a development process. Multisource feedback can then be a way to help managers track improvement in performance as they make progress in their development plans. Now for the major conclusions from the chapter:

- Assessment centers give participants feedback about their performance and suggest directions for their development.

- Assessment centers that are aimed mainly at providing participants with information to guide development are most useful to participants who want the feedback and intend to use it constructively.
- Assessment center results predict later performance measured by 360-degree feedback ratings. The prediction may be enhanced when the 360 ratings are averaged across certain rater groups, showing the value of obtaining job performance ratings from multiple perspectives.
- Assessment results can be fed back to participants to help them determine areas for development. Then 360-degree feedback can help them track the effectiveness of their developmental efforts.
- In addition to the assessment center, there are other methods for assessment and feedback about performance. Computerized assessment offers readily accessible, cost-effective, self-paced methods for self-evaluation. "Practice fields" are games and simulations that allow participants to experiment with new behaviors in settings that are realistic and nonthreatening. These simulations are often incorporated into management development programs to provide feedback and stimulate learning.
- Individuals can seek programs on their own that use practice field simulations, or organizations can commission the design of customized simulations to be used as an organization development intervention.

So far in this section of the book, I have reviewed methods for evaluation. In the next chapter, I turn to ways to support the use of these methods—specifically, the role of the supervisor not only as a prime source of feedback but also as a coach and developer.

Notes

1. Gordon, Mian, and Gabel (2002).
2. Hatten, Glaman, Houston, and Cochran (2002).
3. Gordon et al. (2002).
4. Drasgow, Olson, Keenan, Moberg, and Mead (1993).
5. Drew and Davidson (1993).
6. Drew and Davidson (1993).
7. This example was abstracted from Kaplan (1986).

9

THE SUPERVISOR AS DEVELOPER AND COACH

Feedback must be communicated and interpreted. Here I address what you can do to provide better feedback and facilitate its use. This is the role of the manager or anyone delivering feedback as a coach and developer. I describe how to conduct a meaningful performance review and how to respond when a subordinate is defensive. While many people, even managers whose responsibility is to let their subordinates know how they are doing, shy away from giving feedback, you can learn to make giving feedback a natural part of your management style. You can improve your observation skills, become a more accurate rater, and be more supportive and constructive in giving feedback.

Anticipating Reactions to Feedback

A person's reactions to feedback will depend on how the feedback is presented and on his or her readiness and ability to understand the feedback and change. People are often not sure why they are receiving feedback or what the giver intends by the feedback. At work, when a manager gives a subordinate feedback about his or her performance, the subordinate may be confused about the manager's purpose and goal and may not know how to respond or realize what's at stake—for instance, the subordinate's pay or job stability. The subordinate may not be ready to change his or her behavior.

Overall, then, the goal of the coach in working is to help recipients recognize performance problems, deal with their emotions (especially their likely fear of failure—an emotion they are not likely to express), and inspire them by pointing out the benefits of change and showing confidence in their ability to change. Over time, feedback recipients will realize that change is important to their identity, happiness, and success. You can help the person you are coaching to recognize that he or she can change. People who believe they can bring about positive outcomes (i.e., are high in self-efficacy) are more likely to see the benefits of trying to change. Some self-re-evaluation may be needed to tip the scales

122

from the cons of trying to change to the pros—that change can indeed be accomplished and have positive results. You can help the person you are coaching recognize resources for change. People must assume responsibility for and commit to change, and recognize that, ultimately, they are accountable for resulting performance improvement. This is empowered self-development. Short of establishing that commitment, they will remain in the pre-action stages, and probably never really go further than contemplation.

Coaches need to understand change processes to target feedback so that the receiver pays attention to it and uses it constructively. If recipients are just becoming aware of their strengths and weaknesses, they need time and help to digest the information, accept it, and understand its implications. Then they will be ready to use subsequent feedback to prepare for change and plan a development strategy. Eventually, as they progress to taking action and tracking their success, feedback takes on new meaning. Ultimately, feedback becomes an integral part of their ongoing change and adjustment. The trick to effective feedback is moving through the initial recognition stage to set challenging, realistic goals for development and track performance improvement in relation to these goals.

Beyond Feedback: Goal Setting

Goal setting is the means by which feedback motivates change. For instance, feedback can show a person what is wrong with his or her behavior and demonstrate ways to correct it (as an Olympic ice skating coach would offer feedback and suggestions to a champion skater or a ski instructor would demonstrate the correct method of downhill skiing to a novice). However, the individual needs to set goals to be motivated to improve his or her performance. The individual has to be committed to the goals. For this to happen, it is helpful if the individual participates in setting the goals. Goals selected by others rarely have a positive effect, at least not in the long run.[1] A coach can point out the risks of not paying attention to feedback results. However, it is up to the recipient to recognize the value of the feedback in directing behavior change and the importance of actually changing. Goals and feedback are mutually supportive.[2] Goals make feedback meaningful, and feedback helps improve goal achievement. Goals have little effect when feedback is not given. Similarly, feedback has little effect if it does not result in goal setting. Moreover, the combination of goal setting and feedback is more effective than either one alone.

To be more specific, goals are one of the key ways that feedback gets translated into action. That is, feedback motivates improved performance by means of goal setting. Feedback without goal setting does little to change performance. Similarly, when feedback is given for multiple aspects of performance, those areas that later improve are those for which goals have been set. Goals focus attention on information that is significant, and they direct subsequent action. Further, goal setting and feedback are important because they have positive and negative consequences. That is, they are followed by reward or recognition.

Goal setting and feedback are not necessarily explicit. Even when goals are not assigned or people are not asked to set goals following feedback, they may do so anyway. Also, even if feedback is not provided explicitly, people may use a variety of cues to get an idea about how well they are doing. They may use internal cues, such as how fast they are working or how hard they are trying. While these cues may be inaccurate, they still play a role in the person's cognitions about performance judgments.

Goals for performance improvement and development should be initiated during the appraisal review session, but this should be only the beginning of goal setting and reviews of progress. Goal setting is a continuous process with several meetings needed to suggest, negotiate, and agree on goals. Also review sessions on goal progress should be held throughout the year, quarterly, monthly, or even weekly depending on the job and person's experience.

Setting goals involves analyzing the gap between where one is and where one wants to be.[3] The supervisor or coach can ask the recipient, "Where do you want to be in a year?" and "What do you have to do to get there from here?" Supervisors can convey their expectations for their subordinates, but the subordinates will not be motivated until they adopt these expectations as their own. Goals need to be few in number, clear, behavioral, and difficult—that is, challenging but not unrealistic. Too many goals will dilute attention and reduce motivation. A clear, behavioral goal will specify what needs to be done. For instance, to encourage a manager to "pay attention to others' ideas," it may be necessary to ask the manager how he or she thinks this can be done. Asking for examples will reduce defensiveness and increase the chances that the manager will take heed. This may entail having a discussion about ways to elicit others' ideas (listen more than speak, restate others' ideas for clarification, and acknowledge others' contributions). Goals should be difficult; otherwise they are not worth achieving. Stretch goals (goals that are difficult yet doable) enhance the internal desire to achieve them. Goals that are impossible, however, reduce motivation and prompt helplessness.

Developmental goals should be more about learning or mastery, not merely performance improvement.[4] Learning goals enhance persistence beyond achievement of a particular level of performance. Supervisors and coaches can help their charges recognize their increased degree of mastery by providing timely feedback, which in turn can lead to further persistence in learning, rather than stopping because a particular level of performance and associated reward were achieved. Furthermore, a learning goal is not about merely taking a given course or completing a new type of task. Development and task performance should go hand-in-glove, occurring together and feeding on each other for continuous learning and continuous performance improvement.

Feedback Intervention Theory

Feedback helps people regulate their behavior as they compare the feedback they receive to the goals they set or the standards that are set for them by the organization. Feedback interventions change the focus of attention and hence lead to behavior changes.[5] That is, the feedback people happen to receive shapes their attention and causes them to change. If the feedback is not important to performance improvement, or if there is no feedback at all, behavior is unlikely to change, and it could change in ways that actually diminish performance. On the other hand, if feedback is targeted to behaviors that are important to success and the recipient detects a performance gap, the recipient is more likely to be motivated to reduce that gap—that is, to change his or her behavior and improve performance.

An important point is that feedback that is directed to behaviors needed to perform the task at hand (e.g., "Shorten your presentation by 5 minutes") is more constructive than feedback that threatens self-image (e.g., "Your presentation skills are lacking").

There are two aspects of the self—your ideal (what you want to be or do) and your ought (what others want you to be or do).[6] Negative feedback that focuses attention on what others want you to do is likely to motivate you to work hard to avoid disappointing others. Positive feedback about tasks that others want you to do provides no incentive for further improvement. However, positive feedback that helps you bring about your ideal self ("Be all that you can be") is likely to motivate you to continue to improve. But when you receive negative feedback about performance on tasks you want to do, the gap between your desired and actual self may seem too hard to overcome, so you give up.

Feedback that relates to previously established goals is likely to direct attention to the task and not to the self. Goal setting augments the power of feedback on performance. People who say they want more feedback are often those who do not have clear goals. Also, without clear goals, the feedback provider's focus may differ from that of the feedback recipient. Moreover, feedback that compares a person's performance to others is less effective than providing information about the degree of performance improvement over time. Comparing a person to others is threatening (it diminishes one's self-esteem), while comparing performance over time focuses on the individual's own goals for improvement (what the individual can become, not what others want the individual to become) and behaviors needed to bring about further improvement.[7] A 360-degree feedback survey or an annual performance appraisal should be tied to previous goal setting and have implications for future goals.

Helpful Hints for Giving Feedback[8]

- *Avoid sweeping statements.* Words such as "always" and "never" only make people angry, and defensive. It is too easy for them to say, "That's not true. I don't *always* . . .!"
- *Focus on major responsibilities and performance standards.* People want to know what is expected of them, not how they compare unfavorably to others.
- *Ask recipients to identify causes of performance problems.* Self-evaluation avoids defensiveness.
- *Provide feedback frequently.* As noted already, performance feedback should not be saved up and dumped on a person once a year during an annual performance review.
- *Discuss behavior or results, not the person.* Focusing on traits (e.g., "You are too passive") is likely to be seen as a personal attack.
- *Specify what needs to be done.* Don't just tell people what they did wrong. Help them establish a direction for improvement.
- *Use both positive and negative feedback.* Positive feedback provides encouragement and enhances motivation. Provide negative feedback in a way that *informs* the recipient rather than attacks the recipient's self-esteem.
- *Coach rather than judge.* Help the recipient of your feedback improve.
- *Fit feedback to the individual.* As I stated earlier, providing information enhances a person's insight into him- or herself and organizational expectations. Some people need more feedback than others, perhaps because of their experience or their ability to discern their effectiveness in the organization. Some people may not realize what is important to you perhaps because it was never discussed openly. Or they may not realize the effect that their behavior is having on others.

A Sample Discussion

Here's a way to *start* the review: "I'd like you to start the discussion. What do you think are the three most important things you accomplished during the last 6 months? [later] What are the things you wish you had done better? What do you think needs improvement? What do you need to help you improve?"

Be prepared for *defensive reactions*—denying the problem, changing the subject, focusing on something else, attributing external blame. Here are some possibilities:

"That's not the way I see it at all! I tried my best, but there was nothing more I could have done. It was out of my control."

"I don't know where you are getting your information, but that's not what happened."

"Several people in the group just don't like me. But I worked as hard as anyone."

"I'm doing my best. I did everything you wanted me to."

"It's unfair to be telling me now you wanted something else. I would have been happy to change if you had only told me."

"I've had plenty of experience, and I know how things work around here. This is the way we've always done it, and I see no reason to change now."

"I agree with you that things didn't turn out as well as they could have. If we only had . . . better information, a new computer system, more coop-eration from other departments, etc. Something should be done about this. Maybe I can work on it now that we all recognize the problem."

Avoid *destructive comments in responses to defensiveness*: don't argue, debate, deny, insist, cite others as the source of the evaluation, generalize, or personalize. For example, don't say . . .

"You're just going to have to see it my way. You really have no choice."

"You better think it over."

"It doesn't matter what you think."

"This isn't the way I feel. I'm just passing on what our boss thinks, and you better come to terms with that."

"How could that be?"

"Face it—you're not cut out for this job."

Here are some *constructive responses to defensiveness*: Recognize and diffuse the problem up front. Agree and move on. Be repetitive. Focus on facts (behaviors or outcomes) rather than personal characteristics. Sug-gest directions for improvement. For example . . .

"I know you don't agree with me. I'm just asking you to hear me out."

"This is how I see it, and you need to know that. Now here's what I recommend."

"Here are some things you could do differently next time."

"Rather than debate the issue, let's work on what you can do differ-ently next time."

These statements may have to be repeated several times before the employee hears them.

Case: Preparing to Give Feedback

John Gallagher, an IT manager, noted the value of preparing to give feedback. He related an occasion when he needed to give a subordinate feedback about a presentation he had recently given. The subordinate was a technical expert in an area that John knew less about. John knew he had to prepare, gaining some better knowledge of the technical subject and also looking up information about presentation style, especially for technical presentations to people who were not technically savvy. John prepared by reviewing the presentation PowerPoint, and reviewing several manuals on the technology. John felt that his preparation made the feedback discussion successful. He showed his subordinate that he was involved and interested in not only the subject but also the subordinate's professional development. John saw that he needed to take into account who was receiving the feedback, and his likely reaction. Each subordinate is different and requires a different technique.

Summary

Feedback provides direction for goal setting, and goals motivate behavior change. Goals need to be challenging yet realistic—that is, accomplishable. They need to focus on behaviors that can be changed, not general personality characteristics that are difficult to define let alone know how to change. Once goals are set, feedback needs to be specific enough and targeted to behaviors that are goal-focused. Otherwise it will be ignored. Overall, feedback should (a) focus on the task (i.e., behavior), not on the person's sense of self; (b) not threaten the recipient's ego; (c) be specific about how to improve performance; (d) link the feedback to prior goals and to future goals; and (e) minimize information comparing the recipient to others and maximize information about ways to improve performance.

Coaching

Performance coaching is the process of helping someone collect and interpret feedback, set goals, and track performance. It is a one-on-one process. Coaching is part of the development process. However, it goes beyond giving feedback and providing resources for learning, such as opportunities to attend workshops or to try new assignments. The term "coach," borrowed from athletics, is someone who helps you focus on behaviors that you can change, both on your own and in interaction with others, often in relation to critical events, such as working on an important assignment or being a newly hired or elected president of an

128

organization. Coaches may be external, and indeed, there is a profession called executive coaching. Executive coaches are often experienced managers who are hired by executives or their firms to work closely with executives to help them think about how they can improve. The purpose of hiring a professional executive coach from outside the firm is to build a trusting relationship in which the executive can talk openly about her- or himself and co-workers. Still, people internal to the firm can be coaches. A coach may become a mentor, providing ongoing guidance to further an individual's career, but this is more of a personal relationship of support and nurturing professional development, whereas coaching is more goal-oriented and focused on improvement during several months' time. Coaches may start with 360-degree performance survey results, review the results with their clients, and help the clients discuss the feedback with co-workers to get more precise feedback, set goals, recognize their accountability for using the feedback, and process changes in behavior.

Feedback from an external coach may be less threatening and command more attention than feedback from a peer. Peers (co-workers in similar positions and organizational levels) may be viewed as competitors for the positive attention and rewards from the supervisor or team leader. So even though peers are present to observe an individual's behaviors firsthand, people may be less likely to trust their perceptions or ideas for improvement. External coaches are more credible. They gather information from peers and others, synthesize the information, provide what you may view as a more objective analysis, and encourage you to think about the feedback mindfully. Indeed, in one study, team members' performance improved more after external coaching than peer coaching.[9]

As an example of external coaching, a company offered its senior managers executive coaches as part of a leadership development initiative. The managers could select coaches from a list provided by the human resources department. The list described each coach's background, including education, corporate managerial experience, and experience coaching managers in different corporations. During the first 3–4 hour meeting, the coach explained the purpose of the coaching and discussed the manager's job and current business and departmental issues. Follow-up sessions were scheduled. Coaches tried to arrange for meetings away from the manager's office (e.g., in a conference room) so that the manager would not be disturbed or distracted. Some coaches met with the manager's subordinates or other co-workers to obtain additional input. Multisource feedback survey results were available, and the manager could ask the coach for help with understanding the results. Some coaches asked the manager to complete measures of leadership style and personality that might be helpful in understanding how the manager handled interpersonal relationships. The coaches worked with managers to set development goals and formulate a plan for meeting those goals. The human resources department paid for the first four sessions—the amount of time usually required to review needs and set developmental goals. After that, managers could elect to continue with the coach, paying the bill from the manager's departmental funds.

Coaching sessions may be formal talks with meeting times scheduled to set them apart from the grind of daily activity. They may also occur in the moment, perhaps immediately following an event or critical incident. If you are a supervisor acting as a coach at a particular time, you should state explicitly that the session is meant to be coaching, and the employee needs to agree that he or she is willing to participate in a coaching session. If this is an informal, spontaneous meeting, you might say, "Let's have a coaching session." "What did you think happened in the meeting?" "How did people react to you?" "Here's what I saw." "Do you agree with my assessment?" "How could you have responded differently . . . more constructively?"

Coaches' Regulatory Focus

Regulatory focus refers to different ways in which people pursue goals. People with a promotion focus give attention to achieving positive outcomes. Those with a prevention focus give attention to avoiding negative outcomes.[10] Leaders and coaches who have a promotion focus can inspire a focus on positive achievement, especially if those they are coaching believe that they can improve their performance. However, if they are coaching people who believe that behaviors cannot be changed easily, then focusing on positive outcomes during the coaching session is not as effective as focusing on avoiding negative outcomes.[11] So, for example, a leader who is optimistic and encourages team members to keep an eye on achieving goals and the positive rewards that will result has a positive effect on team and individual performance, especially when the team members believe they can improve. If they are skeptical about the ability to achieve their goals, then reminding them about what will happen if they fail to achieve their goals will be more effective.

Steps for Effective Coaching

Coaching is harder than giving feedback. It is easier to say what is right or wrong with performance than it is to identify ways to correct a performance problem. Coaching is essentially problem solving applied to a performance problem. Here are some steps for effective coaching discussions:[12]

> *State the purpose*: Be direct (e.g., "I want to talk about the report you gave me yesterday").
> *State the performance problem*: It helps to have observations or measures. Describe the expected performance, the actual performance,

130

and the effects of the actual performance on the job (e.g., "The vice president wanted the report to include a time series analysis of the company's financial performance, but you didn't do that"). Also, admit that there are multiple perspectives.

Get reactions: Ask the person you are coaching for his or her perspective ("What do you think?" "Do you agree with me?"). Keep the discussion on track. Don't get sidetracked by ancillary issues (e.g., a response such as, "Other reports don't include the information and I recall their authors were given a chance to present the results in person to the vice president. I hope you'll let me have that chance.").

Analyze the causes of why the performance is unsatisfactory: Explore possible causes of the performance problem. Ask the person you are coaching to identify factors he/she has control over that may be causing the problem (e.g., "Maybe you don't know enough about the database or software to get what we need here"). Consider external factors that may have caused the performance problem (e.g., "The computer systems were down").

Seek a collaborative solution if possible: Ask for ideas about how to solve the problem (e.g., "How can we fix this?"). Be patient, and consider all ideas. Offer your own course of action if the staff member is uncertain what to do. Summarize the agreed-to course of action (e.g., "Okay, so we agree. You'll ask Bill for help in analyzing the data, and you will revise the report this weekend.").

Provide assistance and follow-up: Establish what assistance the person you are coaching will need in the future. Determine what each of you will do for follow-up and subsequent performance review (e.g., "Let me have the revised report on Monday morning. I'll read it right away, and we can discuss it right after lunch.").

Case: Generational Differences and Coaching

Sue Bolinger, an operations manager in a telecommunications firm, manages a group of ten. Sue has worked for the company for 16 years and is in her early 40s. She reports to a district manager, Joan Kaminski. Joan has an MBA degree and is in her early 30s. Joan has worked for the company for 3 years and has been moving up quickly. Sue has a positive attitude about feedback. She says that Joan is a wonderful supervisor and she has the utmost respect for her even though she has far less actual work experience. Joan encourages open dialogue and has created an environment of trust. They have direct communication, and Sue feels that she has learned a lot working for Joan the past 6 months. Joan treats feedback as form of coaching, and Sue sees it the same way. Joan's feedback is specific to Sue's job and team. Sue doesn't see this as micro-managing. Sue feels that the feedback could just as easily be called "guidance." Joan listens to Sue without interrupting. Joan's feedback is communicated not only verbally, face-to-face, but also in actions, when she gives Sue additional responsibilities, showing that she has confidence in Sue's ability. However, Sue admitted that some of her fellow managers who also report directly to Joan do not see Joan's feedback in the same positive light. Rather than interpreting Joan's performance discussions as constructive, they complain to Sue that Joan doesn't know what she is talking about. Sue thinks they are threatened by Joan's success as a young manager in the company's development program for high-potential managers. They say that Joan will make changes and be promoted out of the department and not have to live with the consequences of bad decisions. Instead of learning from and with Joan, and seeing her as a coach who is concerned with their development, as Sue is doing, they prefer to be disgruntled. Of course, they don't let Joan know how they feel, but they do so indirectly by saying little when Joan gives them feedback and doing little to change. Joan has complained to Sue that she is frustrated and wonders why the other managers can't have a constructive, direct discussion about performance the way she and Sue have. So Sue has tried to reverse the coaching relationship, giving Joan some advice—to be patient, listen, recognize that the managers may be jealous, and that there is a natural generation gap that will take time to overcome.

Coaching Improves the Value of 360-Degree Feedback

A study of 1,361 executives in a large, global company showed the importance of coaching to improve the value of multisource feedback.[13] All the executives received feedback from their boss, peers, and subordinates and then set two to four goals for improvement. About a fourth of these executives worked with external coaches (consultants selected by the human resources department) to help them interpret their feedback and set goals. The executives were not assigned randomly to the coaching but were in departments that participated in the coaching process. Human resources managers matched coaches to executives based on the coach's prior managerial experiences and the coach's experiences working with clients in similar situations. Each executive worked with a coach for three or four sessions over a period of 6 weeks or so. The coach was given the executive's feedback results before the first meeting with the executive. About half the executives who were coached completed a brief online questionnaire about their reactions to the coaching soon after it took place. The company administered a "mini-360" survey 8 months after the first survey to obtain ratings of the extent to which the executives had made progress toward their goals. Executives who had been coached and those who had not were rated in this survey. The survey actually listed each executive's specific goals and asked for ratings of improvement on each one. Then, 1 year after the first survey, there was another survey completed by most of the original sample of managers.

The results showed that 86% of the executives who had the chance to work with a coach wanted to work with a coach again, and 78% wanted to work with the same coach. The executives generally believed that their coaches had done a good job. Those who worked with a coach were more likely to set specific goals, share their feedback, and solicit ideas for improvement from their managers, compared with those who did not work with a coach. Contrary to prediction, executives who worked with a coach were rated lower in goal progress by their peers and managers 8 months after the first survey. This could have been because the expectations were higher for those who worked with a coach or because the coach actually slowed down performance improvement by taking more time to set the goals. After 1 year, executives who had been coached improved more in ratings from their subordinates and managers than executives who had not been coached but there was no significant difference for peer ratings. The number of meetings with the coach was not related to changes in performance ratings.

Another finding from the study was that there were differences between coaches—for example, some coaches produced more positive effects than others. Coaching was not a uniform process. While the company had worked hard to identify competent coaches, train them in the purpose and content of the feedback survey, and match them to executives, the coaches varied in their approaches. Some began their coaching by reviewing the feedback results with the executive. Others spent time asking the executive about current business issues and challenges and then related the feedback results to coping with these current problems. (This was a way to capture the executives' attention by focusing on business issues at hand rather than general development needs.) Still other coaches asked the executives with whom they worked to complete various personality measures—for instance, measures of the tendency to be introverted or extroverted. These coaches may have spent less time on the 360-degree feedback results than on the particular personality measures they favored. Overall, idiosyncratic coaching styles are likely to influence the value of coaching.

Case: Using Emotional Intelligence

Shirley Strauss is an attorney in independent practice. In her late 50s, she has built her practice during the last 25 years and now employees two other attorneys, four paralegals, and two secretaries. Shirley tries to give her people regular feedback whenever the need arises. When employees ask for feedback, especially when their performance has been okay or even exemplary, she thinks about why— do they really want feedback or are they insecure and want some reassurance, or are they trying to focus Shirley on what they do well? When Shirley has something negative to say about an employee's performance, she considers how the employee will take the feedback. Some people prefer feedback to be direct and intellectual, not beating around the bush, whereas others need to be reached through their emotions. In all cases, though, the feedback must be honest and accurate. People should not offer non-essential gratuitous advice, provide personal views, or offer their own hunches. Shirley's experience has been that when people actually care about the person to whom they are speaking, their guard is often let down, and that is a recipe for trouble—they mean well, but they try to be Dr. Phil, which is the kiss of death.

Accountability for Giving and Using Feedback

Accountability applies to providers and receivers of feedback. As a provider, accountability refers to being responsible for making careful judgments. Feedback providers who take this responsibility seriously may keep their own notes about their observations as critical incidents occur and then draw on those notes when asked to make ratings, write comments, or write an extensive performance evaluation. Admittedly, though, this is rare. On the job, supervisors generally respond to the rating task when it occurs, especially in the case of multisource feedback, which asks subordinates to rate supervisors and peers to rate each other. (Supervisors should expect that they will be asked to evaluate their subordinates, and they should take preparatory notes and keep documentation over time to support their judgments.) Even though these ratings are anonymous, raters, as committed team and organization members, should still feel responsible for providing ratings that are useful.

Recipients who take responsibility for using the feedback seriously may seek additional information; ask for assistance from the raters, their supervisor, or a coach in interpreting the information; incorporate the feedback in planning their development, and follow up by tracking changes in their behavior and, hopefully, improvement in their performance over time. The feedback process itself and associated support from the organization and supervisor in the form of coaching, training, and job assignments will help drive home the value and importance of the feedback to raters and recipients.

Case: Focusing on the Positive in Giving and Receiving Feedback

Jim Grafton is a computer programmer in his mid-40s. He supervises a team of five other programmers and reports to a supervisor who manages seven other teams similar to his. In giving feedback to his subordinates, Jim tries to find something positive in order to boost confidence. He addresses performance problems by sharing stories of his experiences in dealing with similar issues. He then uses these stories as a mechanism to suggest ways to improve and alternative ways to solve problems. He admitted that he is not a good receiver of feedback. He finds criticism hard to accept. However, he finds that positive feedback motivates him to work harder. He feels "unworthy" of praise, and this stimulates him to do even better and live up to his manager's positive view of him.

Summary

Coaching is a development process. It may start with feedback—for instance, from a multisource feedback report, a performance review, or information from the person who is coached. External coaches are often hired to help senior managers work through feedback and establish development plans. This coaching relationship may continue as the manager uses the coach as an objective sounding board for ideas, a counselor to help with work relationship problems, and/or a sage advisor. Managers can become coaches to the people who report to them. As such, they go beyond formal performance reviews to provide guidance and resources for their subordinates' performance improvement and career development. Being a coach does not mean that the manager gives up other, more directive aspects of the managerial role, such as delegating work and making tough staffing decisions. In other words, the manager and the subordinate need to understand the boundaries of the coaching role—when the manager is acting as a coach, providing individual and interpersonal support, and when the manager is acting as a decision maker, providing direction and control. This can be a fine line that the manager may need to clarify explicitly at the start of one-on-one feedback/performance management discussions. In general, the research on coaching suggests that coaching is a valuable adjunct to feedback, but more extensive research is needed in this area to understand the effects of different approaches to coaching and the conditions under which these approaches are most likely to be successful.

Conclusion

This chapter explored conditions for enhancing feedback acceptance and use. The person's readiness to change is important to accepting feedback. Using feedback to set goals is important to making feedback worthwhile. The formal performance review and informal performance discussions can target behaviors, track goals, and motivate further accomplishment. Here are points to remember:

- Information is likely to be perceived more accurately and be accepted when it follows a number of conditions—for instance, it comes from a source who the recipient views as knowledgeable and trustworthy, it comes soon after the behavior, and it is positive, frequent, and specific.
- A goal is the gap between where one is and where one wants to be. Goal setting is the means by which feedback motivates change. Ongoing feedback helps individuals calibrate their degree of goal accomplishment and the level of effort needed to reach the goal.
- Individuals must participate in setting their own goals. Participation leads to commitment to the goals. Assigned goals don't work.
- Goals should be few, clear, behavioral, and difficult in order to motivate learning and behavior change.
- For continuous development, goals should be focused on learning and mastery, not performance improvement.
- Feedback interventions should focus on the task (i.e., behavior), not on the person's sense of self. Also, feedback should be specific about how to improve performance, be linked to prior goals and to future goals, minimize information comparing the recipient to others, and maximize information about ways to improve performance.
- Coaching sessions may be formal talks with meeting times scheduled to set them apart from the grind of daily activity.
- In-the-moment coaching can be a very effective way to change behavior because it is immediate and closely tied to actual behaviors that can be discussed.
- Coaching increases the positive benefits of 360-degree feedback.
- Accountability motivates the rater. People who feel accountable by having to justify their ratings to someone else generate more accurate ratings.

This chapter concludes the second section of the book. The first section focused on how people perceive themselves and each other and give and use feedback. This second section described methods for evaluation as the source of feedback and ways managers support the use of feedback. In the third section of the book, I turn to the present context for feedback—issues of culture, team and organization feedback, and technology for collecting and delivering feedback—and finally, I end the book with how to develop a feedback-oriented, continuous learning organizational culture.

Notes

1. Dalton and Hollenbeck (2001).
2. This section is based on London (1995b); Locke and Latham (1990, Chapter 8) provide an extensive review of feedback and goal setting.
3. Dalton and Hollenbeck (2001).
4. Dalton and Hollenbeck (2001).
5. Kluger and DeNisi (1996, 1998).
6. Higgins (1987).
7. Kluger and DeNisi (1998).
8. Silverman (1991).
9. Sue-Chan and Latham (2004).
10. Higgins (1987).
11. Sue-Chan, Wood, and Latham (2012).
12. Adapted from Hillman, Schwandt, and Bartz (1990, p. 26).
13. Smither, London, Flautt, Vargas, and Kucine (2002, in press).

Section III

EXPANDING THE POWER OF FEEDBACK

10

FEEDBACK ACROSS THE GLOBE

In a multinational company, a common performance appraisal and
feedback process communicates the key performance dimensions across
units of the company. This should be of value in helping teams and individuals recognize common objectives, which, in turn, should facilitate
collaboration within and between organizational units.[1] Managers in
multinational companies need to have competencies that allow them to
be independent and entrepreneurial, taking advantage of local business
opportunities, rather than be guided solely by corporate planners who
are removed from the marketplace.[2] They also need competencies that
allow them to develop interdependent connections with other subsidiaries and headquarters. They need to focus on the task, establish effective
interpersonal relationships, and build trust.

360 Feedback in Multinational Organizations

Multisource feedback can be valuable to expatriates in multinational
companies who are not familiar with their host culture.[3] The feedback
can help them understand the expectations of the different sources of
feedback and be more realistic in setting performance goals. Multisource
feedback captures the high complexity of the global work environment,
and this may help managers adapt to their new environment. While to
some extent multinational subsidiaries adapt to the culture of the company's headquarters—establishing a common corporate culture across the
multinational organization—there is also the possibility that differences
in cultural values may affect the importance of performance dimensions.
As a result, some dimensions of performance may be more important in
one national culture than another.

One study collected 360-degree feedback data from 23 sites of a single
high-tech organization over a period of 2 years.[4] The performance survey
included 31 items. Self-, subordinate, peer, customer, and supervisor ratings were obtained for 408 mid-level managers. Factor analysis of the items
across all ratings revealed four dimensions of performance: task-oriented

leadership, people-oriented leadership, strategy development/planning, and change/innovation management. The study also examined differences between the favorability of the ratings on the factors between managers in different countries. Task-focused leadership did not vary between countries, perhaps because of the individualism of Western cultures and the high uncertainty avoidance of Eastern cultures.[5] Managers in the U.S. were significantly higher than managers in other countries on people-focused leadership. The researchers interpreted this as a result of the high power equalization that typifies management in the U.S.[6] Managers in Far Eastern countries were higher than Anglo, Nordic, Latin, and U.S. managers on strategic planning (a dimension that would be important to global strategy). This may be because Far Eastern countries emphasize the development of new markets. Also, managers from the U.S. and Far Eastern countries were significantly higher on the change/innovation dimension than managers from other countries, perhaps because of the competitive spirit in the U.S. and the need to harmonize and adjust in the Far East. In addition, managers from countries that are characterized as individualistic, particularly the U.S., tended to rate themselves higher than other sources rated them.

Managers from different cultures may perceive performance-related behaviors and traits differently, and, as a result, the relationships among the items and the factors underlying these relationships may differ between cultures. This would call into question the ease of "internationalizing" a rating instrument, even when the translations are carefully done to ensure common understanding of the items. (This translation process usually entails translating the items to another language and then translating them back to the original. After several iterations of translation and back-translation by different linguists, equivalence can be determined. This can be a painstaking process, especially when the survey is translated into several different languages.) Without examining the equivalence of factor structure across cultures, mean differences may result in misguided or inaccurate conclusions because the items mean different things in different cultures. This may occur when people from different cultures use different categories of thinking or different constructs to define and interpret behavior.[7] To examine this, a study obtained subordinate performance ratings for managers in a U.S.-based transportation company.[8] The study included managers from U.S. operations and in-country nationals working in corporate offices in Great Britain, Hong Kong, and Japan. In terms of cultural values, the managers from the U.S. and Great Britain were higher in individualism and lower in power distance than those from Hong Kong and Japan. Norms (e.g., mean levels of performance on items) within a country should be presented to the managers to help them interpret their results. Feedback workshops should discuss cultural factors that may influence the results.

Also, country differences should be considered in understanding performance results across the company and the need for training. Some companies may wish to implement a communications campaign across subsidiaries to develop a common understanding of performance dimensions. Other companies may wish to recognize these differences and determine how they can be advantageous to the firm, rather than training to eliminate them. So, for instance, a company may select and train managers for transfer on the cultural differences so they can adapt and develop effective working relationships more quickly. Also, understanding these differences will help managers work with other firms (partners and customers) within the culture, as well as facilitate collaboration in joint ventures between cultures.

Cultural Differences in Self-Evaluations

While leniency in self-ratings is common, it is not universal. However, this may stem from a bias in favor of individualism in Western culture and in other societies. For instance, Taiwanese workers show a "modesty bias" with lower self-ratings than ratings obtained from supervisors.[9] This may be due to a collectivism bias coupled with high deference to authority in the Taiwanese culture. However, a study of blue collar workers in Nanjing, China (the People's Republic), found a leniency bias in self-ratings compared to peer and supervisor ratings.[10] This suggests that culture is not homogeneous and may be differentiated by many factors (country, industry, mode of operations and organization, and so forth).

Case: Clash of Cultures

Bo Wang is a Chinese mechanical engineer employed by an automobile manufacturer who recently purchased a Swedish car company. Sent by his firm for a 6-month assignment to Sweden to collaborate on a joint project, he was assigned to a team directed by Viktor Albertsson, an experienced engineer and executive. Bo's English is excellent, as is that of most of his new co-workers in Sweden, although the Swedish team tended to communicate in Swedish when Bo was not involved in the conversation. Bo felt isolated. To him, teamwork and team performance were key. Viktor, on the other hand, treated everyone equally but focused on each person's individual performance. After 3 weeks in Sweden, Viktor gave Bo some feedback. He felt that Bo was not concentrating on the engineering work. He was trying too hard to help each member of the work group. Viktor didn't see the group as a team so much as individuals who had their separate and clear roles.

Think about how this would work in reverse. Suppose Viktor had been assigned to work in China, where collective work is highly valued. He might feel he is doing a good job concentrating on his assignment, working individually and providing input to the team as needed. He might not receive direct feedback, since his management wouldn't want to make him, as a guest, lose face or feel underappreciated or insulted by not valuing his expertise. They might appear to agree with his design ideas and then proceed to ignore them. At the end of each week, they might gather around a computer to examine a plot of the team's output for the week, number of completed projects, and progress on ongoing projects. They might celebrate with a late-night meal, replete with numerous toasts, and expect Viktor to participate. Viktor will realize that the excellence of his individual work is not as key, and learn to feel satisfaction from the team's accomplishments, of which his work is a part.

Case: Crossing Continents between Individualistic and Collectivistic Cultures

After graduating from college with a B.S. in finance from a U.S. university, Fu Pen Yao, a native of Beijing, was hired by a major international investment bank to work in the regional headquarters in the U.K. Fu Pen's manager met with Fu Pen and his co-workers on the derivatives team each morning to review the day's activities, and at the end of each day, which tended to be a long 10–12 hours, to review performance. His manager went around to each person, discussing the accomplishments or lack thereof and asked the other team members what they thought. Fu Pen became used to receiving and giving feedback, clearly and sometimes in harsh tones. The work was demanding and each day had to show value for the bank. After 2 years, Fu Pen secured a higher-level position with a Chinese bank. He was thrilled to be returning home in a highly paid position, especially for someone so young. He was given his own team of subordinates to manage, and he followed the same management style he had become used to in the U.K.—meeting with his team early in the morning to set goals and late in the day to give feedback. He was dismayed when his team members said nothing in these first meetings unless Fu Pen asked them a specific question. They seemed embarrassed when he asked them for their opinions about other team members' performance. Their participation was lively only when Fu Pen presented results for the team as a whole. Then they expressed pleasure at the team's overall high performance and made suggestions when the team's overall performance did not meet Fu Pen's expectations. Fu Pen discussed this with a friend he knew from his high school days who worked for another company. He told Fu Pen that he had been away too long and that he had never really had a chance to see how work gets done in Chinese firms. He reminded him about what happened when they were on the high school football team. The coach never singled out an individual player in front of the others. If the coach had a suggestion for one of the players, the coach would take the player aside and have a private discussion. Even this was rare. The focus was always on the team.

Cross-Cultural Training

Multinational firms must prepare managers to operate effectively in other cultures. As might be expected, cultural insensitivity leads to failure of expatriates. Cultural awareness helps people recognize their own values, analyze contrasts with other cultures, and apply the insights gained to improve interpersonal effectiveness. Cross-cultural training may apply a number of different methods.[11] For instance, the training may describe the target culture through lectures, readings, videos, and other media. Simulations and role plays may be used to give managers practice functioning in the new culture. Self-assessments may be used to build self-awareness, increasing managers' understanding and acceptance of themselves, thereby giving them greater ability to adjust in another culture.

A popular method of cultural awareness training uses role-playing encounters between a U.S. citizen and a person from another culture with contrasting values.[12] The method highlights awareness of differences but not necessarily skills for enhancing sensitivity.

Case: Feedback in a Global Company

The following case describes Astro International. The company manufactures and distributes wireless Internet communications equipment, such as handheld 3-by-5-inch video screens for paging, email, Internet search, and telephone. They also operate wireless networks throughout the world. Astro has a manufacturing division, a marketing and sales arm with equipment sales and service through third-party vendors and direct sales to corporate clients, a service division, a consultation division (for web design), and a large research and development (R&D) division. In addition, the company is starting a new video-on-demand and television satellite-like program distribution division). Astro employs 50,000 people worldwide, and the firm is growing by 15 to 25% in personnel a year. It is headquartered in Melbourne, Australia, performs manufacturing in Thailand and India, employs programmers in India and Israel, has billing and computer processing operations in Ireland and Australia, has sales offices in Great Britain, Spain, France, the U.S., Israel, Japan, and Ecuador, and conducts R&D in Australia and India. Given this rapid growth, the company needs to develop a large cadre of managers who can assume leadership positions quickly.

Astro's human resources department administers a company-wide 360-degree feedback survey. One goal of the survey is to communicate dimensions of importance that are critical throughout the organization and that are the hallmark of the Astro corporate culture. Groups of items give special attention to customer service, rapid delivery and installation, customized network services to corporate clients, and partnerships with telecommunications providers (which are difficult corporate relationships because these are also competitors in some markets). Items also evaluate cross-cultural sensitivity—particularly, the manager's understanding of local markets and customs. Items reflect comfort with different cultures, accurately recognizing cultural differences and influences, empathizing with other cultures, valuing cultural differences, seeking new information and clarifying explanations, avoiding culture-bound behaviors, and being flexible.[13]

The 360-degree feedback survey was administered to 365 top executives across the globe. Surveys were completed by these executives' immediate subordinates, peers, supervisors, and customers. Many respondents worked in geographic locations in other cities and countries than the executive's home base. Data were collected electronically. An email message requested participation and pointed raters to a web site for confidential entry of ratings. The ratings submitted through the web site were automatically scored. While the company managers generally spoke English, this was not necessarily the case for customers. So the surveys were available in English, Spanish, and Japanese. Careful translation and re-translation procedures were followed to ensure equivalence of meaning. Also, focus groups of lower-level managers reviewed the surveys and discussed the meaning of each item to be sure the item was clear and understood in the same way across cultures. The email and web site came up in English, offering the respondent a choice of languages for the instructions and actual survey.

Coaches were given the survey reports and asked to review the results and to prepare for in-person, one-on-one feedback sessions with the executives. The coaches were selected by the human resource departments in key offices around the world. The coaches were consultants in private practice and consulting firms and had considerable cross-cultural experiences in business and counseling. The coaches were sent to a workshop in Australia to familiarize them with the company, cultural differences that emerge in Astro's business, the pressures executives face—with an emphasis on the difficulties of cross-cultural interactions—and the contents of the 360-degree feedback survey itself. The coaches flew into the home country of the executive for the initial one-on-one meeting. Then they maintained contact with the executives by email and telephone. The headquarters' human resources department paid for 2 hours' preparation, the initial 2-hour meeting, and three 1-hour follow-ups. The goal of the feedback and coaching was for executives to establish a development plan. Executives who chose to do so could continue the coaching relationship by paying the coach from their own budget.

There were several challenges in this coaching process: (a) matching executives to coaches based on experiences, age, and cultural understanding; (b) ensuring development plans were formulated by the executive with the coach's support (coach shouldn't do the work for the executive); (c) ensuring the coaches didn't use their own favorite methods (e.g., ask the executive to complete a particular personality instrument) but stuck to the script of working with the 360-degree feedback data and helping the executive establish a career development plan; (d) warning the coaches not to get enmeshed in the executives' immediate business problems; and (e) getting the coaches out to the field soon after the results were available—the company was evolving so rapidly that if several months elapsed, the organization would have changed and the issues confronting the executives could be different.

To determine the effectiveness of the feedback and coaching, executives completed a follow-up survey asking about the feedback and the help they received from their coach. The reactions were generally very positive. Also, 20% of the executives contracted with the coach for additional time. The company planned to track changes in 360-degree survey results during the next 2 years to determine if improvements were achieved and maintained by the executives.

Overall, the human resource department estimated that the initial favorable reaction suggested the process was favorably received. The cost was equivalent to sending the executives to a training session that may have lasted several days. However, the customized feedback and personal attention was greater than would have occurred at a typical training session (unless the training incorporated feedback and coaching, which some executive development programs do—at greater cost, of course). Further follow-up was needed to evaluate the program's cost-effectiveness. An added benefit was that the performance evaluations could be used to identify top executives for future growth. This was not done in the first administration. The executives were assured that the data and coaching would be used solely for their development, not for making decisions about them.

The process was not without problems. Some executives were too reliant on their coaches. They called them often, explained their business problems, and asked for advice. Interestingly, executives in Japan and Israel did not welcome their coaches, and coaches had trouble setting up appointments and found the interactions brief and perfunctory. Executives in Japan found the coaching process intrusive and embarrassing. Those in Israel felt they didn't need a coach who intruded on their independence. Coaches in Thailand and Japan reported that the feedback results were not very useful since all the ratings were generally positive, while the executives rated themselves uniformly low. Were the executives being overly modest and the raters overly lenient, and were there actually few differences in various dimensions of performance? Some coaches took too long to get ready and be deployed. Travel expenses were high (as much as the cost of coaching in some cases—e.g., $4,000 for the coach and another $2,000 for travel was not unusual). Where possible the same coach was assigned to more than one executive in an area and trips were coordinated to see several executives at a time. However, this was not always possible because of executives' availability. Also, executives in the same city or country were not always good matches for the same coach. Some executives asked the coach to continue work in their departments by meeting separately with a number of the executives' subordinates to identify ways to help them enhance their teamwork. In this way, coaching expanded from attention to the individual executive's needs for performance improvement to organization development.

Astro intended to extend the process to lower-level managers. It developed a 360-degree survey for 2,500 middle managers and translated it into six different languages. Instead of external coaches, executives and managers were asked to serve in the coaching role for their immediate subordinates. Managers were sent reports of their results by email with a message encouraging them to review the results with their supervisor or regional human resource manager.

This larger survey feedback initiative was not without problems. Some executives were not ready to be coaches and were not receptive to managers' requests for guidance. Also, some managers, particularly in Japan and China, were reluctant to share their results with their boss. Another problem was movement of personnel due to corporate growth. By the time the results were in, the manager or the manager's boss had changed assignments, so continuity of the process was difficult in the context of rapid corporate change. So Astro refined the process to emphasize self-development even more and to encourage managers to take responsibility for their own development, with the 360 survey results as a support tool.

Conclusion

Here, I have covered a few recent studies that address the effects of culture on performance ratings, particularly in the use of multisource feedback, and giving and receiving feedback. Cultural issues are likely to be increasingly important in understanding how people rate others and use feedback to set goals for development and improve their performance. Here are some conclusions to draw from the material covered in the chapter:

- Multisource feedback can be a useful way for expatriate managers to understand cultural differences in performance expectations. Cultural differences may influence how people are rated in performance evaluations. For instance, U.S. managers tend to be more people-focused than managers in other cultures. Far Eastern managers tend to be higher in strategic planning. Managers in the U.S. and Far East tend to be higher than managers in other countries on change and innovation. Managers from the U.S. tend to rate themselves more leniently than managers from other cultures. Relationships among performance dimensions (the factor structure) may not be the same in all cultures. Moreover, culture may affect the level (e.g., leniency) of performance ratings.
- People in different cultures may interpret the elements of performance and how they work together differently, and they may vary in rating tendencies or biases. Given this possibility, which needs to be substantiated by further research, feedback to managers should include in-country norms to help managers understand their results within the context of their own culture. Also, the company's performance management program should explain the meaning of performance dimensions used in appraisal methods and multisource surveys, and managers should have a chance to discuss the meaning of these dimensions before they are asked to rate others and before they receive feedback on their own performance.
- Managers who rate and provide feedback to employees in different cultures may benefit from information and training on sensitivity to

cultural differences. Items in a performance evaluation survey can reflect the company's needs for cross-cultural understanding.

- Measures of cross-cultural sensitivity can be the basis for selecting managers for development and rapid advancement in fast-growing global enterprises.
- When implementing feedback and coaching in a multinational firm, care must be taken to ensure that the measures and process are perceived in the same way in different cultures. Also, there may be cultural differences in the value of the feedback and willingness to share results with coaches or their supervisors.

This chapter recognized that feedback in today's organizations often occurs in a multicultural context. The next chapter recognizes that feedback occurs within the context of team and organizational performance. Individuals need feedback not only about their own performance but also about the team and/or organization as a whole and how they can contribute to team and organizational performance.

Notes

1. Evans, Pucik, and Barsoux (2002); Galunic and Eisenhardt (2001).
2. Bartlett and Ghoshal (1997).
3. Berson, Erez, and Adler (2002).
4. Bartlett and Ghoshal (1997).
5. Hofstede (2001).
6. Berson et al. (2002).
7. Hofstede (2001).
8. Gillespie (2002).
9. Farh, Dobbins, and Cheng (1991).
10. Yu and Murphy (1993).
11. Park and Harrison (1993).
12. Harris and Moran (1987).
13. Items were derived from London and Sessa's (1999) conceptualization of cultural sensitivity.

11

FEEDBACK IN TEAMS

Teams or groups involve people with diverse expertise and backgrounds bringing their knowledge, skills, and experience to bear on problems and projects. Note that there is a difference between a team and a group. The term *team* suggests collaboration, indeed a tight, working relationship in which members depend on each other to achieve a set of goals or level of performance. A group is merely two or more individuals who are not necessarily mutually dependent. Often, team members work together in the same office, or can easily come together for periodic meetings, even if some travel is involved. The team members are sometimes separated by wide geographic distances, and other modes of meeting and communicating may be necessary instead of meeting face-to-face and in person; examples are teleconferences, conference telephone calls, email, Internet chat rooms, and combinations thereof. The team members may come together for short periods of time in order to accomplish specific, limited tasks, such as selecting a new CEO or designing a new data system. In other cases, the team may be responsible for an ongoing process or function, such as advertising a product or worldwide distribution of a product. The complexity of these tasks requires that the team members work interdependently. The importance of these tasks requires that members share responsibility for the work and the accountability for meeting the organization's performance goals. Effective teams should have their own goals, criteria for success, and means of evaluation. Methods to facilitate team interaction about these goals, the team process, and success tracking will enhance team performance and effectiveness.

Business is global. Many organizations have departments, subsidiaries, or partners around the world. This raises questions about whether there are cultural differences in the way people evaluate performance and give and receive feedback and the competencies people need to manage effectively across cultures. This is an area ripe for research to guide the development of performance management programs in global enterprises.

This chapter examines the issues and existing research results, offers case studies, and suggests directions for training to sensitize managers to cross-cultural differences and cultural biases that influence their judgments about people. The first part of this chapter examines feedback in different types of teams and in relation to changing team dynamics, focusing on the team and the individual within the team. It describes how the team members develop a shared mental model that enhances cooperation and mutual trust. I offer ways to facilitate feedback in teams. I also address the use of feedback in virtual teams (those with geographically dispersed members who communicate using a variety of communications media) and negotiating teams.

Types of Special Project Teams

In organizations, teams may be task forces, quality circles, and quality improvement teams. Such teams occur with increasing frequency in organizations.[1] The team becomes more productive as the members begin coordinating tasks and sharing information about themselves and others.[2] Therefore, it is important to consider the effects of self- and interpersonal insight on team interaction processes and performance.[3]

Consider how interpersonal feedback occurs in different types of work teams.[4] There are teams that give advice or provide an avenue for employee involvement (e.g., committees, review panels, and quality circles). There are teams that produce a product or service (e.g., assembly teams, flight attendant crews). Other teams work on a project (e.g., research teams, planning teams) while others engage in action or negotiation (e.g., sports teams, entertainment teams, expeditions, negotiation teams, surgery teams, and cockpit crews).

Teams that give advice, produce a product or service, or work on a project benefit from fluidity and loose coupling. Teams that engage in action and negotiation must perform as tightly coupled systems most of the time. Ensembles are teams that produce a particular effect or product.[5] The members of ensembles are highly interdependent. Therefore, unrestricted, mutual feedback from everyone on the team, leaders and members alike, is particularly important to the development of the ensemble as a tightly coupled system.[6] The product of the ensemble has a distinctive quality or synergism beyond any one of the individual members. Having highly expert ensemble members does not mean that the ensemble's performance will necessarily be excellent. While coupling is a function of the nature of the work, the members have to work at achieving a tightly coupled system.

Team Dynamics and the Use of Feedback

In general, there are several key uses for feedback in a team.[7] Feedback can identify team development needs and help the organization identify teams that need help, such as teams that are floundering and not getting tasks done. This information, in turn, can be used to channel limited resources (e.g., for training) to teams that can benefit the most. Feedback can be an occasion to increase member involvement and control over team outcomes by asking them to analyze their own feedback data and prioritize areas for improvement. Having to face concrete feedback, and support from a facilitator, encourages the team to deal with problems directly rather than ignore them or blame them on outside forces. The organization must be used to collecting and using feedback (e.g., survey feedback surveys with results aggregated at the team level). Also, the organization must support team building by, for instance, providing team process consultants or training team leaders.

Team task demands and interaction patterns among team members mean that members must respond to stimuli from multiple sources. People generally have a common understanding about appropriate team behavior; essentially a team norm. This is a basis for the development of habitual behavior patterns. In fact, different teams have similar patterns of behavior. Teams develop these interaction patterns early in their "lives," and they maintain this pattern even after the situation changes. For example, one study found that teams assigned a tight time deadline early in their limited existence maintained a fast rate but with low quality and with an interaction pattern that was highly task-focused.[8] The pattern continued into later trials even though they no longer had the tight time deadline. Conversely, teams that began working against a less stringent time deadline worked at a slower rate but with higher quality and with an interaction pattern that was more interpersonally focused. This pattern continued on later trials despite shorter time deadlines. Under task conditions for which early trials yielded an experience of qualitative difficulty, teams tended to slow down on later trials and may thereby have increased the quality of their work.

Team members can give each other feedback that helps them understand the emerging behavioral patterns. Also, newcomers to the team may receive feedback quickly. This helps them understand how to be an effective team member in relation to other members' roles and abilities. Through various means of socialization and social control, team members convey their expectations for the new member.

Feedback can be important to team process and performance, just as it is to individuals. Teams that receive feedback on their task achievement and/or interpersonal behaviors that do not match an ideal are more likely to change their behavior and improve team performance, whereas teams that do not receive feedback are not as likely to change their behavior and improve performance.[9] Whether feedback leads to performance improvement will depend on many factors, including the team members' defensiveness and willingness to accept the feedback.

Team feedback is a potentially threatening experience for the supervisor or facilitator responsible for giving the feedback and for the team members. After all, the supervisor or facilitator providing the feedback has to look all the team members in the eye. (This isn't the case when the feedback is an impersonal computer printout of data.) The team members hear the same thing, and will later compare their views of the feedback. As such, the supervisor is on the spot publicly. Here, the supervisor should focus on providing information about team performance, not each individual member's performance. This works well when there is team-level information—for instance, total number of units produced by the team, or projects completed. It also works well when the team members are interdependent, and the team's output is a function of a team effort.

Process feedback focuses on elements of how the team members interact with each other.[10] Consider three of the major elements of team process based on interaction process analysis.[11] One is *dominancy*—the amount of team members' talkativeness, leadership, and influence, at one extreme, and submissiveness, quietness, and obedience, at the other. Large differences between the most and least dominant people in teams should be detrimental to team process and task performance. Another element of team process is *friendliness*—the amount of cooperation and loyalty at one extreme, and withdrawal and antagonism at the other. Behaviors should be primarily team-oriented and friendly as opposed to individually oriented and unfriendly. Yet another element of team process is *expressiveness*—the amount of joking, nurturing, and affection at one end of the continuum, and emotional control, task-orientedness, and attention to rules at the other end. Teams should have a reasonable balance of task-oriented and socio-emotional behaviors, though task-oriented behaviors should dominate.

One study had teams of observers make systematic ratings of each team member's behavior on these three performance dimensions.[12] The teams received the observers' ratings of team process along each dimension with a set of norms against which to compare their results (e.g., for Dominance: "Team discussions should not be dominated by one or two people. There should not be more than an 8-point difference between the most dominant and the most submissive team members."). Each team member knew his or her own score on each dimension. After the feedback, the teams had time to discuss their process feedback and determine how they could improve during a subsequent task. The researchers found that small behavior changes could be manipulated using the feedback and information about ideal ratings on process dimensions compared to teams receiving only task performance feedback followed by an unstructured discussion.

Reacting to this study, other researchers suggested that stronger effects might occur by concentrating on specific goals given to the team as a whole and each member's personal goals.[13] Specific goals should be assigned, rather than merely giving ideal ranges. Teams assigned difficult goals perform better than those assigned moderate or general ("Do your best") goals.[14] The team's overall goals and each member's goals (and commitment to these goals) could actually be measured to be sure the goals were internalized prior to team performance. Team members' perceptions of the team's ability to do the task (induced by providing the team with norms of excellent performance prior to doing the task) also enhance performance. Furthermore, team feedback may be differentially relevant to team members, depending on their results. So, for instance, only members at the extremes on dominance would need to act differently in order to change the distribution of dominance behavior in the team. However, the team process discussion about dominance differences gives everyone a chance to participate and influence the most and least dominant members.

Public feedback in teams can have a positive effect on team members' learning goals, regulatory responses (e.g., team members' confidence in the team's ability to accomplish its goals), and ultimately performance. Consider a study of 131 teams of three college students engaged in a simulation.[15] Team members who received public feedback were more likely to indicate they wanted to learn for the sake of mastery (i.e., to acquire knowledge and improve their skills). This, in turn, was positively related to positive regulatory processes and performance outcomes for the team.

Case: Team Feedback

Tyler Shapira is an IT manager in his 50s. He manages a team of 10 programmers. He stated that the most effective feedback he has experienced occurred in a team context. He believes that feedback is easier when team members are motivated to do the job, and everyone on the team is working to make the product better. If team members are not engaged in their work, negative feedback will be viewed as criticism rather than constructive suggestions for improvement. Giving feedback to a team can be effective when everyone has a common goal, and the feedback refers to the team's performance, not the performance of specific individuals. He gives feedback during regular team meetings. Team members provide updates on their projects, and they expect feedback and discussion from Tyler and their colleagues. The feedback Tyler and the team members give to one another is respectful. There are no personal attacks, and discussions are about problem solving, not airing complaints.

Summary

Feedback can be as important to team functioning as it is to individual performance. Information about team performance can identify team development needs and assist the company in pinpointing teams that need facilitation or leadership. Feedback in teams comes from a supervisor, the team leader, and/or team members. Process feedback refers to information about how the team is functioning—for instance, how well members are interacting with each other—whereas task feedback refers to the work that gets done and the outcomes produced. Attention should be given to how process feedback is used. Members should be asked whether they found feedback to be valuable. The interplay between the effects of feedback to individuals and to the team should be considered. For instance, positive feedback to one team member in front of others may disrupt team identity.

Teams Develop Shared Mental Models

Team effectiveness is a function of team members developing a shared understanding or mental model of expectations about team members' abilities and behaviors, common knowledge, and mutual interpretations of events.[16] This requires team members to know each other well and to communicate their expectations, observations, and intentions. They may do this explicitly or implicitly as the team progresses. The overlap between team members' expectations is positively related to the speed with which team norms develop and begin to affect team performance. In effective teams, members share a set of knowledge that facilitates interaction. This knowledge set includes a shared understanding of their teammates' roles, a shared understanding of the team task and required interactions, and a shared understanding of the potential situations they may encounter. These shared understandings help the team members to explicitly or implicitly coordinate their behavior in response to situational demands. Implicit coordination refers to coordination without explicit communication that articulates plans and behavioral routines. Explicit coordination involves direct communication among team members about their interactions and performance. The more team members have worked together and are familiar with each other's common modes of behavior, the less they may need to communicate explicitly. However, when the need arises, they are willing to ask for and accept assistance and performance feedback.[17]

Feedback is the flow of the information that affects the speed of development of a mental model and the extent to which the contents are accurately shared. When a team is first formed, coordination is affected by the prior experience of the members, the nature of the task, and the perceived demands for interaction. This is the start of a shared mental model. Feedback is the mediating process for forming mental models. If perceptions are accurate, the team is likely to make progress quickly. If perceptions are inaccurate, the team may spend time in early meetings to share ideas and expectations and develop a shared understanding of the task and each other's capabilities. Alternatively, the team may forge ahead without forming a shared understanding, and the result may be frustration, disappointment, and wasted time. So unless team members know each other well at the outset, sharing information will be important to members remaining in the team and the team's effectiveness. When team members do not know each other well, they need to be highly sensitive to each other's responses—for instance, the extent to which they are agreeable or disagreeable or their degree of knowledge and skill. The team members need to be motivated to care about each other and send messages that they can understand. This is more likely when team members are aware of each other's level of knowledge (which would be likely if they received the same training together or had a chance to talk about the team's goals). Moreover, information transmission must be accurate and accepted. The team members must trust each other to provide meaningful feedback that is untainted by ulterior motives or individual agendas. Inaccurate information will prevent coordination.[18] This is likely if there is a low level of trust, disagreement about the team's purpose and goals (e.g., what has to be done by when), or misunderstanding about the level of each team member's knowledge and skills.

When a team is fraught with conflict, participating as a member of the team is likely to be frustrating and, of course, the team is not likely to make much progress. However, conflict can have a benefit when frustrated members take a step back to distance themselves from the team and think about what's going on. The team members become more objective and accurate in their perceptions of the team. This can lead to discussions about team process and sources of conflict. Team members can become adept at assessing the team's activities and giving each other feedback. Ultimately, this can help make membership in the team more rewarding and help the team improve its performance.[19]

In summary, teams develop a shared mental model of expectations about team members' abilities and behaviors, shared knowledge, and shared interpretations of events. This shared model helps the team function effectively. Team members get to know each other well, communicating their expectations, observations, and intentions. Early in the team's formation, the members' prior experiences and the structure and demands of the task influence the degree of coordination and initiate the shared mental model. The team is more likely to do well from the start if the team members have had common experiences that lead them to share expectations. If not, the members may quickly hit roadblocks, such as lack of communication or the emergence of conflicts, because they don't share common expectations or have different goals and because they don't raise these differences. A facilitator can assist the team in communicating issues that affect the team process and help the team members establish common understanding and expectations for behaviors and goals that become a shared mental model and that establish mutual trust. (I will say more about team facilitation later in the chapter.)

Collecting Feedback Data in Teams

Unlike individual performance, the performance of the team may refer to issues of process (such as cooperation and conflict resolution) and/or outcomes or achievements, such as the quality of the team's products and the speed of production. Feedback for teams may focus on a team's process, development, and/or achievement. There are several ways to collect and deliver team performance data. Supervisors can evaluate their team as a whole and provide the team with periodic feedback about how the team operates. The supervisor must take care to address team behavior and deal with individual members' performance in one-on-one private meetings with each member. Special performance surveys can be used to gather data from key observers, constituents, or customers about the operation and effectiveness of the team as a whole. Performance surveys—for example, multisource surveys—may be used to collect data on each member individually. The team members can then discuss the average and variation (range of low to high scores) on each performance item or dimension. While this average does not necessarily reflect the performance of the team as a whole, it provides useful information for team discussion and development.

Data about a team's general effectiveness and working relationships can lead to team discussions about the team's strengths and weaknesses and areas for improvement. As a consequence, the team may participate in developmental or team building activities, such as experiential training, to understand the value of effective teamwork and how it can improve—for instance, ways to open lines of communication, face problems, and teach team members about collaboration.[20] In general, feedback data can help the team commission training that is customized to the team's needs. The feedback can also help the team members prepare for the training—for instance, in recognizing why it is needed and being open to learning.

Use of Multisource Surveys in Teams

Multisource surveys can be used by teams to assess team-level strengths and weaknesses.[21] Survey items can ask whether the team has the right mix of skills, manages conflict well, and meets objectives. The survey can also ask about the team leader—for example, the clarity of the leader's goals and directives. Customers, co-workers, and supervisors can complete the survey. Team members can rate the leader, and the leader can rate the team as a whole, as well as the individual members in the team.

Summary

There are several ways to collect and deliver team performance data. Multisource feedback surveys, with ratings from team members, supervisors of the team members, and the client(s) of the team, can evaluate strengths and weaknesses of the team. In addition, a survey can ask questions about whether the team has the right mix of skills, resolves conflicts, has clear goals, and meets objectives. The data can be averaged within different rater sources (e.g., all team members, all customers, all supervisors), and the team can discuss the results, perhaps with the assistance of a facilitator. Users of the team output can evaluate the output's quality and timeliness. Team members, the supervisor, or a process facilitator who directly observes the team in action can evaluate the team process, such as whether time is wasted on side issues that detract from the task at hand, perhaps because of poor communication or disagreements about leadership or scheduling.

Facilitating Team Feedback

There are several ways to help ensure that the team uses the feedback constructively.[22] The facilitator may work with the leader individually to present the results and to suggest different behaviors the leader can try to help the team members work together better. This could be very helpful if the results reveal that the leader is a cause of the team's problems. Alternatively, the facilitator may work with the team as a whole by leading a discussion about the results, the reasons for them, and what the team can do about them. Note that the facilitator may be a professional in the field of organization development who is called in by the leader or a top executive to work with the team. In the absence of a professional facilitator, the team leader or even a team member may assume the facilitator's role, taking responsibility for designing a method to review and interpret the results with the team members and lead a joint effort to design a plan for development and improvement. When team leaders take on this role, they need to be willing to acknowledge their own shortcomings to the team and to create conditions that allow participation without fear of retaliation.

Feedback is likely to work best when the issues addressed are within the control of the team members. On the one hand, if the problems arise from other organizational issues (e.g., lack of timely or accurate data, or lack of cooperation from other parts of the company), the team members are likely to be frustrated. On the other hand, if the problems arise from issues that the team members can do something about, and they are going to remain together long enough to make the required changes, they are likely to feel ready to try different courses of action that will make a difference. Moreover, they are likely to develop a shared commitment to become a better team.[23]

The Tendency for Teams to Over-Evaluate Their Performance

Jourden and Heath discovered that team members develop a "positive illusion" about their team's performance, estimating that their team's performance is above the 50th percentile.[24] There are several reasons why members of a team may over-evaluate the performance of their team. Members may encourage each other when the team seems to be doing poorly. They affirm each other's value, giving each other helpful suggestions. As the team's task progresses, they may convey to each other how much they are learning together. Ross and Allen studied the relationship between the extent to which team members report this type of information exchange and post-performance evaluations of the team's performance.[25] The subjects were 55 undergraduate psychology students who were randomly assigned to one of 11 three-member teams or five four-member teams to work on a model bridge building task. Before the task, the members ranked how well they expected their team to perform on the task relative to a hypothetical set of 10 other teams (how the team would rank among 10 randomly selected teams). After the task, they ranked their team's actual performance on the same measure. They also completed a 14-item measure of the degree to which they experienced information exchange behaviors in their team (e.g., "The team made me feel as if my ideas made sense" and "We gave each other constructive feedback on our ideas"). The items were averaged to form a reliable information exchange measure. The measure of information exchange was positively correlated ($r = 37$, $p < .01$) with the post-performance ranking after controlling for the pre-performance ranking. The results indicate that team members who perceive more information exchange are likely to rank their team's performance higher than those who perceive less information exchange.

Team Goal Setting

A team should establish team goals for each performance period. The team should discuss potential goals, and the supervisor should facilitate the goal setting in relation to organization-wide objectives. The goals should be challenging—neither impossible nor too easy. The members' involvement in formulating the team's goals should enhance their commitment to the goals. Members' public declaration of willingness to work on and achieve the goals should enhance their feeling of obligation to accomplish them.

If team goals are set and team performance is reviewed, it stands to reason that there should be a team reward. As with individual performance review, the team award should be discussed and distributed sometime after (preferably soon after) the team performance review. The tie between performance achieved as a team and the reward should be explicit. Also, a policy should be established for how to distribute the team reward.

Assuming supervisors have discretion in compensation policy, some supervisors agree at the time team goals are established to split a monetary award equally among all team members. Other supervisors may say they will split the team award according to each team member's contribution. Team members may be asked to rate each other's contribution as a basis for the distribution. Such a policy has the potential for destroying team unity, and an equal distribution is probably most equitable. Keep in mind that team performance review and reward should be coupled with individual performance review and reward. As such, the supervisor can recognize outstanding individual performance and reward it accordingly after appropriate review. Such review may include collecting information from co-workers (e.g., as part of a multisource rating system).

Individual Feedback in Teams

The team setting can also be valuable for giving feedback to individuals if it is done with careful facilitation. This is common after business simulations in management development programs. Here's an example of an appraisal session that stems from a team building process and feeds back peer ratings on a behavioral observation scale:[26] Job analyses are conducted and behavioral observation scales constructed; hence the behaviors rated reflect specific job behaviors and requirements. Also, the scales are developed by employees for employees, so the raters and ratees understand the items as critical job behaviors. Another advantage of the process is that the behavioral scales remind raters about what behaviors are important to think about in providing their ratings. Open-ended questions ask what the ratee should continue doing on the job and what the person should start doing, stop doing, or do differently. Team sessions are then held. Each person's appraisal is given in a 1–2-hour time period. A psychologist or a person skilled in team process facilitates the feedback by first asking the individual if he or she has any questions regarding his or her colleagues' evaluations. Colleagues are requested to offer comments regarding the evaluations. Peers are coached by the facilitator on how to emphasize what the person is to do differently in the future. The person assessed is then asked to summarize what was "heard" and to set specific goals as to what he or she will do differently as a result of this feedback. Subsequent discussion focuses on another individual in the team until every person has received feedback and has set goals.

Summary

A facilitator can help the team focus on certain feedback—particularly areas the team can do something about. Also, the facilitator can help the team leader determine strategies that will help the team stay on track. Facilitators and/or team leaders serving in the role of facilitator can help team members accurately calibrate the performance of the team (avoiding the tendency to believe the team is better than other teams). They can also help the team set goals and conduct discussions of individual members' behavior in the team and contribution to team goals.

The Role of Feedback in Team Negotiation Processes

The goal in teams is to cooperate in a way that will generate an effective product. Consider another type of interaction where individuals or teams are attempting to resolve conflict with one or more other individuals or teams.[27] Negotiation or bargaining sessions are good examples. During negotiation sessions, opposing parties gather information to test the viability and/or acceptability of their own positions. Good scenario planning, trial runs, and feedback become mechanisms for making good decisions in negotiations.[28] Negotiators use feedback to adjust their behavior and offers. But this feedback is not likely to be straightforward. More likely, it is biased or ambiguous. Opposing parties do not readily reveal their strategies and reactions to others. They may even try to mislead the opposing negotiator. Also, negotiators are likely to be biased in how they perceive the opposing party's reactions. Even experienced negotiators may misjudge cues from the opposing party.

In traditional, positional bargaining, good feedback between teams is avoided; one team doesn't want to divulge what it has learned. So negotiators do not exchange information about their interests during the negotiation process.[29] However, feedback is important to avoiding faulty judgments in conflict and negotiation situations.[30] Feedback has a self-correcting function that allows negotiators to compare their present strategy to a more favorable ideal.[31] Outcome feedback is knowledge of the results of a decision, while cognitive feedback is information about relations in the environment, such as information about the task and one's own and others' thought processes (e.g., weights people give to different dimensions of possible outcomes).[32]

Good feedback is important in principled negotiations in which negotiators have a common understanding that they can (and want to) reach a win-win settlement. This requires understanding one's opponent's interests. Feedback may come from experience; however, it may help to have information about the opponent. To test this, one study compared negotiators who were given information about their opponents (as they may gain in a principled negotiation) with those who did not have this information (a typical positional negotiation).[33] After an initial negotiation, the negotiators in the cognitive feedback condition were given information about their opponent's payoff schedule for different possible outcomes, whereas other negotiators were given only information about the payoff resulting from the negotiation. Negotiators who received the cognitive and outcome feedback made more accurate judgments about their opponent's interests and subsequently negotiated outcomes that were better for both parties. The feedback allowed negotiators to develop an effective strategic conceptualization of the negotiations. This suggests the value of building such feedback into ongoing, principled negotiations such that both parties are briefed about each other's emerging interests, perhaps by an independent mediator or a consultant who is hired separately by each side.

Before negotiation, members of each party's bargaining team often consult with each other and plan effective strategies. After a bargaining session, they are likely to give each other feedback, processing their perceptions of the opposing team's reactions.[34] They may also discuss the negotiation process with the opposing team. While this may be unlikely, it would be a chance to raise points of misunderstanding and clarify points of difference between opposing parties. Establishing a regular forum for discussion so that the opposing parties can consider issues that arise in disputes that cut across other aspects of relationships between the parties is a good idea. An example would be the union and management representatives meeting together regularly in "common interest forums."[35]

Summary

Feedback is a contributor to better-performing teams. Members give each other advice before the negotiations begin and feedback afterwards, thereby sharpening their perceptions of the opposing team. Discussions with the opposition may clarify points of differences and identify commonalities that may foster faster agreements and higher gains for both parties than might have occurred without these discussions.

Conclusion

This chapter first reviewed how feedback can enhance team performance. Feedback can prompt a team's examination of its strengths, weaknesses, and areas for improvement, just as it does for individuals. Team feedback provides members with information about the team as a whole and the behavior of individual members. Feedback is important for members to have an accurate understanding of the expectations they have of each other, the goals of the team, and how the members work together to get work done. Here are key conclusions:

- Team feedback is valuable in informing team members about the performance of the team as a whole. This is appropriate when there is information about the team's performance and team members are interdependent. Team goals should be established during team discussion. With sufficient care, the team setting can be useful for giving feedback to individuals. This works well during developmental programs where team members in a nonthreatening environment can give each other constructive feedback.

- Team effectiveness depends on team members developing shared mental models that facilitate coordination. Shared mental models include expectations about behaviors and skill levels, awareness of team members' knowledge and skills, and a shared understanding of the task and goals. Explicit communication about expectations and goals at the outset promotes the development of shared mental models. Feedback about behaviors and performance during the task enhances the development of these models and facilitates coordination and task accomplishment. Inaccurate expectations and feedback will thwart shared understanding and the capability of the team to coordinate.

- Feedback is as important in virtual teams as it is in face-to-face teams. The use of feedback in virtual teams may depend on the richness of the communications media and the leaders' style of management. Transactional leadership focuses on goal-centered feedback, building conditional trust. Transformational leadership focuses on developing a common understanding of feedback and its meaning for team development, building unconditional trust. During initial stages of team development, low media richness and transactional leadership may help jump-start trust building. As the team progresses, increased media richness and transformational leadership may facilitate team development.

- Feedback is important in negotiating teams to provide insights into the opposition and bargaining situation that individual members may not have alone and to communicate perceptions between opposing parties as a way of reaching more rapid resolution and higher gains on both sides.

Notes

1. Hackman (1990); Saavedra, Earley, and Van Dyne (1993).
2. Luft (1970).
3. For more information on this topic, see London (1995b, Chapter 7).
4. Sundstrom, De Meuse, and Futrell (1990).
5. London and London (1996).
6. Gersick and Hackman (1990).
7. Hallam (2001).
8. Kelly and McGrath (1985).
9. McLeod, Liker, and Lobel (1992).
10. Wells (1992).
11. Bales (1950, 1988).
12. McLeod et al. (1992).
13. Locke and Latham (1992).
14. Whitney (1994).
15. Kozlowski, DeShon, Schmidt, and Chambers (2002).
16. Fiore, Salas, and Cannon-Bowers (2001).
17. Smith-Jentsch, Campbell, Milanovich, and Reynolds (2001).
18. Fiore et al. (2001); Hardin and Higgins (1996).
19. Breugst, Patzelt, Shepherd, and Aguinis (2012).
20. Hallam (2001).
21. Hallam (2001).
22. Hallam (2001).
23. Hallam (2001).
24. Jourden and Heath (1996); Heath and Jourden (1997).
25. Ross and Allen (2002).
26. Initially outlined by Locke and Latham (1990).
27. This section was adapted from London (1995b, Chapter 8).
28. Neale and Bazerman (1991).
29. Thompson (1991).
30. Thompson and Hastie (1990).
31. Thompson and DeHarpport (1994).
32. Balzer, Doherty, and O'Connor (1989).
33. Thompson and DeHarpport (1994).
34. Ury, Brett, and Goldberg (1988).
35. London (1988).

12

TECHNOLOGY AND FEEDBACK

Advanced technology allows the collection of abundant information, which can occur at the expense of individual privacy. It allows people to learn from new sources of information, including feedback. Here I consider different technology-based formats that can be used for performance feedback: electronic performance management using objective performance indicators, learner-controlled instruction, online performance management, and online feedback and coaching.

Sources of Objective Performance Information and Self-Reflection Tools

Electronic Performance Monitoring

Advanced computer technologies allow close tracking and scrutiny of employees' behaviors. Millions of people are subject to electronic performance monitoring at work, not to mention that our use of the Internet is monitored by search engines, online shopping sites, and social media. Consider some examples of employee monitoring. For truck drivers, remote monitoring tracks location, speed, on-time deliveries, and even elements of the condition of the truck (tire pressure) and possibly the driver (e.g., heart rate, response time, and attentiveness). For hospital personnel, detailed patient recording systems can determine the amount and type of patient contact for each health care provider. For factory workers, work station monitoring can determine quality (accuracy) and quantity (pace) of output. For educators, student test scores can be tracked and summarized by teachers, controlling for initial student abilities. For attorneys and management consultants, time tracking systems are important for billing, and they also indicate the type and amount of work performed.

While this book has emphasized when and how feedback can be valuable, an open question is how monitoring, especially electronic monitoring, affects the employee's productivity and feelings of stress. Monitoring may improve individual performance of people who are highly skilled

166

because such people tend to perform better when they are observed. This is called the "social facilitation" effect.[1]

Case: Tracking Objective Performance Indicators

Keith Saltzman, 63, owns a boutique stock brokerage with 48 employees. He doesn't see the value of feedback discussions. Each employee knows his or her specific roles, and they are measured by clear performance indicators, especially the brokers, whose performance is a function of their trades for clients. The analysts he employs are also measured by the number of reports they produce and their use by the brokers, which is measured by brokers accessing the reports on the company's computer system. Feedback comes in the form of bonuses in relation to the sales and trades. Analysts work for the brokers, and brokers share their compensation with the analysts based on pre-specified percentages, just as the brokers receive direct commission from their sales. However, given the recent recession and slow recovery, the brokers and analysts have depended more on their smaller base salaries. If a broker or analyst goes above and beyond their current client base—for instance, establishing new industry expertise that brings in more clients—Keith will give the person a one-time extra bonus—a "spot award"—recognizing the value to the firm. Feedback, then, is purely monetary. This is the nature of the business. Keith is wary about positive verbal feedback. He might like someone and feel the person is working hard and works well with others in the firm, but if the person is not performing—making trades or generating useful information that supports sales—the bottom line speaks for itself. Keith is quick to point out that he doesn't tolerate any office abnormalities, such as screaming or sexist and/or racist comments, and he has fired brokers for such unacceptable behavior.

Learner-Controlled Instruction

Self-paced or "open" learning, also called self-directed learning, refers to people working on their own to learn new skills and acquire knowledge. Assessment and feedback are generally built into the process in order to help people determine what they should learn and whether they have learned it. Self-paced material may be presented in written form, on a computer with CD-ROM, on audio- or videotapes, or on an interactive video system. Open learners have autonomy to decide what they study and how, when, where, and at what pace. Learners control the time spent on material, the amount of review of explanatory material and feedback, the revision of responses, and the way they explore and test new concepts.

As an example, a British firm incorporated open learning into training programs for junior managers on such topics as communication, problem solving, budgeting, hiring, and health and safety.[2] The topics were selected after extensive needs analyses for first-line managers in many different organizations. The trainees participated in the program during a 4-month period. They attended a 3-day introductory session, a 2-day workshop at the halfway point, and a 2-day review at the end. The rest of the time, trainees studied on their own, including 5 hours of paid time each week. Each module contained a workbook, an audio cassette, and exercises to be completed along with self-testing questions and quizzes. Exercises and assignments were submitted to an assigned tutor for assessment and feedback.

Despite the self-paced design, this was a fairly structured program. Participants were given the modules and they merely had to go through them on their own. Tutors provided guidance and oversight. Other programs are less directive. They require the participant to select topics for study based on their own interests, views of their capabilities and knowledge, and assessment of career opportunities.

Online Career Planning and Development

Computers provide avenues for individuals to direct their own development needs. One such program, called "Smart Software," has five components: One, called *Career Review*, asks questions about career progress and key learning experiences that occurred on the job. A second component, *Motivation to Develop and Career Aspirations*, asks questions that promote the respondents' understanding of their future career direction—not specific jobs, but the creation of alternatives for where and how they could apply their skills. A third component, *Competence-Based Job Analysis*, asks respondents to rate certain behavioral competencies in terms of their importance to their current role. This results in a weighted competence framework that allows the respondent to compare his/her assessment to his/her immediate supervisor's assessment. A fourth component, *Competence-Based Self-Assessment*, uses "insight" questionnaires to evaluate strengths and weaknesses in areas identified as important in the prior job analysis. A fifth component, *Development Strategies*, asks respondents to identify the three main areas they wish to develop. The software then offers appropriate literature that provides key principles in such areas as strategic thinking, problem solving, interpersonal communications, and motivating others.[3]

Overall, self-paced learning, often utilizing computer technology, is a cost-effective, flexible method. It can be accessed by the individual whenever he or she has the time and inclination. Feedback is provided from automatic scoring as the individual progresses. Also, it is applicable to small and large firms alike, since excellent software programs, videos, audio tape, and written material are increasingly available.

Online Performance Management

In addition to using web-based and smart technologies (e.g., "apps") to administer multisource feedback surveys, companies are using the technology to also offer self-assessment, e-learning, informal learning guides, online and telephone coaching, and career development workshops. For instance, companies can purchase subscriptions to TalentAlliance.com for their employees. The site offers assessments and leadership 360-degree feedback, career coaching, links to distance learning opportunities, career information, and job opportunities (the latter is especially useful to companies in the process of downsizing). The assessments module contains a leadership 360-degree feedback process and self-diagnostic instruments to help employees gain feedback and understand their strengths, work preferences, and career goals. The career coaching module provides telephone contact to a coach for one-on-one career consulting services. The available services are customized to the needs of the company, and Talent Alliance advertises that by utilizing these virtual solutions, clients can experience the same quality career coaching services as face-to-face meetings. The web site offers a "coach's corner" that offers a range of practical tips, exercises, and suggestions for helping managers prepare for performance reviews and coaching sessions with subordinates.

Recognizing the value of feedback and self-assessment through online technology, the consulting branch of the accounting firm Deloitte & Touche developed a web site to support its consultants' skill development, including their team leadership, sales, and responsiveness to clients. Tied to a 360-degree feedback survey and in-person coaching, the site provides self-assessments, guidelines for informal learning, and directions for development planning and follow-up. The professionals proceed through each site at their own pace, contacting their coach to discuss assessment results and development plans as they progress.

Overall, the web provides tools to help managers and professionals take more responsibility for their own career development, including obtaining feedback and finding help with understanding and using it and recognizing that learning is a continuous process. Sites can be customized to enhance their value to the company and the individuals using them. The materials and assessments can reflect corporate strategies and competency requirements. Individuals can use the materials at their convenience and in relation to their needs and goals. Sites can be related to the company's other performance management tools and training, such as the annual performance appraisal process and courses or workshops provided by the corporate training department. Informal learning guides encourage managers to take advantage of the opportunities for skill development available during their normal course of work, encouraging them to seek informal feedback rather than waiting for multisource survey results or their annual performance review with their supervisor.

Just-in-Time Multisource Feedback

Email, Internet, and smart phone and tablet technologies open the possibility of collecting performance ratings electronically, making feedback more "real-time." This has been used successfully for 360-degree feedback. Indeed, managers can actually construct their own survey, send an invitation to respond and the web site or app link by email, collect the data on the web through the cloud, and receive the results electronically relatively quickly. This is called "just-in-time" feedback because managers can start the process when they feel they have a need for feedback.

Here's how online multisource feedback can work: Consider a manager who is responsible for leading a large project with team members spread across the country or the globe. She may want periodic feedback about team conditions, perhaps at key junctures of the project—maybe because there was a problem (e.g., a deadline was missed) or she simply has a sense that things could be going better and she wants some idea of how she can improve the situation. She logs on to a team performance management page on the company's human resource web site or app and then clicks a link entitled, "Create Your Own 360-Degree Feedback Survey." The site guides her through the initial steps in the process. She selects survey items from a list of possibilities categorized by area, such as Clarity of Communication, Task Orientation, Interpersonal Relationships, Customer Contact, and Strategy Setting. She clicks the questions she wants included in the survey. Then she selects raters. The system asks her to select a minimum of three to a maximum of ten raters per group (peers, subordinates, supervisors, and/or customers). She types in their names and email addresses, or the system ties to the company's human resource database so all she has to do is type in their names. The system then creates the customized survey and automatically sends an email to the designated recipients, telling them the purpose of the survey, who requested it, and how they can respond online. The web address to the survey is embedded in the email, so the recipient can go onto the site at a convenient time. Recipients complete the survey on the web, and when they are done they click "submit." The system averages the ratings from each source for each item and produces a report. Mean results are not provided for a given item unless a minimum of three people responded to the item. The report includes the mean ratings on each item along with company norms (the average rating received on the item by a sample of managers at the same organizational level across the company). The report is sent directly to the manager herself and not to her supervisor, coach, or human resource department representative. The manager may decide to share her results with others or not. The purpose of the report is purely developmental. A danger from such convenience is that some managers—especially those who are insecure—may overuse this option or do it frequently.

The company may use a similar procedure to administer a multisource survey for all managers. In this case, the items, chosen by top executives or a representative group of managers, would be the same for all feedback recipients. The managers would receive an email from the human resources department, requesting their participation and asking them to indicate names of respondents. The report might be sent to the managers' supervisors if the intention was to use the results to make administrative decisions about the managers. In general, this becomes a simple, cost-effective means of administering a survey across a large company.

Electronic Feedback and Coaching

With the advent of instant messaging, texting, email, voice-over IP, Skype, and Skype-like applications, not to mention the old-fashioned telephone, there is an abundance of ways to keep in touch and convey performance information. This is especially important because of the prevalence of geographically dispersed project teams and work groups. These technologies bridge the psychological distance imposed by the virtual work situation. An open question is, what are the psychological effects of electronic feedback on the recipient and the sender? When relationships are in the formation stage, we might expect that instant messaging, email, and the telephone would be positive ways to give feedback and provide suggestions for behavior change. Email might even be better than telephone. The reason is the simpler and more direct the media, the more attention is focused on the clarity of the message itself. Information is less likely to get lost, confused, or misinterpreted than in a media-rich environment.[4] And does technology bridge or cause further gaps between people of different cultures who are working in different geographical locations who may have different roles, different educational backgrounds and discipline expertise, and different employers? These are all elements of virtual distance that can create rifts, conflicts, and misunderstandings.[5] Conveying feedback in a way that is not face-to-face may be easier. However, if there are no face-to-face meetings, and the coach has only limited, partial information about the coachee based only on virtual performance (i.e., behavior and performance seen through various electronic media), then electronic communication may pose barriers to delivering and discussing performance feedback.

Face-to-face communication, while more personal, is fraught with a multitude of cues that communicate a variety of explicit and implicit messages simultaneously, including words, voice inflections, gestures, and facial expressions. The potential for misreading these cues is great, as is the potential for richer and more complete information. Reactions are likely to be a function of existing relationships (e.g., trusting or not). Givers of negative feedback may worry about the receiver's hurt feelings and defensiveness. Givers of positive feedback may worry about how they will be perceived—for instance, as ingratiating or manipulative. Receivers of negative feedback may try to hide their hurt, perhaps inadvertently communicating a cavalier, careless attitude. Receivers of positive feedback may try to be humble but may convey a haughty attitude by their aloofness or by taking the information in stride. Email can cut through the game playing. However, email can also be a way to mask true feelings by the careful use of words and may generate misleading conclusions.

Writing about the hazards of email in the *New York Times*, business columnist Adam Bryant observed that "emails are too easily misinterpreted, with often-disastrous consequences for the culture of the organization, because they can damage whatever connective tissue exists between colleagues."[6] Talking in person or over the phone avoids dangerous misunderstandings, and you develop relationships and trust. Email doesn't convey tone and expression—whether you are irritated or joking, for instance, even if people know you. "People change when they talk in person about a problem, not because they chicken out, but because they have the benefit of seeing the person, seeing their reaction, and getting a sense of the person."[7]

When people know each other well, they have an easier time reading each other's nonverbal behavior, and using email to deliver weighty information, such as negative feedback, may be perceived as the cowardly way out. Also, coaching by instant messaging or email may not work well unless the parties have excellent typing skills and the time to convey their true thoughts in depth. Of course, in long-distance work relationships, electronic communication media are the next best thing to being there.

There is a lot we don't know about how people react to online feedback—for example, do managers feel more comfortable giving feedback in email messages than in person? Is telephone communication of feedback viewed as more personal and appropriate for feedback than email? Do feedback recipients prefer to hear negative feedback in person? Do the answers to these questions depend on whether the feedback is positive or negative? Is the message clearer when it is delivered in person or in writing? Are people more or less defensive when they receive negative feedback in a written message rather than in person? Email correspondence creates a record that could be retained and forwarded to others. Do people view this means of communication as less confidential?

Is this a problem in managing geographically dispersed team members with whom communication is often by email? Can managers learn how to communicate more effectively by email, especially ways of delivering clear feedback and useful coaching? The answers to these questions would suggest training methods and guidelines for managers to use the various communications media available to best advantage.

Case: Technology—Too Much of a Good Thing

Jake Fielding, age 42, is a professor of political science at a community college. He has always been an "early adopter" when it comes to new technology. He relishes purchasing the latest computing and telecommunications technology and related gadgets and trying new software and apps. He is an avid user of LinkedIn, Facebook, and Twitter, and he uses these social media in all aspects of his life—family, friends, and work. Instead of meeting with his colleagues at work, even if they are in the next office, he is likely to send emails or instant messages whenever thoughts occur to him. He tends to be forthright in expressing strong opinions anyway, and this comes across loud and clear on his professional web page and his weekly blog on industry trends. To Jake, the technology brings him closer to anyone and everyone he cares about, people he knows well and interacts with regularly, and people he doesn't know personally—his 1,272 Twitter followers and 822 "friends" on Facebook. Jake has made a name for himself as an educator. He doesn't hesitate to let a "friend" know if he or she has expressed an opinion he doesn't agree with. He is quick to criticize. Jake sees this as part of his job as an academic. However, he has developed a reputation for being hard to talk to, closed-minded, and intimidating. In meetings, Jake tends to focus on his smart phone while discussions go on around him. Actually he is using his phone to search on topics and gather information that might inform whatever is being discussed. But others see this as disinterest. Younger faculty and especially his students see him this way. Few students dare to turn up for his office hours. Although to Jake, technology brings his world closer to him while widening his sphere of influence, those with whom he interacts see him differently.

Summary

Technology opens opportunities for obtaining feedback data (e.g., electronic monitoring) and for self-paced learning. Indeed, email and the web can be used for online performance management, including the collection of multisource feedback ratings and access to a host of job information and even customized advice and coaching.

An open question for research is the effects of feedback under various organization conditions. The nature of feedback—its importance, ease of delivery, and likelihood of acceptance—may depend on the climate in the organization and the immediate work pressures. Are people more receptive to feedback, and are supervisors more comfortable giving feedback, when the task demands are high—for instance, when there is a work-related crisis of some sort (e.g., meeting a customer deadline), the competition is stiff, and/or the organization is in the process of restructuring at a rapid pace? Under these conditions, everyone may have a sense of urgency. After every meeting, people may talk to their colleagues about how it went, how others reacted to them, and what they can do better next time.

The effects of organizational stress on feedback may interact with individuals' personalities, such as their self-esteem. Some people facing tough conditions may be more sensitive to criticism than usual. They may recognize the critical nature of their actions and decisions and be more self-critical. This does not mean, however, that they will necessarily welcome feedback and be open to coaching. Indeed, they may be more defensive when they hear negative feedback from others. They may avoid conversations about their performance and not want to hear suggestions from others.

Feedback in Virtual Teams

Many organizations do much of their business in team environments. This is because complex work that is distributed across regions, often across the country or across the globe, requires input from different disciplines and functions. The advent of new communications technologies, such as wireless telephone, email, and Internet connections, allows people to work in virtual or geographically distributed teams. These teams may rarely, if ever, meet face-to-face. Members interact with each other in real time (synchronously) or at different times (asynchronously). The shift toward using virtual teams in organizations raises several fundamental questions, such as how do interpersonal perceptions evolve, how does trust develop, and how are leaders perceived by team members?[8] More particularly, how do leaders of virtual teams learn about and develop its members' needs, show consideration, inspire, create innovative thinking, and act as a role model for team members? The virtual team, similar to the face-to-face team, has to establish norms of interacting, agree to a mission, appreciate each member's capabilities, share feelings, develop mutual trust, and gain a sense of cohesiveness. Members of a virtual team have less opportunity to interact face-to-face, and so team development becomes a significant challenge.

Virtual teams face substantial problems.[9] Since they cannot take advantage of social and nonverbal cues, developing deep interpersonal relations among team members takes substantially longer, if it occurs at all. Team members will have trouble establishing a common image in their minds of what is required of them, their roles, and how they must work together to accomplish the team's mission. They will have trouble developing the interpersonal perceptions that are the foundation for building trust.

Elements of transactional and transformational leadership can help virtual teams to develop norms and expectations to guide their future interactions.[10] For example, transactional leaders clarify acceptable and unacceptable team behaviors, specify the team's goals, and provide feedback. By setting goals and rewards for accomplishing them, transactional leaders motivate the team members to achieve agreed-upon levels of performance. The leader and team members share information with each other about their task objectives, who is responsible for what, and who deserves recognition. This contributes to members' initial sense of conditional trust.

In contrast, transformational leaders develop unconditional trust by augmenting transactional leadership. The transformational leader instills confidence among team members about their ability to work together to overcome challenges and accomplish team goals. They communicate messages and feedback that convey how team members can go beyond their own self-interests for the sake of the team. Every member is encouraged to contribute to the team's goals, and feedback focuses the extent to which this is happening.

Feedback in virtual teams is another means of developing mutual trust. The richness of media in collaborative technologies (LISTSERVs, chat rooms, electronic bulletin boards, instant messaging, and simple email and conference calls, including teleconferencing) allows for immediate feedback to individuals and to all team members in a variety of ways. Using a variety of cues and channels in the media-rich environment provides ways for the leader and team members to personalize their communications to each other and have in-depth interactions. The result is a perception of mutual ability, benevolence, and integrity among team members. The formation of trust may be hindered when media richness is low and facilitated when it is high.[11] However, for early interactions, lean media may help members categorize each other more quickly and understand each team member's potential contribution to the team without the stereotypes from gender, race, or other factors that get in the way in face-to-face teams. As such, initially low media richness may help prevent stereotypes getting in the way of team interaction. The team can focus on task relevant feedback and establish an initial sense of conditional trust. As richer communications media are used and the team develops, unconditional trust will emerge. Research is needed to link media richness with virtual team interactions and interpersonal perceptions. Also, research is needed to examine the effects of leadership style (e.g., transactional and transformational), team composition, and media richness on members' communication patterns and productivity of virtual teams.

In summary, given advancing communications and computer technologies, virtual teams are increasingly prevalent in organizations. They provide a means of using talent regardless of where people are located. Early in the team's history, the virtual team can benefit from using just one or two media channels. Simple media and clear communication can help team members categorize each other more quickly, understand each team member's potential contribution to the team, and provide feedback without the stereotypes getting in the way. As trust develops, richer media can be beneficial in promoting the team's development and productivity.

Conclusion

Technologies can facilitate providing feedback, coaching, and opportunities for self-determined learning. Organizations can establish environments that use feedback effectively to promote continuous learning that matches the organization's need for change. Here are some final conclusions:

- We can expect abundant feedback from objective, technology-based sources of information. This poses some threat and raises the challenge to develop useful computer-based modes for involving people in self-management for continuous performance improvement.
- People are increasingly responsible for their own assessment of their skills, evaluation of opportunities and needs, and acquiring the skills and knowledge required for continued success. Self-paced learners have autonomy to decide what they study and how, when, where, and at what pace. This raises exciting opportunities for cost-effective ways to deliver education effectively. However, these methods must take into account the need to motivate people to evaluate their own strengths and weaknesses, learn on their own, set performance goals, and track their performance.

Notes

1. Zajonc (1965).
2. Warr and Bunce (1995).
3. James (1994).
4. Avolio, Dahai, Dumdum, and Sivasubramaniam (2001).
5. Sobel-Lojeski (2009).

6. Bryant (2014a, p. 4). Also, see Bryant (2014b) for a more in-depth analysis of how leaders use feedback in the process of creating a culture of innovation.
7. Quote from Nancy Aossey, chief executive of the International Medical Corps, cited in Bryant (2014a, p. 4).
8. Avolio et al. (2001).
9. Avolio et al. (2001).
10. Avolio et al. (2001).
11. Avolio et al. (2001) suggested this.

13

BECOMING A FEEDBACK-ORIENTED, CONTINUOUS LEARNER

This chapter is about how you can create an environment that supports feedback for continuous learning for yourself and those with whom you work. An environment that empowers self-development is a feedback-oriented organizational culture.[1] I begin the chapter by describing what I mean by a feedback-oriented organizational culture. This includes support for feedback from supervisors and co-workers. It also includes what you can do for yourself to be aware of your performance and be your own coach. Ultimately, you can develop a strong feedback orientation—seeking and using feedback to learn and improve your performance continuously. I consider how the changing nature of work, such as new technical knowledge and skills, attention to lowering costs, and the prevalence of teamwork and organization change, increases the importance of self-directed learning and being sure you are making a contribution to accomplishing team and organizational goals. I recognize that factors such as age and personality may influence a person's readiness to accept and use performance feedback. I conclude with a review of the power of feedback for creating a continuous learning organization.

What Is a Feedback-Oriented Culture?

A feedback-oriented organizational culture is one in which people are comfortable with giving and receiving feedback, and feedback is an integral part of the performance management process. Your organization, whether a company or a volunteer club or not-for-profit organization, can develop a feedback culture in a number of different ways:[2] It can support nonthreatening feedback by instituting multisource feedback surveys for use in development but not decision making. It can train supervisors to be better coaches to their employees, ready to help their employees interpret feedback results and use the data to set goals for development. Also, the organization can strengthen the link between performance improvement resulting from development and valued outcomes, such as pay increases or promotion. That is, in developmentally oriented feedback cultures, people are rewarded for performance improvement, and goal setting, participation in development activities, and continued performance review are encouraged. The same principles apply in nonwork settings as well, such as home and community volunteer organizations. At home, family members can focus on behaviors they believe can improve, suggest sources of information to help people recognize their strengths and weaknesses, and have frequent discussions about "how things are going." Discussing behaviors and actions we like and dislike about ourselves and others can be part of daily life; we don't have to wait for a traumatic episode or family counseling to unearth them.

Generally, a feedback culture comes from (1) enhancing the quality of feedback, (2) emphasizing the importance and value of feedback, and (3) providing support for using feedback.[3] The quality of feedback can be increased by realizing the power of our words and focusing on actions and behaviors, not personality characteristics and abilities. Behaviors can be pinpointed without being judgmental or critical of personal characteristics. The quality of feedback can also be increased by ensuring there are clear expectations and goals and providing time to discuss and clarify the feedback results—for instance, encouraging discussions in which you ask and answer each other's questions. At work, employees can ask questions when their supervisor gives them feedback or managers can be encouraged to share their feedback survey results with their peers and subordinates and discuss the meaning of the results.

Performance appraisal and review processes are not likely to be effective if the climate is not supportive of feedback exchanges. Conversely, a poorly run and formulated performance appraisal and review process can be overcome if managers have created an environment that supports feedback exchanges.[4] An important element of the supervisor's role is to develop a culture of coaching, learning, and development. Supervisors do this when they are trained to understand the value of feedback and how to give and receive meaningful and useful feedback. Stated another way, they need feedback about feedback—how well they are doing in delivering feedback. They can get this from their subordinates and/or in management development workshops. Senior leaders can be role models of giving accurate and useful feedback to the managers who report to them. Managers need to fully comprehend the goals, expectations, and measures used to evaluate performance. They need to learn to make the time for sharing feedback not just in a formal appraisal but also in informal ways every day.[5]

Case: Dealing with a Performance Problem

Mel Franklyn has owned a dry cleaning business for more than 30 years. He realizes the adverse (hot) working conditions his employees endure. He wants his employees to know they are appreciated. If he must give them criticism, he tries to control his tone. He is soft-spoken by nature. When he gives employees feedback, he stresses the importance of their job to his business and the quality of their work, and he reminds them that without customers, there is no business, which in turn means no job. Customers must be treated well, and a personal touch makes all the difference. He described an older woman who worked for him who tended to be impatient and terse with customers. Mel spoke to the employee, and she responded that she understood. A few days later, a customer complained that the employee called her ignorant because she let her child wander around the store. Mel thanked the employee for her tenure, paid her the wages due, and severed their employment relationship.

Support for Feedback

Your organization can highlight the importance of feedback by having top executives participate in and model a multisource process, asking their subordinate managers to rate them and then receiving a feedback report and participating in development activities. Parents can do the same for their children, and spouses for each other. As such, they become role models for the feedback process. Encourage the importance of informal feedback and give feedback to others "in the moment"—immediately after a critical event.

At work, support for feedback may include providing skilled facilitators or coaches to help feedback recipients interpret the meaning of the feedback, set goals for development, and collect data to track changes in their performance over time. Coaching is a central management responsibility in corporate cultures that value feedback. Managers are rewarded for devoting time and energy to coaching their subordinates. The amount of time they spend coaching and the quality of that time can be measured by asking employees about their supervisor's coaching behavior in attitude and multisource feedback surveys. In addition, organizations support feedback by providing opportunities for development. In other words, the organization needs to support not only the delivery and discussion of feedback and developmental goal setting but also the availability of training programs, special job assignments, and other ways to enhance development.

Self-Coaching

You can learn to evaluate your own performance and consider ways you can improve. One way to do this is to list the critical behaviors that are important to your job or elements of your job, such as your work on a team. List behaviors you believe are important. Test them by talking to your supervisor, co-workers, or team leader. Or if your company uses a performance appraisal measure that includes specific behaviors, use this tool. Then review your own performance periodically, maybe once a month or after an important event, such as a key team meeting during which you participated actively or gave a presentation. Consider behaviors that went well and those you may want to improve. Think about what you can do to improve. You can be just as effective in finding ways to improve your performance and give yourself as much help as an external coach.[6] This takes self-discipline, of course, which many of us do not have. From an organization's standpoint, providing training and reminders to help executives evaluate and coach themselves can be far less expensive than external coaches. Also, since organizations are not likely to invest in external coaches for managers who are not senior executives, training in self-coaching can be a cost-effective method to stimulate performance improvement in a business unit.

Case: Creating a Feedback-Oriented Culture

Michelle Turner is a human resource manager in her early 40s. She believes that feedback should be given often, and as close to any event (good or bad) as possible. As a human resource manager, she knows the importance of documenting performance, particularly performance problems, since reasons for a dismissal, if it comes to that, need to be documented. Beyond compliance, however, Michelle feels that constant communication about performance builds honest and trusting relationships. She has encountered situations when an employee has erred, only to come forward and have a discussion with her about the error. She attributes this to the feedback provided in good times and bad, and trusting relationships.

Michelle pointed out an experience with an employee who was having trouble with a particularly difficult issue. During discussions, the employee was able to understand the source of difficulty and provide a plan to improve. She believes this can happen only when feedback is given constantly, is nonthreatening, is given for reasons of growth and development, and takes place in an environment where the relationship is based on trust. Often supervisors believe they have provided feedback while the subordinates may feel that they have been involved in a status update meeting. This is not clear feedback, obviously.

Your Feedback Orientation

A feedback culture will be enhanced when you develop a stronger feedback orientation. Some people have high growth/curiosity traits. They welcome feedback naturally. They have a sufficiently thick skin (high self-esteem) to seek feedback regardless of its favorability. They don't fear being evaluated. They seek it out and process it carefully and deeply. They want to know what it means and why people feel the way they do about their performance. People who are high in feedback orientation are sensitive to how others view them, and they care what other people think of them. They believe that feedback offers insights that may help them become more effective. In other words, they believe that feedback is, indeed, useful. Moreover, they feel accountable to use the feedback since their colleagues or customers bothered to provide it and since the company clearly wants them to take advantage of feedback as a guide for improving their performance.

The feedback environment includes the following elements:

1. *Source credibility* is the feedback source's expertise and trustworthiness as a provider of feedback (e.g., "My supervisor [co-worker] is generally familiar with my performance on the job").
2. *Feedback quality* is the consistency and usefulness of the feedback (e.g., "My supervisor [co-worker] gives me useful feedback about my job performance").
3. *Feedback delivery* is how considerate the feedback provider is of the recipient's feelings (e.g., "My supervisor [co-worker] is supportive when giving me feedback about my job performance").
4. *Favorable feedback* is the frequency with which positive feedback is provided and is consistent with the recipient's self-perceptions (e.g., "My supervisor [co-worker] generally lets me know when I do a good job at work").
5. *Unfavorable feedback* is the frequency with which negative feedback is provided and is consistent with the recipient's self-perceptions (e.g., "My supervisor [co-worker] tells me when my work performance does not meet organizational standards").
6. *Source availability* is the amount of contact the recipient has with the feedback source and the effort the recipient needs to expend to receive the feedback (e.g., "My supervisor [co-worker] is usually available when I want performance information").
7. *Promotion of feedback seeking* is the supportiveness of the supervisor and/or co-worker of feedback seeking (e.g., "My supervisor [co-worker] encourages me to ask for feedback whenever I am uncertain about my job performance").[7]

The stronger the feedback environment, the higher employees' organization citizenship behavior (e.g., altruism and courtesy, rated by their supervisors) and the lower their absenteeism, especially for individuals who are committed to the organization (i.e., they identify with, are involved in, and are emotionally attached to the organization).[8] That is, favorable feedback environments affect behaviors that go beyond performance improvement to influence how people relate to each other as they contribute to the organization. If supervisors understand how their daily interactions with subordinates influence subordinate work behaviors, then supervisors may be able to generate more favorable work behaviors and improve cooperation and teamwork. Supervisors may need to be reminded that they should consistently encourage their subordinates to seek feedback, and that this will increase employees' favorable perceptions of the feedback environment. In turn, this should limit absenteeism and increase employees' citizenship behavior.

Case: Recognition for Extraordinary Performance

Don Kravitz, in his mid-60s, is a professional data analyst in a large city's housing and human services department. He is one of 30 employees in his department, and he has no subordinates. He receives an annual performance appraisal, which shows that his work is consistently good. Other than that, when his supervisor says something about his performance, it is to criticize him for something. His supervisor has never complimented him on his work. After a recent severe storm, he was invited, along with 200 other employees, to a "thank you" breakfast hosted by the mayor. Don had worked extraordinarily hard to ensure that emergency shelters were available to storm victims. He worked 24/7 for 2 weeks. His supervisor said nothing to him directly, however. Don finds this lack of feedback and especially lack of recognition demoralizing. Other civil service employees don't go the extra mile because they know that management has little control over them. They certainly can't be fired. So managers don't bother to give feedback, let alone recognize outstanding performance.

Feedback and the Changing Nature of Work

Some fields are experiencing rapid changes in jobs, the creation of new positions and roles, and work team re-configurations. Often these changes are imposed with minimal formal education or training. As a result, on-the-job training and feedback become critical to success, and existing employees need to learn how to give feedback to make the new employees effective as they all initiate new roles.

A good example is provided by the health care industry. The nursing shortage in many parts of the U.S. and the concern for lowering health care costs led hospitals to begin changing the mix of licensed and unlicensed employees caring for patients. For instance, the Ochner Foundation Hospital in New Orleans developed the position of nursing care technician, and the Presbyterian Medical Center of Philadelphia created the position of patient care associate. These new personnel work with and for registered nurses (RNs), who delegate and supervise their work. After initial training from the hospitals, these unlicensed assistants learn new skills on the job from RNs. The RNs are trained in good delegation, communication, and teambuilding skills. Giving ongoing feedback is an essential part of enhancing an assistant's skills. Each assistant works with two or three RNs, who have a chance to develop close working relationships with the assistant while allowing for flexible scheduling. Therefore, the RNs need to be consistent in their expectations and feedback, engage in ongoing evaluation of the assistants' role, and revise expectations and relationships as the assistants learn more skills that do not require licensed personnel.

Consider work organization. In the past, employers tended to take responsibility for their employees' development. For example, supervisors decided who received training and when. While today's organizations provide the enabling resources, such as career planning programs and training courses of all types, they don't necessarily assign people to these programs and courses unless there is an immediate business need (e.g., a requirement for employees to learn a new software system). Instead, the organization makes resources available, and employees can decide for themselves whether to take advantage of these resources.

While some people engage in self-directed learning without any precipitating organization or job changes, new organizational conditions can ignite an employee's readiness to act and learn. Organizational factors that require self-directed learning include explicit performance standards, being assigned to work on a new task, or an event that shows an imbalance between job expectations and performance capabilities (i.e., performing a task poorly). Synergistic, voluntary, self-directed learning results from a combination of the motivation to act and learn and the spark of an organizational change, such as a promotion to a new job.

Managers may participate in assessment centers and/or multisource feedback surveys that give them feedback on their abilities and potential to advance to higher organizational levels. The organization can make available information about organizational goals and business directions and the implications of anticipated changes for performance expectations and promotional opportunities. There may be a call to action, for instance, asking for volunteers to be considered for a new subsidiary or work abroad. Here, the opportunity is presented, and you, the employee, must decide what to do—engage in development that prepares you for the opportunity or ignore the opportunity.

Managers can create a supportive climate by conveying information about opportunities, offering coaching, and providing resources for development, such as time away from the office along with tuition and travel expenses to attend training. Also, managers may hold their subordinates accountable for their continuous learning. Employees need to understand what they need to know in order to be valuable to the organization. If they don't keep up, they may suffer the consequences: poorer performance and lower than average salary increases, or possibly a layoff during a downsizing initiative.

Perceiving Support

You probably have a sense about the extent to which others support your learning and are willing to give you feedback that helps you pinpoint behaviors you can change and skills you can learn.[9] This support comes from people you care about sitting down to talk to you about your actions and future. It also comes from resources they are willing to provide to help you. For instance, your boss may be willing to send you to a training course. Your spouse may be willing to go to classes with you at the local community college or be patient with you when you want to take a class and come home with homework. Your friends or co-workers may be willing to show you a new skill and give you pointers to help you improve—whether golf, presentation skills, or some other activity for work or leisure. Knowing that you will be treated fairly and the feedback and advice are given for your benefit and not some other motive (a competitor who would just as soon see you fail) will give you confidence to try. This will also develop a tighter relationship, cementing a friendship or mentor-mentee relationship.

Organizations that empower self-development expect employees to recognize their development needs and take responsibility for their own learning. Employees can do this by actively seeking performance feedback, not waiting for it to arrive. They can compare their self-assessments to the perspectives of others and to predictions of future performance standards and job requirements. That is, they need to determine if they will be ready to meet the needs of the organization today and tomorrow. They should then use these assessments to set development goals and investigate opportunities for development, and then take part in development activities. Empowered self-development is a continuous process. As progress is evaluated, goals are adjusted. New goals are set as old ones are accomplished.

EXPANDING THE POWER OF FEEDBACK

Additional Factors Affecting Feedback

Age Differential

The ease of giving feedback may depend on the ages and roles of the feedback provider and recipient. Supervisors who are considerably older (say 15 years or more) than their subordinates may have an easier time delivering negative feedback, because they can assume a parental or mentoring role more easily than supervisors who are closer in age to their subordinates. Similarly, subordinates may be less threatened by negative feedback from managers who are more senior in age and/or level in the organization. Negative information may be more difficult to discount or ignore when it comes from a more senior, and presumably more respected, manager. Perhaps the subordinate's respect for the manager is more important than age or position effects. Managers who are highly respected for their accomplishments may find that their subordinates are more receptive to their feedback than feedback from managers who are less revered by their subordinates. On the other hand, managers who understand and value the esteem in which others hold them may be reluctant to risk this status by being critical.

Style of Leadership and Feedback

A leader's style of leadership may influence, or be evident, in how he or she delivers and receives feedback. Leaders who are strong in task structure are likely to deliver clear and cogent feedback. They may be less likely to praise accomplishments and more likely to focus on areas for improvement. Leaders who are strong in building interpersonal relationships are likely to be empathetic and considerate of others' feelings, and as such would be diplomatic or tactful in delivering negative feedback and effusive in recognizing accomplishments. These are hypotheses at this point, however. Research is needed to understand how leadership style influences how feedback is delivered and received.

The Dark Side of Feedback: The Effects of Personality on Feedback

There are many ways that personality may influence managerial style. We know that raters may manipulate their ratings to convey certain impressions—for instance, they may evaluate their supervisor leniently because they think their supervisor will repay them in kind, even though the ratings are anonymous.[10] An open question is whether managers' personalities influence how they rate others' performance. Are vindictive people likely to use their feelings to get back at others, essentially undermining the

186

manager they are rating and simultaneously sabotaging the performance evaluation system? Do they use their ratings to ingratiate themselves with the people they are rating? How does the rater's personality relate to the quality of the ratings or written responses to open-ended questions? Do some raters deliberately provide wrong, incomplete, or no information?

The effects of negative personality on feedback are problematic when it comes to in-person feedback. That is, controlling how and what a bitter, angry, or vindictive supervisor may say or do is more difficult than identifying and removing biased survey ratings. However, subordinate ratings may be useful in identifying leaders with performance problems that are likely to be caused by negative personality traits. Higher-level management can monitor these individuals' performance with particular attention to how they treat their subordinates and the decisions they make about their subordinates. The fairness and accuracy of their decisions can be evaluated and, if necessary, called into question. Training or, ultimately, disciplinary action may be needed. This is how leaders with personality deficiencies are eventually unmasked and derailed.[11]

Personality is related to job performance. People who are micromanagers, aloof, cautious, and high-strung tend to receive lower performance ratings.[12] This isn't surprising since these individuals are probably not well liked. Flawed interpersonal strategies may arise from a person's distorted beliefs about others. Interestingly, people who are viewed as colorful (i.e., engaging yet distractible) tend to receive positive ratings.

In summary, there is a dark side to performance ratings and feedback. Negative personality characteristics may portend career derailing. This may be good in pinpointing people who are in need of development, but probably the people who are least likely to be responsive to the feedback. These people may actually undermine establishing a feedback-, development-oriented culture, or at least make establishing such a culture more difficult, especially if they head large departments.

Case: Feedback in the Moment Can Have a Backlash

Jane Morrison, a woman in her 60s, is an account manager for an office equipment company. While she was on the phone one day to a client, one of her male co-workers was shouting at another co-worker, also male. She put her hand over the phone and sharply asked the man who was shouting to take the discussion to another room. When she completed her call, she called the man who was shouting back into the office and told him his behavior was disrespectful to her and the co-worker and conveyed a negative impression to the client on the phone who might have overheard the shouting. Jane let him know that that type of behavior was not appropriate in a work setting. Her co-worker was taken aback by being called out and told her this was none of her business. He later apologized to the man he had been arguing with, but ignored Jane during the next few weeks even though their desks were only 6 feet away from each other. Jane decided to write him a note of apology for expressing her feelings. He failed to acknowledge the note. Their subsequent conversations were civil, but barely friendly.[13]

Creating a Learning Organization

Some organizations work hard to continually develop performance capabilities. These "learning organizations" emphasize *generative learning*— "an emphasis on continuous experimentation and feedback in an ongoing examination of the very way organizations go about defining and solving problems."[14]

The Role of Feedback in Creating Positive Performance Cycles

Feedback is the key to self-correcting adjustment in effort and performance and avoiding downward spirals.[15] Knowing whether you succeeded or failed is not enough. Feedback must provide accurate, timely, and specific information about how your behavior led to performance improvement. Inaccurate or delayed feedback may cause you to use inappropriate performance strategies in the future. That is, the person must understand the cause-effect relationship between his or her behavior and subsequent performance. This is why negative feedback should be provided without threatening the person's self-image. Similarly, positive feedback should be given in a way that fosters attention to the effort-behavior-performance linkages, rather than general flattery. Breaking tasks into small components can be an effective way to obtain manageable information and experiment with new behaviors without undue risk. Small losses can be analyzed carefully and new behaviors tried. Small wins can be repeated and be followed by incrementally more complex actions.

Learning to Use Feedback

Negative feedback alone will not necessarily lead to a constructive response. Instead, it may lead people to be defensive or merely to ignore the information. Negative feedback won't have much effect on people who are low in self-awareness. These individuals are likely to tune out unfavorable information about their performance. However, people who have low performance who are guided through the feedback in a way that

188

makes them pay attention to, and reflect on, the performance data are likely to avoid the same mistakes later. When confronted with unfavorable feedback, subordinates are likely to be defensive, deny the problem, or blame situational factors beyond their control, including the supervisor's unrealistic expectations and demands.

Feedback Seeking, Empowerment, and Trust

When you feel empowered to make decisions and take actions on the job, this is likely to increase the trust you have in your supervisor, which in turn contributes to your seeking feedback to improve your performance.[16] Generally, employees who are empowered and feel more intrinsic reward from doing their job trust their supervisor more than employees who are not empowered.[17] If you are high in empowerment, you are likely to say that your work is important to you (meaning), you are confident in your ability to do your job (competence), you have significant autonomy in determining how you do your job (self-determination), and you have considerable control over what happens in your department (impact).[18] Your supervisor creates the environment that allows you to feel empowered and holds you accountable for your job performance. The trust you have in your supervisors reduces the risk you feel in asking for feedback. Employees who trust their supervisor and have a sharing relationship with their supervisor feel free to share ideas, feelings, and hopes and approach their job with professionalism and dedication.[19] Being empowered and held accountable increases your proactive behavior—your willingness to take action to do what's necessary to perform well.[20] This includes seeking feedback. Employees are likely to perform better when they trust their supervisor.[21] Supervisors who create an environment that empowers their subordinates are more likely to be receptive to requests for feedback and give feedback that demonstrates the trust they have in their employees to use the information. Employees who value the relationship they have with their supervisor respect the suggestions and information he or she offers for performing better. They apply this knowledge to do better on the job.

Conclusion

This chapter showed how organizations encourage feedback and enhance employees' favorable disposition toward feedback. In a feedback-oriented, continuous learning environment, rather than deny, ignore, and/or withhold feedback, employees and managers seek, provide, and discuss performance feedback and learning needs on an ongoing basis, creating positive performance cycles. However, negative feedback can become a self-fulfilling prophesy, and some people's negative personality characteristics are likely to thwart the value of feedback. Organizations need to work hard to create environments that support learning; feedback, goal setting, and development are keys to successful learning. I conclude this chapter and the book with the following points:

- Jobs, roles, and work group structures are being transformed to impose new demands on employees. These changes emphasize work processes that cross functions, departments, and organization levels. People need to learn new competencies to work in these environments. They must learn how to design new positions and support the feedback and development of employees in the new and evolving positions.
- An organization environment that empowers self-development promotes the collection and use of feedback (e.g., through a multisource feedback survey and the availability of coaches). Also, the organization can make available information about organizational goals and business directions and the implications of anticipated changes for performance expectations and promotional opportunities.
- A feedback-friendly or feedback-oriented corporate culture is one in which managers and employees are comfortable with giving and receiving feedback, and feedback is an integral part of the performance management process. A feedback-oriented culture can be developed by (1) enhancing the quality of feedback, (2) emphasizing the importance of feedback in the organization, and (3) providing support for using feedback.
- Employees who are high in feedback orientation like feedback, do not mind being evaluated, and actually seek feedback. They are sensitive to how others view them and they care what other people think of them. Feedback-oriented corporate cultures promote employees' feedback orientation.
- Reactions to feedback may depend on the ages, leadership style, and personality of the feedback provider and receiver. Performance ratings are generally highly related to the personality of the person rated, indicating that ratings are a way to identify people with dysfunctional characteristics. Also, these characteristics may negatively influence the validity of the ratings these managers make about others.
- As people learn to use feedback, they can set goals to avoid negative results and establish positive cycles of reinforcement for performance improvement.

Notes

1. London and Smither (1999).
2. London and Smither (2002).
3. London and Smither (2002).
4. Dahling and O'Malley (2011).

5. Peterson (2009).
6. Sue-Chan and Latham (2004).
7. Steelman, Levy, and Snell (2002); see also Steelman and Levy (2001).
8. Norris-Watts and Levy (2002).
9. Whitaker (2011).
10. Kozlowski, Chao, and Morrison (1998).
11. McCall and Lombardo (1983).
12. Fleming and Holland (2002).
13. Based on a letter written to Walker (2013).
14. Senge (1990); McGill, Slocum, and Lei (1992, p. 5).
15. Lindsley, Brass, and Thomas (1995).
16. Huang (2012).
17. Zhu, May, and Avolio (2004); Moye and Henkin (2006).
18. Spreitzer (1995).
19. McAllister (1995).
20. Grant and Ashford (2008).
21. Mayer and Gavin (2005); Madjar and Ortiz-Walters (2009).

REFERENCES

Aguinis, H., Gottfredson, R. K., & Joo, H. (2012). Delivering effective performance feedback: The strengths-based approach. *Business Horizons, 55,* 105–111. doi:10.1016/j.bushor.2011.10.004

Anderson, L. R. (1990). Toward a two-track model of leadership training: Suggestions from self-monitoring theory. *Small Group Research, 21*(2), 147–167.

Anderson, L. R., & Thacker, J. (1985). Self-monitoring and sex as related to assessment center ratings and job performance. *Basic and Applied Psychology, 6,* 345–361.

Ashford, S. J. (1986). The role of feedback seeking in individual adaptation: A resource perspective. *Academy of Management Journal, 29,* 465–487.

Ashford, S. J. (1989). Self-assessments in organizations: A literature review and integrative model. *Research in Organizational Behavior, 11,* 133–174.

Ashford, S. J., & Tsui, A. S. (1991). Self-regulation for managerial effectiveness: The role of active feedback seeking. *Academy of Management Journal, 34*(2), 251–280.

Atwater, L. E., Ostroff, C., Yammarino, F. J., & Fleenor, J. W. (1998). Self-other agreement: Does it really matter. *Personnel Psychology, 51,* 577–598.

Atwater, L. E., Rousch, P., & Fischthal, A. (1995). The influence of upward feedback on self and follower ratings of leadership. *Personnel Psychology, 48,* 35–59.

Avolio, B. J., Dahai, S., Dumdum, R., & Sivasubramaniam, N. (2001). Virtual teams: Implications for e-leadership and team development. In M. London (Ed.), *How people evaluate others in organizations* (pp. 337–358). Mahwah, NJ: Erlbaum.

Bales, R. F. (1950). *Interaction process analysis: A method for the study of small groups.* Cambridge, MA: Addison-Wesley.

Bales, R. F. (1988). A new overview of the SYMLOG system: Measuring and changing behavior in groups. In R. B. Polley, A. P. Hare, & P. J. Stone (Eds.), *The SYMLOG practitioner: Applications of small group research* (pp. 319–344). New York: Praeger.

Balzer, W., Doherty, M., & O'Connor, R., Jr. (1989). Effects of cognitive feedback on performance. *Psychological Bulletin, 106,* 410–433.

Bandura, A. (1982). Self-efficacy mechanisms in human agency. *American Psychologist, 37,* 122–147.

Bandura, A. (1986). *Social foundations of thought and action: A social-cognitive view.* Englewood Cliffs, NJ: Prentice-Hall.

192

Barnes-Farrell, J. L. (2001). Performance appraisal: Person perception processes and challenges. In M. London (Ed.), *How people evaluate others in organizations* (pp. 135–153). Mahwah, NJ: Erlbaum.

Baron, R. A. (1988). Negative effects of destructive criticism: Impact on conflict, self-efficacy, and task performance. *Journal of Applied Psychology, 73,* 199–207.

Barrick, M. R., & Mount, M. K. (1991). The big five personality dimensions and job performance: A meta-analysis. *Personnel Psychology, 44,* 1–26.

Bartlett, C. A., & Ghoshal, S. (1997). The myth of the general manager. *California Management Review, 40,* 92–116.

Bass, B. M., & Yammarino, F. J. (1991). Congruence of self and others' leadership ratings of naval officers for understanding successful performance. *Applied Psychology: An International Review, 40,* 437–454.

Bassman, E. S. (1992). *Abuse in the workplace: Management remedies and bottom line impact.* Westport, CT: Quorum Books.

Belschak, F. D., & Den Hartog, D. N. (2009). Consequences of positive and negative feedback: The impact on emotions and extra-role behavior. *Applied Psychology: An International Review, 58,* 274–303. doi:10.1111/j.1464-0597.2008.00336.x

Berson, Y. R., Erez, M., & Adler, S. (2002, April). 360-degree feedback on managerial performance across cultures. Paper presented at the 17th Annual Meeting of the Society for Industrial and Organizational Psychology, Toronto.

Blakely, G. L. (1993). The effects of performance rating discrepancies on supervisors and subordinates. *Organizational Behavior and Human Decision Processes, 54,* 57–80.

Boice, R. (1983). Observational skills. *Psychological Bulletin, 93,* 3–29.

Botwood, L. (2002, April). Feelings about feedback: Predicting affective reactions from work goal orientation. Paper presented at the 17th Annual Meeting of the Society for Industrial and Organizational Psychology, Toronto.

Bouskila-Yam, O., & Kluger, A. N. (2011). Strength-based performance appraisal and goal setting. *Human Resource Management Review, 21*(2), 137–147.

Bracken, D. W., Timmreck, C. W., Fleenor, J. W., & Summers, L. (2001). 360 feedback from another angle. *Human Resource Management, 40,* 3–20.

Brett, J. F., & Atwater, L. E. (2001). 360° feedback: Accuracy, reactions, and perceptions of usefulness. *Journal of Applied Psychology, 86*(5), 930–942.

Breugst, N., Patzelt, H., Shepherd, D. A., & Aguinis, H. (2012). Relationship conflict improves team performance assessment accuracy: Evidence from a multilevel study. *Academy of Management Learning & Education, 11,* 187–206.

Brink, K. E. (2002, April). Self-efficacy and goal change in the absence of external feedback. Predicting executive performance with multi-rater surveys: Who you ask matters. Paper presented at the 17th Annual Meeting of the Society for Industrial and Organizational Psychology, Toronto.

Brown, S. P., Ganesan, S., & Challagalla, G. (2001). Self-efficacy as a moderator of information-seeking effectiveness. *Journal of Applied Psychology, 86*(5), 1043–1051.

Bryant, A. (2013, December 20). Corner office: Spencer Rascoff. *New York Times* (Business section), p. B2.

Bryant, A. (2014a, January 5). Management be nimble. *New York Times* (Sunday Business section), pp. 1, 4.

Bryant, A. (2014b). *Quick and nimble: Lessons from leading C.E.O.'s on how to create a culture of innovation*. New York: Times Books.

Cannon, M. D., & Witherspoon, R. (2005). Actionable feedback: Unlocking the power of learning and performance improvement. *Academy of Management Executive, 19*, 120–134.

Carlson, E. N. (2013). Overcoming the barriers to self-knowledge: Mindfulness as a path to seeing yourself as you really are. *Psychological Science, 8*, 173–186. doi:10.1177/1745691612462584

Cascio, W. F. (2012). *Managing human resources: Productivity, quality of work life, profits*. New York: McGraw-Hill/Irwin.

Church, A. H. (2000). Do higher performing managers actually receive better ratings? A validation of multirater assessment methodology. *Consulting Psychology Journal: Practice and Research, 52*, 99–116.

Cohen, R., Bianco, A. T., Cairo, P., & Geczy, C. (2002, April). Leadership performance as a function of multisource survey feedback. Paper presented at the 17th Annual Meeting of the Society for Industrial and Organizational Psychology, Toronto.

Colquitt, J. A., LePine, J. A., & Noe, R. A. (2000). Toward an integrative theory of training motivation: A meta-analytic path analysis of 20 years of research. *Journal of Applied Psychology, 85*(5), 678–707.

Dahling, J. J., & O'Malley, A. L. (2011). Supportive feedback environments can mend broken performance management systems. *Industrial and Organizational Psychology, 4*, 201–203.

Dalessio, A. T. (1998). Using multisource feedback for employee development and personnel decisions. In J. W. Smither (Ed.), *Performance appraisal: State of the art in practice* (pp. 278–330). San Francisco: Jossey-Bass.

Dalton, M. A., & Hollenbeck, G. P. (2001). After feedback: How to facilitate change in behavior. In D. W. Bracken, C. W. Timmreck, & A. H. Church (Eds.), *The handbook of multisource feedback* (pp. 352–367). San Francisco, CA: Jossey-Bass.

Dobbins, G. H., & Russell, J. M. (1986). The biasing effects of subordinate likeableness on leaders' responses to poor performers: A laboratory and field study. *Personnel Psychology, 39*, 759–777. doi:10.1111/j.1744-6570.1986.tb00593.x

Drasgow, F., Olson, J. B., Keenan, P. A., Moberg, P., & Mead, A. D. (1993). Computerized assessment. *Research in Personnel and Human Resources Management, 11*, 163–206.

Drew, S. A. W., & Davidson, A. (1993). Simulation-based leadership development and team learning. *Journal of Management Development, 12*(8), 39–352.

Elliot, A. J., & Harackiewicz, J. M. (1996). Approach and avoidance achievement goals and intrinsic motivation: A mediational analysis. *Journal of Personality and Social Psychology, 70*, 461–475.

Evans, P., Pucik, V., & Barsoux, J. L. (2002). *The global challenge*. New York: McGraw Hill.

Facteau, C. L., Facteau, J. D., Schoel, L. C., Russell, J.E.A., & Poteet, M. L. (1998). Reactions of leaders to 360-degree feedback from subordinates and peers. *Leadership Quarterly, 9*(4), 427–448.

Farh, J. L., Dobbins, G. H., & Cheng, B. S. (1991). Cultural relativity in action: A comparison of self- ratings made by Chinese and U.S. workers. *Personnel Psychology, 44*, 129–147.

Farr, J. L. (1996). Informal performance feedback: Seeking and giving. In H. Schuler, J. Farr, & M. Smith (Eds.), *Personnel selection and assessment: Individual and organizational perspectives* (pp. 163–180). Mahwah, NJ: Lawrence Erlbaum.

Fedor, D. B., Rensvold, R. B., & Adams, S. M. (1992). An investigation of factors expected to affect feedback seeking: A longitudinal field study. *Personnel Psychology, 45,* 779–805.

Fenigstein, A., & Abrams, D. (1993). Self-attention and the egocentric assumption of shared perspectives. *Journal of Experimental Social Psychology, 29,* 287–303.

Ferris, G. R., Judge, T. A., Rowland, K. M., & Fitzgibbons, D. E. (1994). Subordinate influence and performance evaluation process: Test of a model. *Organizational Behavior and Human Decision Processes, 58,* 101–135.

Fiore, S. M., Salas, E., & Cannon-Bowers, J. A. (2001). Group dynamics and shared mental model development. In M. London (Ed.), *How people evaluate others in organizations* (pp. 309–336). Mahwah, NJ: Erlbaum.

Fiske, S. T., Xu, J., Cuddy, A.J.C., & Glick, P. (1999). (Dis)respecting versus (dis)liking: Status and interdependence predict ambivalent stereotypes of competence and warmth. *Journal of Social Issues, 55*(3), 473–489.

Fleming, B., & Holland, B. (2002, April). How dark side personality factors impact performance ratings: A meta-analysis. Paper presented at the 17th Annual Meeting of the Society for Industrial and Organizational Psychology, Toronto.

Fleming, J. B. (1979). *Stopping wife abuse.* New York: Anchor Books.

Fried, Y., Tiegs, R. B., & Bellamy, A. R. (1992). Personal and interpersonal predictors of supervisors' avoidance of evaluating subordinates. *Journal of Applied Psychology, 77,* 462–468.

Funder, D. C. (1987). Errors and mistakes: Evaluating the accuracy of social judgment. *Psychological Bulletin, 101,* 75–90.

Gabarro, J. J. (1990). The development of working relationships. In J. Galegher, R. E. Kraut, & C. Egido (Eds.), *Intellectual teamwork: Social and technological foundations of cooperative work* (pp. 79–110). Hillsdale, NJ: Lawrence Erlbaum.

Galunic, D. C., & Eisenhardt, K. M. (2001). Architectural innovation and modular corporate forms. *Academy of Management Journal, 44,* 1229–1249.

Gardner, W. L., III. (1991, April). The impact of impression management on the performance appraisal process. Paper presented at the Sixth Annual Meeting of the Society for Industrial and Organizational Psychology, St. Louis.

Gardner, W. L., III. (1992). Lessons in organizational dramaturgy: The art of impression management. *Organizational Dynamics, 21*(1), 33–46.

Gersick, C.J.G., & Hackman, J. R. (1990). Habitual routines in task-performing groups. *Organizational Behavior and Human Decision Processes, 47,* 65–97.

Gerstenberg, F.X.R., Imhoff, R., Banse, R., Altstötter-Gleich, Zinkernagel, A., & Schmitt, M. (2013). How implicit-explicit consistency of the intelligence self-concept moderates reactions to performance feedback. *European Journal of Personality, 27,* 1–18. doi:10.1002/per.1900

Gifford, R. (1994). A lens-mapping framework for understanding the encoding and decoding of interpersonal dispositions in nonverbal behavior. *Journal of Personality and Social Psychology, 66,* 398–412.

Gillespie, T. L. (2002, April). Global 360: Balancing consistency across cultures. Paper presented at the 17th Annual Meeting of the Society for Industrial and Organizational Psychology, Toronto.

Goleman, D. (2001). An EI-based theory of performance. In C. Cherniss & D. Goleman (Eds.), *The emotionally intelligent workplace* (pp. 27–44). San Francisco: Jossey-Bass.

Goodstone, M. S., & Diamante, T. (1998). Organizational use of therapeutic change: Strengthening multisource feedback systems through interdisciplinary coaching. *Consulting Psychology Journal: Practice and Research, 50*(3), 152–163.

Gordon, S., Mian, M. Z., & Gabel, L. (2002, April). An exploratory analysis of the validity of multi-rater feedback and assessment center ratings. Presented at the 17th Annual Meeting of the Society for Industrial and Organizational Psychology, Toronto.

Grant, A. M., & Ashford, S. J. (2008). The dynamics of proactivity at work. *Research in Organizational Behavior, 28,* 3–34.

Hackman, J. R. (Ed.). (1990). *Groups that work (and those that don't): Creating conditions for effective teamwork.* San Francisco: Jossey-Bass.

Hackman, J. R., & Wageman, R. (2005). A theory of team coaching. *Academy of Management Review, 30,* 269–287.

Hallam, G. (2001). Multisource feedback for teams. In D. W. Bracken, C. W. Timmreck, & A. H. Church (Eds.), *The handbook of multisource feedback* (pp. 289–300). San Francisco: Jossey-Bass.

Halverson, S., Tonidandel, S., Barlow, C., & Dipboye, R. L. (2002, April). Self-other agreement on a 360-degree leadership evaluation. Paper presented at the 17th Annual Meeting of the Society for Industrial and Organizational Psychology, Toronto.

Hardin, C. D., & Higgins, E. T. (1996). Shared reality: How social verification makes the subjective objective. In R. M. Sorrentino & E. T. Higgins (Eds.), *Handbook of motivation and cognition, Vol. 3: The interpersonal context* (pp. 28–84). New York: Guilford Press.

Harris, M. M., & Schaubroeck, J. (1988). A metanalysis of self-manager, self-peer, and peer-manager ratings. *Personnel Psychology, 41,* 43–62.

Harris, P. R., & Moran, R. T. (1987). *Managing cultural difference.* Houston: Gulf.

Harvey, P. (2013). Why Generation Y yuppies are unhappy. *Huffington Post.* Retrieved from www.huffingtonpost.com/wait-but-why/generation-y-unhappy_b_3930620.html

Hatten, J. T., Glaman, J. M., Houston, J., & Cochran, C. C. (2002, April). Do assessment center scores predict 360 evaluations? Presented at the 17th Annual Meeting of the Society for Industrial and Organizational Psychology, Toronto.

Heath, C., & Jourden, F. (1997). Illusion, disillusion, and the buffering effect of groups. *Organizational Behavior and Human Decision Processes, 69*(2), 103–116.

Herriot, P. (1989). Attribution theory and interview decisions. In R. W. Eder & G. R. Ferris (Eds.), *The employment interview: Theory, research, and practice* (pp. 97–110). Newbury Park, CA: Sage.

Higgins, E. T. (1987). Self-discrepancy: A theory relating self and affect. *Psychological Review, 94,* 319–340.

Hillman, L. W., Schwandt, D. R., & Bartz, D. E. (1990). Enhancing staff members' performance through feedback and coaching. *Journal of Management Development, 9*(3), 20–27.

Hofstede, G. (2001). *Culture's consequences* (2nd ed.). Thousand Oaks, CA: Sage.

Huang, J. T. (2012). Be proactive as empowered? The role of trust in one's supervisor in psychological empowerment, feedback seeking, and job performance. *Journal of Applied Social Psychology, 42*(S1), E103–E127. doi:10.1111/j.1559-1816.2012.01019.x

Ilgen, D. R., Fisher, C. D., & Taylor, M. S. (1979). Consequences of individual feedback on behavior in organizations. *Journal of Applied Psychology, 64,* 349–371.

Jacobson, N. S., & Margolin, G. (1979). *Marital therapy: Strategies based on social learning and behavior exchange principles.* New York: Brunner/Mazel.

James, S. (1994). Recent advances in management development: Self-directed, continuous development through "Smart Software." *Journal of Management Development, 13*(7), 35–39.

Johnson, J. W. (2001). The relative importance of task and contextual performance dimensions to supervisor judgments of overall performance. *Journal of Applied Psychology, 86*(5), 984–996.

Jourden, F., & Heath, C. (1996). The evaluation gap in performance perceptions: Illusory perceptions of groups and individuals. *Journal of Applied Psychology, 81,* 369–379.

Judge, T. A., & Ferris, G. R. (1993). Social context of performance evaluation decisions. *Academy of Management Journal, 36,* 80–105.

Kanter, R. M. (1977). *Men and women of the corporation.* New York: Basic Books.

Kaplan, R. E. (1986). What one manager learned in "The Looking Glass" and how he learned it. *Journal of Management Development, 5*(4), 36–45.

Karl, K. A., & Kopf, J. M. (1993, August). Will individuals who need to improve their performance the most, volunteer to receive videotaped feedback? Paper presented at the Annual Meeting of the Academy of Management, Atlanta.

Kayes, A. B., & Kayes, D. C. (2011). *The learning advantage: Six practices of learning directed leadership.* Basingstoke: Palgrave-Macmillan.

Kelly, J. R., & McGrath, J. E. (1985). Effects of time limits and task types on task performance and interaction of four-person groups. *Journal of Personality and Social Psychology, 49,* 395–407.

Kenny, D. A., & DePaulo, B. M. (1993). Do people know how others view them? An empirical and theoretical account. *Psychological Bulletin, 114,* 145–161.

Klimoski, R. J., & Donahue, L. M. (2001). Person perception in organizations: An overview of the field. In M. London (Ed.), *How people evaluate others in organizations* (pp. 5–43). Mahwah, NJ: Erlbaum.

Kluger, A. N., & DeNisi, A. (1996). Effects of feedback interventions on performance: A historical review, a meta-analysis, and preliminary feedback intervention theory. *Psychological Bulletin, 119,* 254–284.

Kluger, A. N., & DeNisi, A. (1998). Feedback interventions: Toward the understanding of a double-edged sword. *Current Directions in Psychological Science, 7*(3), 67–72.

Kopelman, R. E. (1986). *Managing productivity in organizations: A practical, people-oriented perspective.* New York: McGraw-Hill.

REFERENCES

Korsgaard, M. A., Meglino, B. M., & Lester, S. W. (1997). Beyond helping: Do other-oriented values have broader implications in organizations? *Journal of Applied Psychology, 82,* 160–177.

Kozlowski, S.W.J., Chao, G. T., & Morrison, R. F. (1998). Games raters play: Politics, strategies, and impression management in performance appraisal. In J. W. Smither (Ed.), *Performance appraisal: State of the art in practice* (pp. 163–205). San Francisco: Jossey-Bass.

Kozlowski, S.W.J., DeShon, R. P., Schmidt, A. M., & Chambers, B. A. (2002, April). Effects of feedback and goal orientation on individual and team regulation, learning, and performance. Paper presented at the 17th Annual Meeting of the Society for Industrial and Organizational Psychology, Toronto.

Krasman, J. (2011). Taking feedback-seeking to the next "level": Organizational structure and feedback-seeking behavior. *Journal of Managerial Issues, 23,* 9–30.

Kumar, K., & Beyerlein, M. (1991). Construction and validation of an instrument for measuring ingratiatory behaviors in organizational settings. *Journal of Applied Psychology, 76,* 619–627.

Langer, E. J. (1992). Matters of mind: Mindfulness/mindlessness in perspective. *Consciousness & Cognition: An International Journal, 1,* 289–305.

Larson, J. R., Jr. (1984). The performance feedback process: A preliminary model. *Organizational Behavior and Human Performance, 33,* 42–76.

Larson, J. R., Jr. (1988). The dynamic interplay between employees' feedback-seeking strategies and supervisors' delivery of performance feedback. *Academy of Management Review, 14,* 408–422.

Latham, G. P., & Locke, E. A. (2006). Enhancing the benefits and overcoming the pitfalls of goal setting. *Organizational Dynamics, 35,* 332–340.

Latham, G. P., & Wexley, K. N. (1981). *Increasing productivity through performance appraisal.* Reading, MA: Addison-Wesley.

Lawler, E. E., III. (1999). *Rewarding excellence.* New York: Wiley.

Leonard, E., & Williams, J. R. (2001, April). An empirical examination of accountability perceptions within a multi-source feedback system. Presented at the 16th Annual Meeting of the Society for Industrial and Organizational Psychology, San Diego.

Levy, P. E. (1991, April). Self-appraisal and attributional judgments. Paper presented at the Sixth Annual Meeting of the Society for Industrial and Organizational Psychology, St. Louis.

Li, N., Harris, B., Boswell, W. R., & Xie, Z. (2011). The role of organizational insiders' developmental feedback and proactive personality on newcomers' performance: An interactionist perspective. *Journal of Applied Psychology, 96,* 1317–1327. doi:10.1037/a0024029

Lindsley, D. H., Brass, D. J., & Thomas, J. B. (1995). Efficacy-performance spirals: A multilevel perspective. *Academy of Management Review, 20*(3), 645–678.

Locke, E. A., & Latham, G. P. (1990). *A theory of goal setting and task performance.* Englewood Cliffs, NJ: Prentice Hall.

Locke, E. A., & Latham, G. P. (1992). Comments on McLeod, Liker, and Lobel. *Journal of Applied Behavioral Science, 28,* 42–45.

Lombardo, M. M., & Eichinger, R. W. (2000). High potentials as high learners. *Human Resource Management, 39,* 321–330.

London, M. (1985). *Developing managers*. San Francisco: Jossey-Bass.

London, M. (1988). *Change agents: New roles and innovation strategies for human resource professionals*. San Francisco: Jossey-Bass.

London, M. (1995a). Giving feedback: Source-centered antecedents and consequences of constructive and destructive feedback. *Human Resource Management Review, 5*, 159–188.

London, M. (1995b). *Self and interpersonal insight: How people learn about themselves and others in organizations*. New York: Oxford University Press.

London, M. (2001). The great debate: Should multisource feedback be used for administration or development only? In D. W. Bracken, C. W. Timmreck, & A. H. Church (Eds.), *The handbook of multisource feedback: The comprehensive resource for designing and implementing MSF processes* (pp. 368–385). San Francisco: Jossey-Bass.

London, M., & London, M. (1996). Tight coupling in high performing ensembles. *Human Resource Management Review, 6*(1), 1–24.

London, M., & Mone, E. M. (2009). Strategic performance management: Issues and trends. In J. Storey, P. Wright, & D. Ulrich (Eds.), *Routledge companion to strategic human resource management* (pp. 245–261). London: Routledge.

London, M., & Mone, E. M. (in press). Designing feedback for performance improvement. In J. C. Passmore, K. Kraiger, & N. Santos (Eds.), *The Wiley Blackwell handbook of the psychology of training, development, and feedback*. New York: Wiley.

London, M., & Sessa, V. I. (1999). *Selecting international executives: A suggested framework and annotated bibliography*. Greensboro, NC: Center for Creative Leadership.

London, M., & Smither, J. W. (1995). Can multi-source feedback change self-awareness and behavior? Theoretical applications and directions for research. *Personnel Psychology, 48*, 803–840.

London, M., & Smither, J. W. (1999). Empowered self-development and continuous learning. *Human Resource Management, 38*(1), 3–16.

London, M., & Smither, J. W. (2002). Feedback orientation, feedback culture, and the longitudinal performance management process. *Human Resource Management Review, 12*(1), 81–101.

London, M., & Tornow, W. W. (1998). Introduction: 360-degree feedback—More than a tool! In W. W. Tornow & M. London (Eds.), *Maximizing the value of 360-degree feedback: A process for successful individual and organizational development* (pp. 1–8). San Francisco: Jossey-Bass.

Luft, J. (1970). *Group processes: An introduction to group dynamics*. Palo Alto, CA: National Press Books.

Mabe, P. A., & West, S. G. (1982). Validity of self-evaluation of ability: A review and meta-analysis. *Journal of Applied Psychology, 67*, 280–296.

MacKenzie, J. (2013). *Magid Generational Strategies reveals America's newest generation*. Retrieved from http://magid.com/pluralist-generation-press-release

Madjar, N., & Ortiz-Walters, R. (2009). Trust in supervisors and trust in customers: Their independent, relative, and joint effects on employee performance and creativity. *Human Performance, 22*, 128–142.

Marikar, S. (2013, December 22). A generational divide. *New York Times,* p. 16.

Maurer, T. J., & Tarulli, B. A. (1994). Acceptance of peer and upward performance appraisal systems: Considerations from employee development, job analysis, and leadership. Unpublished manuscript. Georgia Institute of Technology.

Mayer, R. C., & Gavin, M. B. (2005). Trust in management and performance: Who minds the shop while the employees watch the boss? *Academy of Management Journal, 48,* 874–888.

McAllister, D. J. (1995). Affect- and cognition-based trust as foundations for interpersonal cooperation in organizations. *Academy of Management Journal, 38,* 24–59.

McCall, M. W., & Lombardo, M. M. (1983). *Off the track: Why and how successful executives get derailed* (Technical Report No. 21). Greensboro, NC: Center for Creative Leadership.

McCauley, C., & Lombardo, M. (1990). Benchmarks: An instrument for diagnosing managerial strengths and weaknesses. In K. E. Clark & M. B. Clark (Eds.), *Measures of leadership* (pp. 535–545). West Orange, NJ: Leadership Library of America.

McGill, M. E., Slocum, J. W., Jr., & Lei, D. (1992). Management practices in learning organizations. *Organizational Dynamics, 21*(1), 5.

McLeod, P. L., Liker, J. K., & Lobel, S. (1992). Process feedback in task groups: An application of goal setting. *Journal of Applied Behavioral Science, 28,* 15–41.

Meyer, H. H. (1991). A solution to the performance appraisal feedback enigma. *Academy of Management Executive, 5*(1), 68–76.

Morrison, E. W. (2002). Newcomers' relationships: The role of social network ties during socialization. *Academy of Management Journal, 45,* 1149–1160. doi:1.2307/3069430

Morrison, E. W., & Bies, R. J. (1991). Impression management in the feedback-seeking process: A literature review and research agenda. *Academy of Management Review, 16*(3), 522–541.

Morrison, E. W., & Vancouver, J. B. (1993, August). The effects of source attributes on feedback seeking. Paper presented at the Annual Meeting of the Academy of Management, Atlanta.

Moye, M. J., & Henkin, A. B. (2006). Exploring associations between employee empowerment and interpersonal trust in managers. *Journal of Management Development, 25,* 101–117.

Murphy, K. R., & Cleveland, J. N. (1991). *Performance appraisal: An organizational perspective.* Needham Heights, MA: Allyn & Bacon.

Nadler, D. A. (1979). The effects of feedback on task group behavior: A review of the experimental research. *Organizational Behavior and Human Performance, 23,* 309–338.

Napier, N. K., & Latham, G. P. (1986). Outcome expectancies of people who conduct performance appraisals. *Personnel Psychology, 39,* 827–837.

Neale, M. A., & Bazerman, M. H. (1991). *Cognition and rationality in negotiation.* New York: Free Press.

Nickerson, R. S. (1999). How we know—and sometimes misjudge—what others know: Imputing one's own knowledge to others. *Psychological Bulletin, 125,* 737–759.

Nisbett, R. E., & Wilson, T. D. (1977). Telling more than we know: Verbal reports on mental processes. *Psychological Review, 84,* 231–259.

Norris-Watts, C., & Levy, P. E. (2002, April). The feedback environment and work outcome variables. Paper presented at the 17th Annual Meeting of the Society for Industrial and Organizational Psychology, Toronto.

Operario, D., & Fiske, S. T. (2001). Causes and consequences of stereotypes in organizations. In M. London (Ed.), *How people evaluate others in organizations* (pp. 45–62). Mahwah, NJ: Erlbaum.

Organ, D. W. (1988). *Organizational citizenship behavior: The good soldier syndrome.* Lexington, MA: Lexington Books.

Park, H., & Harrison, J. K. (1993). Enhancing managerial cross-cultural awareness and sensitivity: Transactional analysis revisited. *Journal of Management Development, 12*(3), 20–29.

Peterson, D. B. (2009). Coaching and performance management: How can organizations get the greatest value? In J. W. Smither & M. London (Eds.), *Performance management: Putting research into action* (pp. 115–156). San Francisco: Jossey-Bass.

Reilly, B. A., & Doherty, M. E. (1989). A note on the assessment of self-insight in judgment research. *Organizational Behavior and Human Decision Processes, 44,* 123–131.

Reilly, B. A., & Doherty, M. E. (1992). The assessment of self-insight in judgment policies. *Organizational Behavior and Human Decision Processes, 53,* 285–309.

Reilly, R. R., Warech, M. A., & Reilly, S. (1993, April). The influence of self-monitoring on the reliability and validity of upward feedback. Paper presented at the Annual Meeting of the Society for Industrial and Organizational Psychology, San Francisco.

Rogers, C. R. (1980). *A way of being.* Boston: Houghton Mifflin.

Rose, D., & Farrell, T. (2002, April). The use and abuse of comments in 360-degree feedback. Paper presented at the 17th Annual Meeting of the Society for Industrial and Organizational Psychology, Toronto.

Ross, E. M., & Allen, N. J. (2002, April). Evaluation of task performance: Do groups make a difference? Paper presented at the 17th Annual Meeting of the Society for Industrial and Organizational Psychology, Toronto.

Rousch, P. E., & Atwater, L. E. (1992). Using the MBTI to understand transformational leadership and self-perception accuracy. *Military Psychology, 4,* 17–34.

Russo, J. E., & Schoemaker, P.J.H. (1992). Managing overconfidence. *Sloan Management Review, 33*(2), 7–17.

Ryan, A. M., Brutus, S., Greguras, G. J., & Hakel, M. D. (2000). Receptivity to assessment-based feedback for management development. *Journal of Management Development, 19*(4), 252–276.

Saavedra, R., Earley, P. C., & Van Dyne, L. (1993). Complex interdependence in task-performing groups. *Journal of Applied Psychology, 78,* 61–72.

Salvemini, N. J., Reilly, R. R., & Smither, J. W. (1993). The influence of rater motivation on assimilation effects and accuracy in performance ratings. *Organizational Behavior and Human Decision Processes, 55,* 41–60.

Sanders, M. M. (1993). Situational constraints through the cognitive looking glass: A reinterpretation of the relationship between situations and performance judgments. *Human Resource Management Review, 3,* 129–146.

Sargeant, J., MacLeod, R., Sinclair, D., & Power, M. (2011). How do physicians assess their family physician colleagues' performance? Creating a rubric to inform assessment and feedback. *Journal of Continuing Education in the Health Professions, 31,* 87–94.

Sargeant, J., Mann, K., Sinclair, D., van der Vleuten, C., & Metsemakers, J. (2008). Understanding the influence of emotions and reflection upon multisource feedback acceptance and use. *Advances in Health Sciences Education, 13,* 275–288.

Sargeant, J. M., Mann, K. V., van der Vleuten, C. P., & Metsemakers, J. F. (2009). Reflection: A link between receiving and using assessment feedback. *Advances in Health Science Education, 14,* 399–410. doi:10.1007/s10459-008-9124-4

Senge, P. M. (1990). *The fifth discipline: The art and practice of the learning organization.* New York: Doubleday.

Shrauger, J. S., & Shoeneman, J. (1979). Symbolic interactionist view of self-concept: Through the looking glass darkly. *Psychological Bulletin, 86,* 549–573.

Silverman, S. B. (1991). Individual development through performance appraisal. In K. N. Wexley (Ed.), *Developing human resources* (pp. 120–151). Washington, DC: Bureau of National Affairs.

Silverman, S. B., Pogson, C. E., & Cober, A. B. (2005). When employees at work don't get it: A model for enhancing individual employee change in response to performance feedback. *Academy of Management Executive, 19,* 135–147.

Smither, W., London, M., Flautt, R., Vargas, Y., & Kucine, I. (2002, April). Can executive coaches enhance the impact of multisource feedback on behavior change? A quasi-experimental field study. Paper presented at the Annual Meeting of the Society for Industrial and Organizational Psychology, Toronto.

Smither, W., London, M., Flautt, R., Vargas, Y., & Kucine, I. (in press). Can executive coaches enhance the impact of multisource feedback on behavior change? A quasi-experimental field study. *Personnel Psychology.*

Smither, J. W., London, M., & Richmond, K. R. (2002, April). Relationships between leaders' personality and reactions to, and use of, multisource feedback: A longitudinal study. Paper presented at the Annual Meeting of the Society for Industrial and Organizational Psychology, Toronto.

Smith-Jentsch, K. A., Campbell, G. E., Milanovich, D. M., & Reynolds, A. M. (2001). Measuring teamwork mental models to support training needs assessment, development, and evaluation: Two empirical studies. *Journal of Organizational Behavior, 22,* 179–194.

Snyder, M. (1974). Self-monitoring of expressive behavior. *Journal of Personality and Social Psychology, 30,* 526–537.

Sobel-Lojeski, K. (2009). *Leading the virtual workforce.* New York: Wiley.

Spreitzer, G. M. (1995). Psychological empowerment in the workplace: Dimensions, measurement, and validation. *Academy of Management Journal, 35,* 1442–1465.

Steele, C. M., Spencer, S. J., & Lynch, M. (1993). Self-image resilience and dissonance: The role of affirmational resources. *Journal of Personality and Social Psychology, 64,* 885–896.

Steelman, L. A., & Levy, P. E. (2001, April). The feedback environment and its potential role in 360-degree feedback. Paper presented at the 16th Annual Meeting of the Society for Industrial and Organizational Psychology, San Diego.

Steelman, L. A., Levy, P. E., & Snell, A. F. (2002). The feedback environment scale (FES): Construct definition, measurement and validation. Unpublished manuscript. University of Akron.

Steiner, D. D., Rain, J. S., & Smalley, M. M. (1993). Distributional ratings of performance: Further examination of a new rating format. *Journal of Applied Psychology, 78,* 438.

Stewart, G. L., Carson, K. P., & Cardy, R. L. (1996). The joint effects of conscientiousness and self-leadership training on employee self-directed behavior in a service setting. *Personnel Psychology, 49,* 143–164.

Stinson, L., & Ickes, W. (1992). Empathic accuracy in the interactions of male friends versus male strangers. *Journal of Personality and Social Psychology, 62*(5), 787–797.

Sue-Chan, C., & Latham, G. P. (2004). The relative effectiveness of external, peer, and self-coaches. *Applied Psychology: An International Review, 53,* 260–278.

Sue-Chan, C., Wood, R. E., & Latham, G. P. (2012). Effect of a coach's regulatory focus and an individual's implicit person theory on individual performance. *Journal of Management, 38,* 809–835.

Sundstrom, E., De Meuse, K. P., & Futrell, D. (1990). Work teams: Applications and effectiveness. *American Psychologist, 45,* 120–133.

Taylor, S. M., Fisher, C. D., & Ilgen, D. R. (1984). Individuals' reactions to performance feedback in organizations: A control theory perspective. In K. M. Rowland & G. R. Ferris (Eds.), *Research in personnel and human resources management* (Vol. 2, pp. 81–124). Greenwich, CT: JAI.

Thompson, L. (1991). Information exchange and negotiation. *Journal of Experimental Social Psychology, 27,* 161–179.

Thompson, L., & DeHarpport, T. (1994). Social judgment, feedback, and interpersonal learning in negotiation. *Organizational Behavior and Human Decision Processes, 58,* 327–345.

Thompson, L., & Hastie, R. (1990). Social perception in negotiation. *Organization and Human Decision Processes, 47,* 98–123.

Tice, D. M., & Baumeister, R. F. (1990). Self-esteem, self-handicapping, and self-presentation: The strategy of inadequate practice. *Journal of Personality, 58,* 443–464.

Timmreck, C. W., & Bracken, D. W. (1997). Multisource feedback: A study of its use in decision making. *Employment Relations Today, 24*(1), 21–27.

Tsui, A. S., & Ohlott, P. (1988). Multiple assessment of managerial effectiveness: Interrater agreement and consensus in effectiveness models. *Personnel Psychology, 41,* 779–803.

Ury, W. I., Brett, J. M., & Goldberg, S. B. (1988). *Getting disputes resolved.* San Francisco: Jossey-Bass.

VandeWalle, D. (1997). Development and validation of a work domain instrument. *Educational and Psychological Measurement, 57,* 995–1015.

VandeWalle, D., Brown, S. P., Cron, W. L., & Slocum, J. W. Jr. (1999). The influence of goal orientation and self-regulation tactics on sales performance: A longitudinal field test. *Journal of Applied Psychology, 84,* 249–259.

VandeWalle, D. M., & Cummings, L. L. (1997). A test of the influence of goal orientation on the feedback seeking process. *Journal of Applied Psychology, 82,* 390–400.

Walker, R. (2013, December 29). The workologist. *New York Times* (Sunday edition), p. 9.

Warr, P., & Bunce, D. (1995). Training characteristics and the outcomes of open learning. *Personnel Psychology, 48,* 347–375.

Wayne, S. J., & Kacmar, K. M. (1991). The effects of impression management on the performance appraisal process. *Organizational Behavior and Human Decision Processes, 48,* 70–88.

Wells, L., Jr. (1992). Feedback, the group unconscious, and the unstated effects of experimental methods. *Journal of Applied Behavioral Science, 28,* 46–53.

Whitaker, B. G. (2011). Linking the feedback environment to feedback seeking through perceptions of organizational support and job involvement. *International Journal of Organization Theory and Behaviour, 14,* 383–403.

Whitaker, B. G., Dahling, J. J., & Levy, P. (2007). The development of a feedback environment and role clarity model of job performance. *Journal of Management, 33,* 570–591.

Whitney, K. (1994). Improving group task performance: The role of group goals and group efficacy. *Human Performance, 7,* 55–78.

Woehr, D. J., & Feldman, J. (1993). Processing objective and question order effects on the causal relation between memory and judgment in performance appraisal: The tip of the iceberg. *Journal of Applied Psychology, 78,* 232–241.

Wofford, J. C. (1994). An examination of the cognitive processes used to handle employee job problems. *Academy of Management Journal, 37,* 180–192.

Wohlers, A. J., & London, M. (1989). Ratings of managerial characteristics: Evaluation difficulty, co-worker agreement, and self-awareness. *Personnel Psychology, 42,* 235–260.

Yammarino, F. J., & Atwater, L. E. (1997). Do managers see themselves as others see them? Implications of self-other ratings agreement for human resources management. *Organization Dynamics, 25*(1), 35–44.

Yammarino, F. J., & Dubinsky, A. J. (1992). Supervisor-subordinate relationships: A multiple level of analysis approach. *Human Relations, 45,* 575–600.

Yu, J., & Murphy, K. R. (1993). Modesty bias in self-ratings of performance: A test of the cultural relativity hypothesis. *Personnel Psychology, 46,* 357–363.

Zajonc, R. B. (1965, July 16). Social facilitation. *Science, 149,* 269–274.

Zalesny, M. D., & Highhouse, S. (1992). Accuracy in performance evaluations. *Organizational Behavior and Human Decision Processes, 51,* 22–50.

Zhong, J. A., Cao, Z. L., Huo, Y., Chen, Z., & Lam, W. (2012). The mediating role of job feedback in the relationship between neuroticism and emotional labor. *Social Behavior and Personality, 40,* 649–656.

Zhu, W., May, D. R., & Avolio, B. J. (2004). The impact of ethical leadership behavior on employee outcomes: The roles of psychological empowerment and authenticity. *Journal of Leadership and Organizational Studies, 11,* 16–26.

INDEX

developmental goal setting 124–8
dominancy 154
dysfunctional behavior 43, 58

electronic feedback and coaching 171–3
electronic performance monitoring
  166–7
emotional intelligence 134
emotional response to feedback 16–17
empathy 75
employee performance monitoring 166
employee selection process 111
employee self-evaluation 41–3
ensembles 152
evaluation errors 90
evaluations, characteristics affecting
  74–5
evaluator expertise 72
evaluator motivation 71–2, 89
event schemas 67
executive coaching 129
expressiveness 154
external coaching 129
extraversion 39

fear of failure 56–7
feedback: acceptance and use 58–61,
  136; accountability for 134–5;
  age differential 186; anticipating
  reactions to 122–3; asking for
  57–61; assessment centers 111–16;
  benefits of 19–21; characteristics
  of effective 8; coaching and 130–1;
  constructive 21–5; data collection in
  teams 158–9; defined 15; dynamic
  nature of 65; electronic feedback
  and coaching 171–3; elements of
  6–9; empowerment and trust 189;
  executive support for 180; feelings
  about 16–19; frequency of 51–2,
  107; generational differences and
  11; in a global company 145–9;
  goal setting and 123–8; guidelines
  for 8; helpful hints for giving 126;
  interpersonal relationships and
  26–8; leadership style and 186;
  learning organizations and 188–9;
  legal implications of 9–10; one-on-
  one 50–2, 83, 106, 172; personality
  and reactions to 38–40, 186–7;
  principles for giving 7; psychology
  of 6; readiness for change 136;

receiving 8; self-awareness and
  36; self-correcting function 162;
  self-paced learning 168–9; self-
  regulation and 28; shared mental
  models and 156–8; sources of 47; in
  team negotiation processes 162–3;
  teams and 8, 151–6; technology and
  166–76; in virtual teams 174–6
feedback culture: age differential 186;
  changing nature of work 183–4;
  effects of personality on 186–7;
  elements of 182; empowerment
  and trust 189; feedback orientation
  182–3; leadership style 186; learning
  and use 188–9; overview 178–80;
  perceived support for 185; positive
  performance cycles and 188; self-
  coaching and 181; support for 180
feedback intervention theory 125–6
first impression tendency 90
frame of reference training 90
frequent feedback 51–2, 107
friendliness 154

games and simulations 117–20
generational differences 131–2
Generation X, Y, and Z 11
goal-directed behavior 19–20
goal orientation, components of 40
goal setting: appraisal systems and 9,
  107; coaching and 123–8; feedback
  and 16–17; for teams 160–1
group feedback 20, 106

halo tendency 89
harassment 9–10
health care industry 184

impression management 61–3, 73–4,
  107
incomplete feedback 34
indirect feedback 50
individual feedback 161–2
individual learning 20
informal feedback: continuous nature
  of 49; impression management
  61–3; managers inclination
  toward 49–50; one-on-one 50–2;
  performance appraisal and 104;
  performance management programs
  and 49; self-regulation and 52–7;
  sources of 48–9

206